APPRENTICE TO POWER

INDIA
1904-1908

By

SIR MALCOLM DARLING

1966
THE HOGARTH PRESS
LONDON

Published by
The Hogarth Press Ltd
42 William IV Street
London W.C.2

*

Clarke, Irwin & Co Ltd
Toronto

Printed in Great Britain by
Butler and Tanner Ltd
Frome and London

To

APRIL

Without whose measureless encouragement and help
this book could not have been written

Contents

Part I APPRENTICE

Preface 9
1 Arrival in India 13
2 Interlude 23
3 First Post 26
4 A Cold Weather in Lahore 33

Part II POWER

5 Rajanpur—On my own 45
6 Rajanpur—The Hot Weather 60
7 Rajanpur—The Monsoon 72
8 The Monsoon, continued 86
9 Fort Munro—The Baluchis of the Hills 97
10 Rajanpur in the Cold Weather 108
11 Rajanpur in the Cold Weather, continued 121

Part III HIS HIGHNESS

12 Dewas—First Impressions 135
13 Personalities 152
14 A Visit to Kolhapur 159
15 In and Around Dewas 171
16 Politics and Friendship 180
17 The Grand Tour—Northern India 198
18 The Grand Tour—Burma 209
19 The Grand Tour—India, Eastwards and Southwards 217
20 Initiations—Return to Dewas 225
21 The Wedding 236
22 The End of a Beginning 248

Preface

Apprentice to Power is an attempt to describe my first three and a half years in India some sixty years ago as a newly joined member of the Indian Civil Service—an experience which, with the passing of the British Empire, can never be repeated. It is based mainly upon letters with the addition, for part of the time, of a diary, and only to a slight extent upon memory. If therefore it has any value, it is its contemporary character, since most of the conversations and incidents recorded in it are taken from what was written within a week of their occurrence, often indeed on the day itself.

The great majority of the letters were written to my mother or A. C., the friend of now over sixty years. In both cases they are too voluminous and too hurriedly written for frequent quotation at any length. But whether they are quoted or paraphrased, I have kept scrupulously to their substance. The same applies to the diary. This falls into two parts. The earlier covers the emotional ups and downs of a very unsettled first year. The later is much less personal and consists largely of information gathered at haphazard during the last year about the way of life of the Hindus amongst whom I was living. To the best of my recollection, neither part has been seen by anyone but myself. As to the letters, once posted I never thought to see them again.

As to myself and India, I arrived there knowing something about its history but nothing about its peoples. I had heard that my paternal grandfather (born 1782) had done two voyages there and back as Medical Officer on an East Indiaman; also that my father (born 1816) had declined the offer of a Cadetship in the East India Company's service and taken orders instead. Much later came a more personal connexion. This was to meet two of my father's first cousins, Alfred and James Lyall, on their retirement from the Indian Civil Service, in which each had risen to be the Head of a Province, Alfred of the United Provinces (now Uttar Pradesh) and James of the undivided Punjab. This roused in me an urge to follow, however modestly, in their footsteps, all the stronger for

Alfred Lyall having become my guardian on my father's death when I was twelve.

But one thing I had not reckoned with. In the competitive examination for entry into the Indian and Home Civil Services I was placed high enough to be offered a post in the India Office. This I had never thought possible and it led to one of the most perplexing decisions of my life. The arguments for staying at home were strong; notably that my mother was a widow and that the elder of her two sons was already in the Indian Civil Service. To her lasting credit, as I wavered this way and that, she never said a word to influence my choice.

During the first year of my apprenticeship I was often tempted to regret it. But I gradually became acclimatised to the change, and by the end of the story that follows my apprenticeship had become less to the all-powerful Government of India than to India itself.

It only remains to thank those who have helped me in the writing of this book. I am under deep obligation to E. M. Forster for reading most of Part 3 and for the suggestions that followed; also for allowing me to quote more than once from *The Hill of Devi*. I am much indebted, too, to J. V. Narlikar, Fellow of King's College, Cambridge, for clarifying various points of Hindu religious observance about which I was doubtful. I am specially grateful to Anne Devine for her help with the title and for allowing me to read the whole book aloud to her; also for reading the proofs. Nor must I forget that it was largely my son-in-law Paul van Biervliet's questions about my life in India that embarked me on my task. Finally, the dedication acknowledges my greatest debt of all.

M. L. D.

La Madeleine
15 June 1965

Part I
APPRENTICE

CHAPTER 1

Arrival in India*

ON Sunday, November 27, 1904, the *City of Vienna* dropped anchor in Bombay. I was sleeping on deck, and when I woke the sun was rising in a glow of crimson behind the distant hills across a fine open roadstead. It was already hot, and the air was heavy with an exotic fragrance, first met at Port Said. Port Said had given me "a scare of the East—the natives look so revolting".† Happily there was an Indian on board who gave me a very different impression. Hamid Abdul Ali, a native of Bombay and like myself new to the Indian Civil Service, was widely read in French, German and English, with opinions of his own on all he read and a strong sense of humour. For me he was "the most interesting person on board; yet because of the accident which had made him dark instead of fair he stands even more aloof from the ship's company than I do". It was my first hint of the wide social gulf in the India of those days between East and West.

At nine o'clock, with the first gangway down "up rushed a number of husbands who fell into the arms of their faithful wives, where they remained as long as the heat allowed them". Ashore I fell in with Bernard Dobson (son of the poet, Austin Dobson), another I.C.S. recruit. As we were both under orders to report at Lahore, we travelled there together. On arrival, with no one to guide us, we went to "a neighbouring pub", as we heard later of very doubtful reputation. Next morning we hired a carriage and drove in state to the Secretariat. There I learnt that I was posted to Lahore. I was given a note of introduction to X, the Deputy Commissioner, who was to be my chief. We tracked him down to Kutcherry,‡ where he received us in his Court-room. He was "friendly enough with a slight touch of vulgarity". Had I been

* Unless otherwise stated the terms 'India' and 'Indian' apply to the whole sub-continent as they did until 1947.

† All quotations in double quotes are from my diary or from letters either to my mother or to one or other of my friends in England, unless otherwise indicated. The same applies to subsequent chapters.

‡ Local courts of justice.

'boosting about' on my way up? he asked. He assured me, a little menacingly, that there would be quite enough work to keep me going here. He seemed rather overcome with the weight of his own work and complained of the dog's life it was when you had got halfway up. "I shall have to get to like him", I wrote, but that proved impossible. Next day I moved into a tent in the compound of the old Punjab Club, and at meals shared a table with six other Civilians, all but one "men of force and ability".

I hardly knew whether to be pleased or not with my station. People assured me that I was in luck, but it was a little overpowering to be plunged at the very outset into Lahore's "vortex of business and dissipation" with its intolerable number of social duties. Could it, too, be a good place for learning one's work? As the event proved, these forebodings were justified. Everyone was far too busy to spare time for my training; and the Deputy Commissioner, who should have kept an eye on my infant steps, from first to last took no interest in me.

At first I hated every corner of Lahore except my tent. I felt as if I had landed on another planet. "I knew practically no one; everyone thought the other was looking after me; the language was beyond me, and everything was so new and strange that one dared not take a step for fear of doing something wrong. Then there was the eternal driving along dusty roads—Lahore is the dustiest place on earth—and dealing out cards to endless people about whom one cared not a scrap." Worst of all, the country was hideous—flat as a billiard table but without its green, and looking as if it could barely breathe under its coating of dust. Behind all this lay a not unnatural feeling of homesickness, very like, and sometimes as unpleasant as, what I had felt at the age of eight during my first term at a boarding school.

There were, however, compensations. A nobody at home, here one was somebody, with moreover two manservants of one's own, a 'bearer' and a 'chaprassi'—a valet and an orderly. But how to keep them employed? When everything else failed, "I make the bearer take off my boots." The chaprassi was more difficult: "It takes me the whole day to think of something to give him to do, and one day in desperation I sent him to the station for a timetable, though there was one at the Club two minutes away."

During those first weeks in Lahore, and for long afterwards, I saw next to nothing of India's intelligentsia. My contacts with those who knew English were of the slightest and not always without embarrassment for one still ignorant of Indian taboos. One day, for instance, having to visit the Club office, I entered smoking a cigarette. The room seemed full of Sikh beards, and one of the bearded, presumably the head clerk, demanded somewhat brusquely that I should stop smoking, tobacco being forbidden to the Sikh. I complied at once, but wondered afterwards whether his tone had not taken advantage of a new comer's ignorance.

A little later I found myself up against another barrier. I was trying my first case guided by an Indian clerk squatting on a low stool beside me. I had come armed with a packet of sandwiches for lunch, and when I broke off to eat them, I did as I would have done at home and offered him one. He declined respectfully but not without a smile at the naivety of the offer. I cannot remember whether he was a Hindu or a Muslim: if a Hindu, the sandwiches might have contained beef, the forbidden flesh of the sacred cow; if a Muslim, they were equally to be feared for possibly containing the flesh of the unclean pig. These two tiny incidents, especially the second, showed me that relations with one's neighbours in India could not be as free and easy as at home. I had even been warned not to let an Indian enter my tent with his shoes on; for that, to quote my flippant comment, "would be the first sign of another mutiny".

Initiation into the mysteries of my professional life did not go beyond an occasional hour or two in a magistrate's court. This was a sheer waste of time, for the proceedings were in Punjabi, not one word of which I understood. The first case offered me was one of rape. The proceedings were curiously casual—"like a schoolmaster setting punishments after school", with the parties crowding up to the magistrate's table and at times speaking all at once.

Christmas was now approaching and I set off to spend it with my brother in the United Province. One sight on the journey there I have never forgotten. I was brooding over the endless monotony of the Punjab plain and feeling as if I beheld infinity, when my eye was caught by a distant white cloud stretching right across the eastern horizon. Suddenly I became aware of the most amazing sight. The Himalayas stood before me flushed with the setting sun, and instead of infinity I beheld eternity.

* * *

With the New Year real work began. I now had my own Court and with it my first case. A letter describes the scene. "I sit on a dais screened by a railing from the touch of the vulgar. On my table repose vast tomes of law, into which from time to time I peer wisely. My Munshi,* who fortunately speaks English, without which justice would be at a standstill, sits on my right. I am as a babe in his arms. It is fearful to think of the power he wields." My chaprassi, a stout fellow of six feet two, stands in the body of the Court, and with eyes fixed dog-like upon my face, he tries to penetrate my every thought that an order may be carried out almost before it is given. "Now the complainant enters, with hands folded beseechingly on his breast. My first duty is to take down his statement. This he makes in Punjabi, of which I know not one word, but the Munshi does, God bless him." He translates it into Urdu. Even so, I am not much the wiser, but gradually it begins to dawn on me that the man has quarrelled with a neighbour about a rope taken from a well which they own in common. The neighbour, he says, gave him 'three heavy blows'. 'Any marks?' I ask. Whereupon "he strips his upper half (not very much to come off) and reveals a great tawny trunk with two little spots like pin pricks". Applying a wise provision of the law, I dismissed the complaint as frivolous.

Young and light-hearted, I found it difficult to take all this seriously and, as I tell my mother, "though I look very stern, sometimes the Majesty of the Law is seen to smile behind a handkerchief stuffed into its mouth". And indeed there was something grotesque in a young Englishman being set down to administer justice between two Indians in a language he did not understand. The grotesque had, however, its moments of elation. "You should see (says a letter) half a dozen lazy policemen spring smartly to attention as I sail into the precincts of the Court on a bicycle." "Magnificent, too, to hear my chaprassi shout out behind me—'make way, make way'—and quick as lightning the crowd parts in two." It was my first sip of power.

My next case, three days later, was a little more impressive. Six accused and two pleaders entered the Court, the accused charged with house trespass and voluntarily causing hurt. As the parties were nearly related, one of the pleaders suggested that they should compromise. The complainant did not seem very willing but,

* Indian secretary.

advised by my Munshi, I adjourned the case for a week to give time for better feelings to prevail and so prevent, as often happened, a family quarrel developing into a family feud. The delay was in vain, and a week later, after hearing the complainant tell his story with every possible detail but with no evidence to back it, "I gravely gave my verdict—'We acquit you all'." The day ended with my first conviction, a case of theft so petty—a mere three bits of wood—that I discharged the accused as it was a first offence.

Faced with a transfer from Lahore, I had to get a horse, and one was brought round for me to try. I mounted, and in two minutes we were making for his stable at full gallop. Almost there, he turned sharply and I found myself lying on the road no more than bruised but "feeling a complete fool". Three days later I bought a more docile beast for Rs. 250 (16 guineas) "but (says my diary) it doesn't interest me in the least: since last Friday I have a positive aversion to anything equine". The aversion soon passed, but though I had been taught to ride at the age of eight, I never became anything of a horseman and thirty-four years later was still being run away with.

My transfer was to the district of Jhang for two months' "Settlement Training". This meant learning the A B C of the Punjab's complicated Land Revenue system. The young Civilian was allowed four months for this. In my case there were to be two periods of two months each. Six years later when I had long forgotten the little learnt in Jhang, the Secretariat discovered that there were still two months to be done. But before this could start I was sucked into the Secretariat itself. It is hardly an exaggeration to say that during the whole of my first fifteen months in India, apart from this half-hearted attempt to train me in the Land Revenue system, and some weeks spent as Treasury Officer, I was left to carry on as best I could. This did at least encourage independence. Its great disadvantage was that during my apprenticeship I rarely saw the experienced at work.

It was some days before I met my Chief, as he was in camp, but when I did so I took to him at once. Abbott was an Indian Civilian of eleven years' service. Courteous, energetic, and making his work "both his forte and his foible", he had acquired an intimate knowledge of the district and it was a delight to listen to the flow of his information about the land and its peasants. With the latter he was "perfectly natural, laughing and chatting with them, without a touch of the ruler shrouded in his own dignity—most refreshing after all one has heard and seen" and typical of the best kind of British district officer, the kind that has never failed to attract the Indian peasant.

Very different in type was the Muslim Deputy Commissioner, a Nawab* and a member of the Punjab's landed aristocracy. As an Indian in charge of a District, he represented a change which forty-two years later was to end in independence. In every other respect he belonged to the feudal past. When the Financial Commissioner came to Jhang on tour, he gave us all a dinner of ten courses ending in twenty different dishes of sweetmeats; and during the two hours we sat round his hospitable table, he spoke "only about four times", each time in answer to a question.

Typical of the new generation in India was Abdul Latif, a Muslim Civilian of two years' standing who had had a distinguished career at Cambridge. There he won the Whewell scholarship for international law and tied for the post of Secretary of the Union with Montagu, a future Secretary of State for India. In time he rose to be Financial Commissioner. Belonging to a well-known family in Bombay noted for its intelligence and culture, with all the polish of the West about him, he suggested a cultivated Italian rather than the highly educated well-bred Indian that he was. A little later, indeed, he sent me a wire to say that he had changed his name to Alma Latifi. In sheer cleverness, power of thought and breadth of interest he was Abbott's superior. His mind, too, was subtler and more elastic, but in the daily affairs of life he lacked Abbott's grip; also his natural courtesy, due to a touch of self-consciousness, not surprising in an Indian who had to hold his own in a service then almost exclusively British. This came out in his manner to the natives which was "a little browbeating". His personal dignity was perhaps too constant a care. But with all this he had a good heart and I liked him. He, too, was under Settlement training and we naturally kept house together.

The highlight of my stay in Jhang was the Lieutenant-Governor's state progress through the district. It recalled in miniature the marches of the Moghul Emperors from Delhi to Kashmir. It must have been the last, or nearly the last of its kind, for the motor age was soon to reach the Punjab. This naturally I did not realise at the time.

* A Muslim title of distinction.

The L.G.,* as he was familiarly called, was coming from Multan, and we of Jhang had to meet him on the border of the two districts. The last ten miles to our encampment I did on my horse the night before. It was a perfect ride. It started with a green and golden sky in the west. As darkness spread from the east, the plain ahead seemed to have no end and the stars above no beginning. "There is something uncanny in being alone under such a sky." In the ten miles I met only a few peasants, and one camel which suddenly loomed upon me out of the dark.

Early next morning, with the other officials of the district, I rode the six miles to where we were to meet the L.G.—"a bitterly cold morning, and 'le diable', he kept us chafing at the bit a whole hour before he appeared". After greetings we joined in the cavalcade which followed him. This included the Commissioner of Multan, the all-important Chief Secretary, in whose hands our fortunes so often lay, an A.D.C. and a crowd of local notabilities—all mounted; and bringing up the rear, a bodyguard of Indian cavalry. The L.G. and Lady Rivaz headed the procession in a lumbering old landau drawn by four magnificent camels, each with a blue-turbaned rider on its back trailing a scarlet cloak behind him.

It was in this order that we entered Shorkot (once entered by Alexander), passing under a triumphal arch—a one-day's wonder—and greeted by dozens of schoolchildren waving paper flags of many colours. For us it was not a pleasant ride. The pace of the camel, midway between a horse's walk and trot, made it difficult to keep in line with the carriage; either one dropped behind to be smothered in dust (no tarmac roads in those days), or there one was in front smothering His Honour and his Lady.

That evening I dined with 'His Honour'. All went swimmingly until, dinner finished, he proposed a game of bridge. Meeting with no response from the Commissioner, he swung round upon me with—"Are you a bridge player?" The answer was "No, sir". Frustrated but resigned, he disconsolately turned to a neighbouring table and plunged into *Punch*. Moved with compassion, the Commissioner said he would play and I could but say the same. All then went well, very well in fact, for he got the better of the Commissioner and myself—not perhaps a very glorious victory, for the Commissioner had played only twice before.

* Short for Lieutenant-Governor.

Three more marches took us to Jhang. Off each morning at eight-thirty, we walked the first two or three miles before taking to our horses and reached the new encampment in time for breakfast at eleven. Which sounds simple enough, but it meant an entourage of "about 300 men, 500 camels, and perhaps 80 tents" of one kind and another. Those for the L.G. and his party were in duplicate, so that on arrival after each march everything was in readiness for breakfast and the day's work. "You may imagine how the camp hums and gurgles with all these folk and camels about."

A second dinner followed with the L.G. and "oh! the boredom of it sitting there only nibbling your food in case you should be suddenly turned upon with a question and caught with your mouth full". He was a kindly man with no airs and did his best to bring one into the conversation, but such is a very junior officer's awe 'in the Presence' that he can only answer 'Yes, sir'—'No, sir', with now and then a question "tremblingly stuttered".

It was during the L.G.'s visit that I had my first outing with a gun. For escort I had the L.G.'s A.D.C. (Captain Eric Drummond) and for transport the back of a camel. We saw very little game, but I never think of the day without shame. At one point, "when, as it were, I was looking the other way", my gun went off. The A.D.C.'s only comment was—"These things were better done otherwise." Rightly was he known as "the politest man in Asia".

I was left behind in Jhang to start my Settlement training. There had been several awkward questions from the L.G. and the Chief Secretary about my work—what progress was I making? Was I doing anything of use to the Settlement Officer? Abbott "luckily kept his head" and said he could hardly hope for me to be of much use when I had only just come out. Actually I had been in Jhang nearly four weeks and had been given nothing more serious to do than inspect the local library. This was a small dusty room adorned with a daub of Queen Victoria, and on a shelf below Bulwer Lytton, Marie Corelli and Burke stood side by side.

From now onwards it was a case of eight hours a day learning the work of a patwari, the lowest rung in the long Land Revenue ladder leading from the village to the Financial Commissioner. Five of the eight hours were spent tramping through fields of young wheat or over open ploughs—no hedges here—measuring and mapping, and later filling up "countless records". These gave full particulars of owner, tenant, labourer and mortgagee with their several rights and obligations, and also of the amount of wheat and tobacco to be given at harvest to potter, blacksmith, minstrel and barber for their various services to the cultivator. The potter's services were of special importance in this area of irrigation by well and Persian wheel, for in those days the water pots necklaced on the wheels were still made of earthenware and not, as much later, of iron.

Such operations led ultimately to the assessment of land revenue for the next thirty or forty years, and to a record of rights so reliable that in any dispute relating to its contents it was presumed to be correct until disproved.

One of the curiosities of my new life was the importance of a chair. Only a Commissioner could confer the right to sit on one 'in the Presence'. Looking through a file on the subject I read: 'I cannot support Ali Akbar's claim: his brother has already a chair and one chair is sufficient for one family!' Obviously one had to be on guard with one's chairs: and somewhere there was a table of affinities on the subject.

The question to offer or not to offer a chair arose between me and the patwari deputed to guide me in my work. Technically he was not entitled to one, but how could he work at my side without one? And more important, how could I work without him? Happily there was a packing-case about the height of a chair in the verandah where I laboured at my calculations. So we pushed the work-table against it and there he sits. "Thus I maintain my dignity and he gets his seat."

In those far-off days the British Raj inspired such awe in the peasant that you had only to wear a topee to be treated like royalty. One evening I had been out for a ride and two water-carts, each drawn by a yoke of oxen, were jogging along ahead of me when their drivers, suddenly spotting me, leapt from their carts and rushed them, oxen and all, into the ditch, one to the left, the other to the right, so that I could have the road to myself as I passed between them. This kind of thing happened again and again. If, too, a horseman met you on the road—"and they are legion"—he would either alight until you had passed, or turn into a neighbouring field to avoid having to do this. No wonder that this excessive respect for authority went in some cases to the head.

The day came when I had to leave Jhang and return to Lahore.

My two months there had given me a good deal. I had been lucky in my Chief and Indian stable-mate, and I had taken part in the L.G.'s state progress through the district. Most of my work had been out-of-doors, and great had been the delight of the early-morning rides across fields of young wheat "incredibly green". I had lived in breeches and gaiters, and of society so-called I had been "selfishly but blessedly free". So back to Lahore I went, still unfledged and not yet much interested in my work, but slightly more acclimatised to my surroundings.

CHAPTER 2

Interlude

THE Lahore I returned to in March was all roses, and its dust-laden air scented with the fragrance of orange blossom. Less attractive was the examination before me. Four subjects—language, judicial, revenue and treasury—had all to be passed by the higher standard before pay could rise from Rs. 400 to Rs. 500 a month, and powers as a magistrate from one month to two years' imprisonment. I decided to concentrate on the first three, and thanks to a fortnight's cramming and to merciful examiners, I managed to clear all three hurdles.

The climate recalled an English June, but, as April approached, there was something sinister about it. "Since yesterday", says a letter, "we have been living in a perpetual dust-storm and today, with a yellow fog outside, I had to call for a lamp at 3 o'clock." My diary records what followed a week later:

"Woken up at 6.15 to find the room rocking violently—realised it was an earthquake, seized my clock from the mantelpiece, which swayed perilously and lay in bed watch in hand. The shock lasted about a minute, during which it was very violent, feeling like the motion of an express train on a bad permanent way. Nothing actually fell in my room, but the revolving bookcase with 180 books swayed and creaked horribly. I was not surprised as nothing surprises me in this country. Nor was I nervous, since with no experience of earthquakes I did not know whether it was an unusual one or not. For an hour afterwards there were repeated shocks, but far less violent. The experience made me feel quite stupid all day with just a taste of sea-sickness."

At breakfast I was told I had been a fool to stay put; I ought to have dashed out into the open at once in case the house collapsed, as happened to a number in the city, killing thirty or forty people. Part of one I saw later, "half palace, half castle", was completely wrecked. Though oddly expressed there was truth in a wire sent from Lahore—"Here earth quack bad, how there?" But this was nothing to the fate of Dharamsala, a well-known hill station some fifteen miles away. In less than a minute it was wiped out with the loss of many thousand lives. Three members of my Service were amongst the victims. One of them was due to leave for England the next day; another left a wife of twenty-one. Terrible were the tales we heard later from those who were there.

With the examination behind me, I was allowed a week's leave to enable me to accept an invitation to another part of the Punjab. This proved a delightful interlude and gave me my first sight of the Salt Range, the hills that divide the Punjab plain from the uplands of the north. There were to be great doings at Choa Saidan Shah, a lovely valley rich in orchard and wheat with the clearest of burns running through it. The Deputy Commissioner of the district was to entertain a party of guests there. That I was included amongst them was due to Dobson having been attached to the district.

We had gathered there for the annual cattle fair. On its last day the Deputy Commissioner, seated on a dais with the rest of us about him, and with two long lines of local notabilities tailing away from him, gave away the prizes. "The winners were haled before him, tall shy men of the soil, understanding little of ceremony and obeisance. Police officers caught them by the arm and dragged them to the table to have their ten or twenty rupees thrust into their hands." A florid poem singing everyone's praises and three cheers for the King Emperor, the Deputy Commissioner and the Sub-Divisional Officer brought the proceedings to an end.

In the afternoon came the local sports and games. Our dozen pink-and-white faces were lost in a vast ring of fifteen to twenty thousand brown ones. "Every tree groaned with these gay plumaged creatures, and the hillsides shone with them." Competitors had come from the valleys and villages around to try their prowess. Strong, supple and bronzed, with no more than a cloth around the hips, they became all arms and legs as they tumbled each other in the dust, and at the end of each bout the victor leapt into the air with a shout of triumph and waved his victim's turban to the wind. At the final throw the spectators sprang to their feet and raced cheering across the arena in a cloud of dust to greet the victor. Against that background of hills, as bare as those of Greece, there was something "strange, beautiful and exciting about it all", with even an echo, however faint, of preparation for the Olympic Games of old.

The grand finale was the tent-pegging, heralded by a march-past of some thirty cavaliers "with lance erect and steed jingling with bells". Down they swooped in turn, with lance poised low, and cries of 'In the name of God'—'For God and Ali'* followed, if the lance rose tipped with the peg, by a shout from ten thousand throats of "shahbash—shahbash—bravo". Dobson was starter and afterwards wondered that he still lived "with these 30 fellows around him on prancing horses, swinging their lances round their heads in sheer keenness to be off".

The Salt Range is essentially a Muslim tract, and the day's doings had shown the peasant of the northern Punjab—often more soldier than farmer—at his gayest. But Hindu India also claimed a part in the week's doings, and characteristically a religious part. Not far from Choa are the seven temples of Kitas, 'standing on ground made holy, even in the semi-mythic days of the Pandovas, by a crystal stream which gushes out of the stony soil into a pool reputed by the devout to be bottomless, but actually 23 feet deep'.†

It was to bathe in this pool that once a year pilgrims in their thousands flocked there from near and far. It was a stirring sight to see pilgrim and peasant, winding up the hillside turbaned in red, pink, magenta or gold, many on horseback, others with wife and children in great baskets lashed to the backs of camels, and all moving slowly upwards in a cloud of sunlit dust. At Kitas, on the great day of the pilgrimage, all eyes were upon the procession of naked fakirs on their way to the sacred pool, their bodies powdered with ash, their hair matted and coiled, and many of them without even a loin-cloth. And since all processions like to attract attention, they were led by devotees leaping corybantically into the air, slashing at one another with their swords and parrying the counter-thrusts on small wooden shields.

My last evening at Choa I strolled down the valley below it through a glade of willows in their first spring green, where to the song of birds there flowed a limpid stream leaping from rock to rock, sometimes even playing at being a waterfall. It gave me keen delight "to feel once more the 'beauty born of murmuring sound' ". And with that sound in my ears I returned to Lahore ready to face my first hot weather.

* Ali was the son-in-law of the Prophet and a great warrior.

† *Wisdom and Waste in the Punjab Village*, p. 54, by the writer.

CHAPTER 3

First Post

LITTLE did I know what I was in for. In England I had naturally heard that India was a hot country, but even England had its heat waves and I had not found them unbearable. What I had never imagined was a heat wave lasting the best part of six months. As month followed month, one existed but hardly lived. The needs of the body were paramount: how to keep it cool and dry? how to vary its fare and slake its thirst? how to protect it from bite and sting and let it sleep undisturbed?

In those days – we were still in 1905 – there were no electric fans. One had to make do with a punkah swung to and fro over one's head at a pace varying from tempest to dead calm, as shouts to the punkah-coolie rose or fell. The motor-car, too, had not yet arrived to whirl one to and from office or court in the blinding sunlight. Nor until many years later was the icebox displaced by the frig. And undreamt of was an air-conditioned room. In short, many were the days when one could have exclaimed with Moses: "Would God it were even, and at even, would God it were morning."

Of a day in June my diary said – "hot as hell – like Dives we are 'in torments' ". A letter describes what "in torments" meant. "Come here now (it says), 114 in the shade, 92 last night in the verandah at 1 a.m.; come and writhe on a bed – come and toss down peg after peg and still rage with thirst – come and sit in a closed-up room from 9 till 5: go out at 2 and feel the air like a hot iron to your face." Surprisingly, after all that has just been said, the letter goes on to say – "I am enjoying my life much more than I could have thought possible 6 months ago."

There is not much of interest to record about my work during this period. I sat in Court for many hours a day, and like the tribunes of Coriolanus I often wore out "a good wholesome forenoon" (and more) in hearing petty cases and was all too often obliged to "rejourn the controversy of three-pence to a second day of audience",* often indeed to a third or fourth. Witnesses did

* *Coriolanus* (II. i. 77)

not turn up or a summons was not served in time; or, as happened in one case, the accused lost his mother and had to be allowed to go home and bury her.

Most cases were of petty theft—a lamb, a sheaf of corn or a tree had disappeared. A very human case was that of a son accused by his father of striking him "and generally making a mess of the 5th commandment". But after five minutes of gentle remonstrance from the Court they left "in tears and almost in each other's arms".

May 9th was marked by my first sentence of imprisonment—eight days for petty theft. It was not until over two months later that I gave anyone more than this, though early in June, when I was still only twenty-four, my powers as a magistrate had been raised from one to six months' imprisonment.

Sitting in Court day after day was about as bad an introduction to India as could be imagined. Sometimes I seemed to have before me nothing but lying witnesses and long-winded pleaders bent on making the worse appear the better reason and using every kind of legal sophistry for the purpose. There were moments, too, when complainant, accused, pleader, munshi and chaprassi all talked to me at once.

No more encouraging was my first glimpse of democracy at work in the East. It was also my first experience of trying to manage a crowd, and not a very successful one. It was towards the end of April and the occasion was a Municipal election in Lahore. Two of us were put in charge of a ward in the heart of the city. The votes had to be recorded in a room facing a small square but divided from it by a porch and an iron gate. When we arrived at 7.30 a.m. a mob of four or five hundred were already there, all apparently thirsting to vote, and only thirteen policemen to keep them in check. The police did what they could with their two-thonged whips, but the crowd was continually bursting through them and making for the iron gate. We sent for more police, but they were of little use. They had their frenzied moments lashing out to right and left, but only to relapse into groups and chat with each other and the crowd. The whole affair ended with 400 out of 2,000 votes having to be disallowed for impersonation.

Early in July cholera broke out in the city, and 2,000 wells had to be disinfected. I was allotted 600. From well to well I went accompanied by a Municipal Commissioner to deal with domestic difficulties, an orderly to handle the disinfectant, and two watermen to pour it into the wells, one a Muslim, the other a Hindu—a very necessary arrangement in a country where neither Hindu nor Muslim would drink water from the other.

At 6.30 a.m. eight mornings running we foregathered at the Delhi Gate, and then for three or four hours we went from well to well, penetrating "alleys, courtyards, palaces, outhouses and private rooms". The heat was stifling, but how refreshing "to come back and toss down 3 iced ginger-beers". We did about seventy wells a day with ninety-five on the last. Thanks to the sun, greatest of purifiers, and to the general absence of glass windows, there was hardly a smell, though humans, buffaloes and goats were all herded together. On one of our rounds we came to a house with two massive wooden doors. "We knocked and knocked till they slowly began to move on their hinges, and as they swung wide there appeared a little girl reaching up to just above my knee, as nature made her, half wonderingly scratching her chin with the tiniest of fingers. It was a picture for an artist."

Perhaps the worst week of the hot weather is the one just before the rain breaks. Temperatures are not so high, but the moisture in the air adds to the torment. On this occasion the rains were overdue and the moist heat was such that the Government House swimming bath was the only place where one could be perfectly comfortable.

One evening—it was Monday, July 10—a number of us were at dinner in the Club with a distant rumble of thunder in our ears and with lightning playing among the trees around us, when there was a sound of wind in the branches; another dust-storm, we exclaimed, and door and window were closed at once. "It had been a very hot day and now we were without a breath of air. Suddenly there came a strange sound, not of wind, and with a cry of 'the rains at last' all were up from their seats, the doors were flung open—no waiting for servants—and there rushed in a noise of many waters and the fragrance of a re-awakening earth."

For me that was the end of the hot weather; two days later I received a wire ordering me to Dalhousie, the most beautiful of the Punjab's hill stations.

* * *

At Dalhousie I was to take the place of N. H. P., the Sub-

Divisional Officer in charge of the hill station, who had suddenly gone down with enteric.

Dalhousie was not entirely new to me. In June I had been allowed to go there for a short respite from the heat. Ten days had followed of intense delight. Intoxication began with the first draught of mountain air, inexpressibly refreshing after the heat and dust of Lahore. With it came the exhilarating sound of rushing water, followed by a bathe in a pool into which a torrent leapt frothing; and then, at the long journey's end, there was the sight of mountains rising in giant steps to a chain of snow peaks touching 21,000 feet. More modest, but not less penetrating in its charm, was the fragrance of walnut, fir and pine; and, after living for months in bungalows built to shut out great heat, what a change it was to throw windows open to sunshine and air.

In those pre-motor-car days the journey to this demi-paradise was a twenty-hour affair. A train which ran along what is now part of the frontier between India and Pakistan took one to the foot of the Himalayas. There, towards midnight, one boarded a tonga drawn by two ponies. These were driven at such speed that they had to be changed every fifty minutes, and with such violent alternations of pace—from trot to gallop, from gallop to trot—that again and again one was wrenched from sleep. By four-thirty the forty miles to Dunera had been covered. One was off again at eight, this time in a rickshaw with four coolies to pull and push one up the remaining twenty-three-mile ascent to Dalhousie's 7,000 feet. The last eight miles I walked to keep warm, and on arrival at the Commissioner's bungalow, where I was to stay, a fire, which had seemed incredible the day before, was more than welcome.

Next day I became Sub-Divisional Officer,* Dalhousie (S.D.O. for short), but only till N. H. P. recovered. I owed my luck as the chosen stopgap to the shortage of I.C.S. officers available at the moment. Three had perished in the Dharmsala earthquake, and three more had died unexpectedly in the last six months. The post was coveted for its climate by those sufficiently junior to be offered it, especially by the married who would otherwise have been separated from their families by the heat below. Professionally it had little, if any, importance, but for me at twenty-four there was sweetness in its novelty and comparative independence.

* So called because for administrative purposes Dalhousie was a Sub-Division of a District (Gurdaspur).

I was now not only a magistrate but also in charge of the local Treasury and Vice-President of the Municipal Committee. Of treasury and municipal work I knew nothing, and it was typical of such training as I got that my formal treasury training came only some months later. With the help, however, of the Treasurer, a clerk who knew the Treasury Manual backwards, I managed to scrape through the next two months without blotting my copybook.

My first job was to count the treasury's contents: the cash alone came to 1¾ lakhs of rupees (about £12,000).* The following day I was on my way to kutcherry followed by a chaprassi—I now had two, both in scarlet—when I was met by a police constable who with a salute said curtly: 'A lakh and a half of rupees (£10,000) has arrived.' Hurrying to the Treasury I found a force of police sitting at ease on fifty boxes of cash. This had of course to be counted, fortunately not rupee by rupee but by weighing bags of a thousand against one counted in detail. Payments into the Treasury could be embarrassing. One morning when I was still in bed—it was a holiday with the Treasury closed—I was brought 6,000 rupees in notes. These sums, which looked large to the eyes of a tiro, were relatively small. Later in the year when I was in charge of the Lahore Treasury, I found myself responsible for the equivalent of £60,000.

As Vice-President of the Municipal Committee I had its secretary at my elbow to keep me straight. Owing to the absence of the Deputy Commissioner, who was President, I had to take the chair at my first meeting. The Committee consisted of men nearly twice my age—amongst them the Civil Surgeon and a retired colonel. My first appearance was inglorious. 'Have you the files?' I was asked. My heart sank—I had left them behind. "In a moment I was on my pony hurtling homewards along the Mall and back again." All went well. But at the end of the meeting the Colonel, who had been talking non-stop, said: "There was just one more point—he had noticed how recklessly some people rode along the roads. Confusion of the Vice-President."

The municipal work was petty enough but at least it was varied. Everything had to be seen to—roads, bridges, hydrants, drains, and with a rainfall of 90 inches even trees, lest they fell on somebody's house or on a passer-by. A major task was the lighting of the station, till then without a flicker of light at night. Here the

* In those days a lakh was worth £6,666.

great question was—where should the 150 lamp-posts be placed, and how tall should they be, 11 feet or 10? A letter describes one of my busiest days: 1,700 bank notes counted; the rebuilding of the bazaar, much damaged by the Dharmsala earthquake, considered; a transport contractor interviewed to find out for the military—Dalhousie was a military hill station—how many mules, camels and coolies would be available in an emergency. In addition, endless letters, bills and cheques had to be signed, entries in huge treasury ledgers to be initialled and columns of figures added. "I am not very good at this and make mistakes of thousands which are very happily discovered at once. How many remain I don't know."

Fortunately there were days when I could eat my lunch at leisure. But, "alas (says a letter), my reputation is gone. I had Keats with me in Court today, and he was lying on the table when a subaltern came in for money from the treasury, and as he waited, he saw the book and looking inside, exclaimed—'Poetry, by Gosh!' "

It might rain for days, but sooner or later, generally at sunset, the sun would break through the towering clouds and light up the distant snows; and at our feet, far away below, the Punjab plain would reappear brilliant in purple and green, with three rivers sliding out of the valleys like snakes from their lairs. The vastness of the scene was awe-inspiring, and the splendour of colour and light so overwhelming that the feeling it aroused was "almost pain".

But nature had her adagio as well as her maestoso moods. One such a letter describes: "Yesterday was a holiday and I had a glorious walk with a coolie to carry my tea, and a couple of books in my pocket, Homer in one and Daudet in the other. It was an exquisite day with white clouds pouring through the woods and over the ridges above, or lying anchored in the ravines below. The air, too, was full of bird-song and the sound of running water. It was not till 7 o'clock that I reached the upper pastures, 9,000 feet high, where the buffaloes grazed. My coolie proved a sociable fellow. I asked him what was his idea of God: 'Is he a big man?' 'Yes.' 'Has he hands?' 'No one has seen him, but perhaps.' Then he wanted to know how much did it cost to go to England and back? Were there any 'black folk' there? and did I send any money to my family? What, too, was my pay? He thought I walked very quickly and was '*bara achha admi*' (a very nice man) because I talked to him."

That was a lovely spot, and if there before breakfast, one met merry-faced hill-men and women coming down the hill with the morning's milk on their heads, the men clad in sheepskin coats open at the chest, corded at the waist, and stopping short at the knee. They were different from the men of the plains: they had their own tongue, and a more human climate had given them a cheerful attitude towards life.

N. H. P. had now recovered. So most regretfully I returned to Lahore, well aware, however, of my luck in having escaped two months of its hot weather.

CHAPTER 4

A Cold Weather in Lahore

I WAS now becoming acclimatised to my new world. I had met some fifty of my fellow Civilians and been impressed by their ability and sang-froid. At Dalhousie I had seen something of the Army and found them "exceptionally fine fellows", though with a very different background from my own and some of them too absorbed perhaps in regimental life. I had tasted the gaiety and frivolity of Anglo-Indian society; and the death in those few months of six fellows I had known—two of them during my absence from Lahore— had shown me its tragic side. Were they not even to some extent connected? In one respect I still had everything to learn—I was still grossly ignorant of the people and the country.

I soon settled down again, once more at the Punjab Club. This time I shared a room with Gerard Wathen, a lively and charming Epicurean who threw himself as whole-heartedly into his work as into the gaieties of Lahore. He was on the staff of the local Government College and was even newer to India than myself. It made all the difference to me to be living with someone of about my own age and background, who had much the same interests as I had. It was the beginning of a friendship which lasted until his death in 1958.

The first event of the season was Lord Curzon's visit. The struggle with Lord Kitchener over Defence had ended in his defeat and resignation, and he was now awaiting his successor, Lord Minto's arrival. Wathen and I were among the many officials who had to go and meet him at the station. The scene was a brilliant one, with everyone but ourselves, so it seemed, in uniform. I was in a mere frock-coat, that too borrowed from a tailor, since mine had not yet arrived from England. The train came in and Curzon emerged, "his plump rosy cheeks beaming with health". There followed a vision of loveliness which remains with me to this day. It was Lady Curzon, and I suddenly realised why the Greeks had besieged Troy for so many years.

That evening at a Government House dinner the wife of one of our Judges told Curzon, as she related to me later, that she had a son who could not make up his mind whether to try for the Home or the Indian Civil Service. Which would he advise? He was emphatically for the Indian, believing that in India whatever good a man had in himself must sooner or later show itself, whereas at home it may for ever lie buried in office drawers and paper baskets. Moreover, since we do not know why we exist and what becomes of us, the only reason of existence must be to do good, and where can that better be done than in India?

Sight-seeing took Curzon to the Fort with an entourage headed by the L.G., who followed him about muttering 'damned rot'. Coming to the now well-known Pearl Mosque, which was being used by the garrison for some purpose or other, he asked the L.G. what it was. Sir Charles had not the least idea, nor had anyone else when asked in turn. Finally, all impatience, Curzon went up to the British sentry on guard and said—'Can *you* tell me what it is?' 'Indu mosque, sir,' was the cockney reply. The incident had the happy result of making officialdom take a more enlightened interest in the remains of Mogul rule in Lahore.

But the great event of the season was the visit of Their Royal Highnesses, the Prince and Princess of Wales, later to become King George the Fifth and Queen Mary. Amongst the celebrations there was to be an evening fête at the Shalamar Gardens near Lahore. It was to be a most splendid occasion and an opportunity for the citizens of Lahore to share in the celebrations. The famous Mogul Gardens with their fountains and marble pavilions were to be illuminated with 1,000 Chinese lanterns and 250,000 "little lamps". The cost was put at nearly £3,000 and subscriptions were invited to meet it. It was my job to collect them and allot tickets to subscribers. "1,800 lie thick upon my table. There are red tickets and there are pink tickets, there are yellow and there are green, and now 200 blue have just come in. Of the making of tickets there is no end."

As time was short I started giving them out on my own responsibility, believing, with no orders to the contrary, that I was at liberty to do so. Discovering what I was doing, Mr X., the Deputy Commissioner, took over all the arrangements and left me to carry them out. The original scheme had been to allot tickets and enclosures according to the amount subscribed. This was both simple and fair. But it overlooked a vital point — the importance attached in India to position and rank. For example, was a wealthy trader who had subscribed largely to be more considered than an aristocrat or dignitary who had subscribed much less? On this point aristocratic and democratic principles suddenly clashed. Alarmed at the trouble to be expected if he did obeisance to the one at the expense of the other, Mr X. decided at the eleventh hour to trim. His first step was to tell me to tabulate the subscribers according to their subscriptions. As they numbered about 4,000 this was not a thing of a moment.

All this led to four most strenuous days. The first kept me at work from 8 a.m. to 8 p.m., with two short breaks for meals and three more hours of work after dining out. The second day was worse. Again I was at it the whole day with only half an hour for breakfast and ten minutes for lunch. At 8.30 p.m., after a two-hour Committee meeting, I dined with Mr X. It was the only time he ever asked me to a meal, and he only did so at ten minutes to eight, and then solely to discuss the ticket problem after dinner. But I had first to accompany him to an Indian theatre for a performance in his honour. After watching it for an hour, we went into a small room, where five of us — Mr X., three Indians and myself — sat round a table and pored over the newly tabulated list of subscribers to decide who was sufficiently important to be given special consideration. At 1 a.m. an Indian drove me home, not to sleep but to work out the re-allotment. He left me at three "half staggering with sleep". I went on till seven-thirty, when I changed from dress into day clothes. It was now the third day, but I shall spare the reader further details. Suffice it to say that it was not till 6.30 p.m. on the fourth day that I gave out the last ticket — the last of over 4,000.

A few weeks later X. got his knife into me again. I was in temporary charge of the Lahore Treasury and gave my Head Clerk leave to go and see his mother who was dying. Since he was under me and was to be away only five days, it never occurred to me that I was not entitled to do this. When X. discovered this, he sent me a peremptory note through an Indian in a subordinate service, asking me under what authority I had acted and what pains I had taken to verify it. I could but acknowledge my mistake. It was the way he pointed it out that upset me. "Any gentleman would have told me privately."

The Royal Visit had its lighter side. I was deputed to go to the station on behalf of Government and meet the Nawab of Maler Kotla. The Nawab was the head of a small state in the heart of the Punjab and was coming to Lahore to pay his respects to Their Royal Highnesses. Arrayed in a frock-coat (this time my own), I was driven to the station in the neatest of victorias. There, on a platform spread with red carpet I found a number of State officials assembled to greet His Highness. A letter describes what followed. "The special steamed in and in a moment the place hummed with officials in gorgeous uniforms of red and gold. I was rushing forward to welcome one more gorgeous than the rest thinking he must be the Nawab, when a yet more gorgeous one appeared and yet another, and still not the Nawab. At last a slight insignificant little man hopped out of the royal coach wearing a dirty white collar, scarlet tie, frock-coat, and grey flannel shirt hanging out in front, with tight-fitting trousers to complete the entente between East and West. This was His Highness. I expressed a hope that his health was good, and with that we walked to the most magnificent coach you ever saw—exquisite red satin cushions, heavy gold tassels, vast burnished lamps—4 horses of course and postillions, 2 flunkeys standing up behind, and the portliest and lordliest of attendants seated high up between them. We entered this equipage, and as it rolled away, a mounted escort saluted and fell in behind with flashing sabres. At our side rode an A.D.C. and in front 8 mounted men. During the long drive through the town His Highness was pleased to remark that the dust was much as usual and that probably a great many had come to see the Prince. At his house a guard of honour was present to receive him. Inside I was motioned to a chair and the Vizier, the Foreign Secretary, and the Commander-in-Chief were summoned to be presented. We spoke gravely to each in turn, expressing our hope that they were all as well as their royal master, and with that they retired. A most wonderful man in pink satin embroidered with gold stood at the door, bearing in his hand a scimitar of enormous length — was he perhaps Eunuch in Ordinary to His Highness? But I judged it best not to enquire."

For me the sight of the week was the Review of 5,000 troops with the Head of each State attached to the Punjab leading past his contingent. First came the Maharaja of Patiala, a boy of fourteen looking most engaging in his blue turban, with a sword flashing in his hand and 500 Lancers behind him. Last, and most moving, came the venerable Raja of Nabha, bowed with age and mounted on a splendid charger. He was too weak to carry a sword, and a withered arm was raised to salute the Prince. They all came past at a trot, the camels gliding along in perfect time to 'The Keel Row'. The climax came when the 500 Lancers thundered past *ventre-à-terre*. There was "a distant roar, a cloud of dust, a flash of tearing chargers, and a noise that shook the earth. For a moment war seemed the most splendid thing in the world."

In Court the monotony of false evidence and long-winded pleadings was seldom varied by an interesting case. Two are perhaps worth mentioning. In the first a Maulvi* of some repute had abducted a girl, but when pressed had returned her to her husband. The husband, however, was not satisfied and prosecuted him. This caused a stir, and my Court was thronged for the hearing with members of the husband's *biradari*;† amongst them his aged father, eighty-five years old, "a man with fine features, a white beard and a red cloak". It was essentially a case for settlement out of Court. But the father, speaking as head of the family, said he was an old old man, and he had been outraged before the whole biradari, and the biradari had been outraged, and the biradari was of a thousand men. As he spoke, he tottered and clutched hold of the railing between us. At last it was agreed that the Maulvi should apologise before the biradari in their village. The following Sunday I drove out to it and found the villagers of all ages gathered there. A space was cleared and I sat down with the audience forming a large circle round me. I then discovered that the biradari would not allow the compromise. On the contrary, "they shouted for the Maulvi's blood". I had the six elders of the biradari singled out and placed before me. I talked to them, argued with them, and even appealed to them on religious grounds. I said vengeance was God's, and finding this was in the Koran, I said it was in our holy book too, and between the two of them, it must be right. They agreed with all I said, then added: "Just as God sent his prophets of old to tell the people of his ways so now he has sent you to do us justice in his name." But the justice they demanded was the old Mosaic law—'Eye for eye, tooth for tooth', so back to

* One learned in the Muslim scriptures.

† Literally 'brotherhood', i.e. the tie between members of the same sub-caste.

Court the case had to come, with what result is unfortunately not recorded.

In the second case Mr C., an English pleader of fourteen years' standing, thought he had been insulted by Mr O., an Indian pleader of only six months' standing, and lodged a complaint against him. I suggested to Mr C. that he should accept the apology which Mr O. was perfectly prepared to give. But honour was at stake and he declined. His statement, a very long one, which I duly took down, only showed that Mr O. had been a "little exuberant and indiscreet". I asked Mr C. once more to accept the apology. His reply was to hand me a slip of paper on which he wrote 'Mr O. is a liar'. After some further discussion I took each in turn into my inner room; then bringing them together I somehow managed to effect a reconciliation, and this they clinched by shaking hands in open Court.

Throughout one's service in India the siren voices of flattery were ever in one's ears. In Court they found very varying expression. On one occasion it was to be called 'not a magistrate but a priest'. On another, it was to receive a petition beginning 'O spanking enormity', and ending 'I have only God and Your Honour to help me in this matter'.

Early in January, with all examinations passed, I was made a Justice of the Peace and invested with the powers of a first-class magistrate. I could now jail offenders for two years, have them whipped and fine them Rs. 1,000 (£67). I could also try Europeans but not give them more than three months' imprisonment. Financially I had nothing to complain of: even in Lahore I could live on my pay as long as I kept only one horse and did not play polo.

Such were social conditions in India sixty years ago that it was a full year before I had my first talk with an educated Indian who was not an official, and even then it came by chance. One day in December I had to inspect four factories at some distance from Lahore. After the last inspection the manager of the factory, a broad-minded young Hindu called Behari Lall, came to the station to see me off. While waiting for the train, we sat down on the platform with peasants thronging respectfully round us and discussed religion. Why, he asked, should Indians mind missionaries making Hindus Christians? Every man, he said, had the right to think what he pleased. With marriage, too, what was wanted in

India, he declared, was what the Japanese had done: a Christian marries a Buddhist, and they don't think twice about it. As to English and Indian, he deplored the social gulf and wished Indians could be treated with a little more consideration. Only two days before an elderly European at the Club had told me that Englishman and Indian could never meet as equals—a very common view in those days, and for many years to come.

Three weeks later I had to visit Behari Lall's factory again: a man's arm had been wrenched off by a machine and I had to report on the accident. Once more we talked, this time sitting in front of his house in a large courtyard, where bullocks, buffaloes and pye-dogs, and even a monkey were basking in the sun. Referring to my difficulties in Court, he admitted that witnesses told lies but said, a little optimistically, we should 'elevate' them. In reply to a question he declared that Indians admired love rather than strength. "I instinctively feel (says a letter written on the spot) that the natives are more sensitive to this than Europeans, and far more so than they are given credit for!" This was true, and later on I came to realise more fully the desire, almost the craving, of the educated for a more sympathetic attitude towards them; and the word 'sympathetic' was used in the warm sense of the Italian *simpatico*. They were quick too to detect any touch of hollowness in such sympathy as was offered them. For example, of one Lieutenant-Governor, it was said, in a typical mixture of English and Hindustani—'affability bahut, magar true sympathy kichh nahin'—great affability, but of true sympathy not a jot.

About this time it must have occurred to some sensible person that an odd day in the country on a special mission was not the best way for getting to know the people and their language. Accordingly, in February I was sent out to tour for a week or so and told to keep a diary of all that struck me as I rode from one place to another. On my return the diary was sent up to the Financial Commissioner and earned me the only pat on the back—a very light one—given me by Mr X. I have no copy of the diary but two letters give some account of the tour.

I marched over 100 miles in six days looking at—I can hardly say inspecting—schools, hospitals, Government buildings, Land Records and anything else of that kind that lay on my route, with a criminal case or two thrown in for good measure. At Sharaqpur, a town of some 5,000 inhabitants and the headquarters of a tehsil, after having a look at the Treasury, slaughter house and public gardens, I had to examine the Municipality's finances and discuss with the leading inhabitants a new drainage scheme to cost £1,000. That evening, standing in the verandah of the dark bungalow, I had gathered in front of me thirty or forty of them in long flowing robes and white turbans, shining with a ghostly radiance in the light of a half-moon. The scheme involved a fresh tax and I tried to persuade them that it was worth paying "for the glory of a clean-swept town". That merely led to a general clamour that with a fresh tax their trade would disappear. After half an hour of this I stopped the flow of protest and said, somewhat despotically, I fear, 'This is the order of Government—it is for your good, and we must obey, you and I'—and with that they went.

The discussion and its outcome were an example in miniature of what I had written to a friend—that Government in India was "a paternal bureaucracy based on despotism and run by democrats".

What I enjoyed more was talking with the peasants: "the gulf did not seem so wide then". It was my first opportunity of doing so and the beginning of a love and interest which are with me still. Earlier in the year in Jhang I was too new to the country and too tongue-tied to make any contact with them. But now, day after day, I was in the saddle amongst them, one day for nearly seven hours. Many of them were "great burly fellows of six feet or more, simple cheerful folk, ready to laugh at any joke broad enough for them to understand, and taking kindly to any interest shown in them". All too flattering, too, was the murmur "of awe and admiration" that burst (on one occasion) from the lips of a dozen peasants gathered round me when, after some conversation, I told them I was an "Ishtant Commissioner Sahib" as they called Assistant Commissioners. It was like the 'ah' that bursts from a crowd when the first rocket of a firework display speeds hissing into the night. 'Wonder and satisfaction' rather than 'awe and admiration' would perhaps have better described their feelings, wonder at such a stripling being set over them, and satisfaction that he was interested in their doings. However this may be, there was in those days an instinctive veneration for authority, springing from both hope and fear, hope for its favour and fear of its power.

The peasants were longing for rain to save the spring harvest from blight, and my last night on tour down it came, adding thousands of rupees to the value of their crops. Their beaming faces the next morning were a delight. But Providence, I comment, must be in something of a quandary at times with the grain merchants, "praying all they know" that the drought may continue and the peasants doing the reverse.

Till then the irrigation wells had been at work night and day, and throughout my tour the melody of the Persian wheels rotating their strings of earthenware buckets had been in my ears. Writing one evening, I note that "It is the only sound that comes in through the open door, besides the random bark of a pye-dog: it is the very music of the East—a low continuous moan, almost a dirge, a feeling of suppressed pain, relentless, ceaseless, the kind of chant to come floating across the water from a ship of galley-slaves. There is something grinding in it, yet there is melody, and it is the mixture of the two that fascinates. Wherever you go you hear it: it is the sound that lulls you to sleep, the note that mingles with your waking dreams; in the hot weather, when the air is parched and nature breathless, when you toss on your bed and there is not a sound but this, it is uncanny—it must have driven many mad." That was long before the earthen pot had been generally replaced by one of unmusical metal.

The most interesting place I visited on this tour was Nankana Sahib, where in 1469 Guru Nanak, the saintly founder of the Sikh religion, was born. As one keenly interested in the influence of climate and environment on religion, I was anxious to see the country in which he had grown up, the more so that "in those days man was 'cribbed, cabined and confined'* much more so then he is now". What I saw was a country as desolate and featureless as I had ever seen, perfectly flat, the soil a dull grey clay. Here and there were patches of green, tiny threads winding in and out of the bush where a canal had come, but 450 years ago there could not have been even that. Was it, perhaps, because the gentle Nanak felt the harshness of man's life in such surroundings so acutely that he bade men turn inward and treat all with humility, sincerity and love?

Back I came to Lahore, eager, says a letter, to get to know the peasants and, if possible, to get into touch with educated opinion. For the latter I had to wait, for I was under orders to take charge of a remote Sub-Division on the borders of Sind. But the peasant I should see at his simplest.

* More correctly, 'cabin'd, cribb'd, confin'd'.

"One man I shall miss, my chaprassi, Sultan Ahmed. He is most strangely devoted to me. In camp he would never leave my threshold till I had gone to bed; once only he did so, and that by order, and then he crept away like a dog with his tail between his legs." On another occasion he arrived on duty late. So I kept him on duty longer than usual. Before he left, I explained that this was a punishment. 'It is not a punishment (he said); it is the Sahib's kindness.'

Part II
POWER

CHAPTER 5

Rajanpur – On my own*

'Do you feel fitted to govern Rajanpur?' asked a letter from A. C.? '*Du lieber Himmel*,' I replied, 'I cannot rule myself.' I was only just twenty-five, and a young twenty-five at that, and largely untrained. I had some superficial knowledge of Urdu but none of the two languages spoken in my kingdom – Baluchi and Jhatki – and I was to be so remote from authority that, as the Chief Secretary told me in Lahore, 'You will practically be your own D.C.'†

My kingdom was a strip of country roughly 100 miles long and 30 wide, wedged in between the Indus to the east and the Suleman hills of Baluchistan to the west, and at its southern extremity touching Sind. Technically it was a Sub-Division of Dera Ghazi Khan, the Punjab's only trans-Indus district, but in size, variety and work it was totally different from the Sub-Division I had had brief charge of at Dalhousie. Though so large in area, its population was no more than 100,000. An interesting element in it was the Baluchi tribesmen who had spilt into it from Baluchistan. Two tribes, Mazari and Drishak, had actually settled in the Sub-Division each under its Tumandar or Chief, both of whom, though technically under the Sub-Divisional Officer (S.D.O. for short), were allowed a relatively free hand in the management of their tribal affairs. With a rainfall which averaged only 4 inches a year and sometimes gave but an inch, the Sub-Division was one of the Punjab's hottest and most arid tracts. In short, "it was bound to be a great experience and life will really have begun".

I left Lahore at 10 p.m., "wafted from the station by the salaams of my staff", amongst them "the never-to-be-forgotten Sultan Ahmed in tears". I arrived at the railhead next morning at mid-

* This and the four following chapters are based almost entirely on letters to my mother and two friends, and all quotations, unless otherwise indicated or obviously from another source, are from one or other of these letters.

† Short for Deputy Commissioner (the head of a District) and commonly used accordingly.

day. A nine-mile drive followed and brought me to the Indus. It was still in its winter sleep—the melting of the snows that fed it had not yet begun—and it was less than half a mile wide. Yet here was one of the world's most famous rivers, and to come upon it suddenly as I did gave me a thrill. We crossed it by a bridge of boats and on the farther shore entered Dera Ghazi Khan, the Headquarters of the district, beautifully situated but doomed three years later to be swallowed up by the river.

That afternoon I spent buying furniture and stores, and next day a bullock cart loaded with thirty-three articles set off for Rajanpur 72 miles away. I followed later in the day in a one-horse tonga with the driver astride on a shaft, and my faithful but incompetent bearer, curled up with his calf-less legs on my rifle behind. In 4½ hours, with only one change of horses, we did 30 miles. Another 42 followed the next day over a road at its best like a country track at home, at its worst like a badly ploughed field. And through what a country! A waste of bush and scrub, of sand and clay, broken only here and there by a field of wheat, with however one redeeming feature—the Hills of Solomon 20 miles away and never out of sight. In the last 40 miles we passed only three villages and not a hamlet in between. There were, however, travellers on the road very different from any I had seen before, fine black-bearded Baluchis with long curling hair, many of them ambling along on ponies with ears tipped inwards; strings of camels too, for this was part of the great camel country which stretched almost unbroken from the West Punjab through Iran, Iraq and North Africa to the shores of the Atlantic. Otherwise there was hardly a sign of life, and not a sound of birds.

The first sight of my new abode "chilled me to the bone". I thought that the drive had shown me the worst, but that was beautiful compared with the rows of bungalows and shops crumbling to ruin in silent streets, the wreckage of an abandoned cantonment. But a lovely evening sky made amends, and with nightfall the ugliness disappeared under the magic of moonlight. Even better was the warm welcome given me by Captain Nicolas, my predecessor, and his wife.

With their departure I was left with only one other white man in the station, indeed within 72 miles; and "his face is only white-ish" for he was born and bred in India. Cooper was in charge of Rajanpur's canals and had lived so long alone that he expressed himself with difficulty. "But (I noted) he is quiet and I think I shall like him." And I did. Yet since he had never been out of India and I had hardly been out of Europe, we had little in common and subjects of conversation, even the main one, his dog, were soon exhausted. It did not make matters easier that, when asked to dinner, he would stay until after eleven and only leave then because eight hours in kutcherry had reduced me to speechlessness, if not almost to sleep.

I was now Vice-President of two small Municipalities, chief magistrate and civil judge, head of the local Land Revenue staff, Superintendent of the Jail, and, above all, the representative of the British Raj standing on the lowest step of the long stairway leading through the Deputy Commissioner, Commissioner, and Lieutenant-Governor to the Viceroy himself.

I had arrived on a Saturday. On Sunday I rode through the chief bazaar "to see and be seen of my subjects: it was everywhere one profound salaam" with both hands raised "to shade the eyes from one's meretricious brilliance". Monday, work began with an inspection of the jail before breakfast. Built of mud bricks with walls thirty feet high, it was a very simple affair. In the centre stood a tower from which a sentry could command the whole enclosure. At the moment there were thirty-two prisoners serving sentences and twenty more waiting to be tried. Nothing could have been more cheerless—"not a plant anywhere, just the bare walls and the bare ground, and the glare awful".

Later I would occasionally pass the jail on my evening ride or walk. "Directly I am spied at the end of the road all is bustle—a rushing for arms, a fixing of bayonets, a girding up of loins as the eight constables of the guard and their Sergeant fall in before the iron-grated portal; and at the Sergeant's side the warders, and the head clerk blear-eyed and beer-barrelled, and then as I pass, the order—'Shoulder arms', and I gravely salute."

Other inspections followed during the week: the hospital—"everything very dirty"—the police quarters, and the gardens, three of them in my charge. One had a tank ten feet deep, obviously crying out to be turned into a swimming bath. And in due course it was, with a spring-board, and a thatched roof to shield it from the sun. It was fed from a well worked by a bullock, and close by stood an open pillared arbour overhung by a gigantic banyan tree. The transformation cost the garden fund £7. "It will keep the sahib in a good temper during the hot weather," says a light-hearted letter, "and I am sure all will agree that is cheap at the price." During the coming months it gave me hours of peace and delight.

My first Municipal Committee meeting was a very different affair from the Committee meetings at Dalhousie. It took place in an upper room with blue-washed walls. The eight Municipal Commissioners sat on two benches facing each other, with myself and a large square table at the upper end, and the Secretary in the middle "to bridge the linguistic gulf between us". The proceedings were in a mixture of Urdu and Punjabi. The Commissioners had plenty to say and I let them say it, as the best means of getting my own way. Not that much even so got done – in 2½ hours indeed little beyond fixing the school fees. At one point an old grey-beard rose from his seat and begged leave of the Presence to retire in order to say his prayers.

I had six clerks in my office, headed by a munshi. Pannu Lal had "a black beard and eyes which shrink from you yet seek you furtively when he thinks you are not looking" – rather like a cowed dog but "proud and inflammable". He dressed neatly and wore a black-and-white coat "cut like a frocker", white knee-breeches, a turban and putties. He is most courteous and never speaks unless spoken to. How he lived on his pay of £2. 7*s*. 6*d*. a month with four children, one of them at school and costing eighteen shillings a month, I could only guess.

In the Sub-Division the two most important officials under me were the Tahsildar and the Deputy Tahsildar. They were responsible for the complicated Land Revenue work of the Sub-Division. They were also magistrates, with lesser powers than myself; and under them was a large staff of village accountants called patwaris supervised by Kanungos. Each village had its Lambardar,* and each group of villages a Zaildar. There were more than two dozen of these. All this I mention to explain what "that mysterious word Government" meant in my territory.

My work was of the most varied character and extended from cases of murder to paying blood money for the dead bodies of dangerous animals brought into Court. My first payment on this account was five rupees for a wolf. There was a big post every day, which sometimes took two hours to dispose of – petitions for leave,

* Headman. The larger villages had more than one.

reports of investigations, fines to be imposed, diaries of subordinates to be read, damages to assess, new schemes to be considered and so forth. All this in the vernacular. The reports were read out to me by the munshi and I had to follow them as best I could. Often they involved some point which I did not understand and rules and regulations had to be looked up. The languages were my great initial difficulty. I could follow Urdu when well spoken and not "gabbled and garbled". Most of the peasantry spoke a mixture of Punjabi and Sindhi called Jhatki, but the two Baluch tribes in the Sub-Division spoke Baluchi.

Then there were my visitors. They alone could take up an hour or two after breakfast—lambardars, zaildars, officials, Municipal Commissioners, local notabilities—all with some complaint, claim or difficulty they wished to ventilate, press or discuss, and all to be sent away with the feeling that your one thought was of them. And they were not confined to the morning. One evening, after sitting all day in Court recording evidence in my first murder case—a girl of five had been strangled—I found fifty-seven people waiting in my garden to see me.

An important visitor was Sardar Drehan Khan, one of the two Baluch Tumandars or Chieftains nominally under me—a fine-looking man with a grey beard and enveloped in folds of white raiment in which he walked "at a pace of nearly one mile an hour". Unlike most visitors, he was no flatterer. On a second visit, after seeing my pony, he called it a most ill-looking beast, and looking round my room and seeing my books he said I should be as keen on horses as I was on them: a horse was a friend and required as much care as books. This was indeed pertinent advice to one who had never owned a horse before. He followed it up by suggesting it was time for me to be learning the language, by which as a Baluch he probably meant Baluchi. Of this I was well aware, but I had decided to learn Jhatki first. I have to confess I was glad when he went: he had in fact touched my vanity.*

One Sunday he came to see me with his uncle, with whom he had quarrelled. Refused some repairs to his house, the uncle had gone to live outside his nephew's jurisdiction and in doing so had put him to public shame. Now they wanted to have it out

* On my re-visiting Rajanpur thirty-three years later, he came to see me, a very old and impressive figure. Meanwhile he had done much for his tribesmen.

before me. The uncle was a venerable figure with a vast head, a long-flowing beard and sightless eyes, as it might have been Oedipus himself. He was full of his wrongs and talked long and loudly about them, "yet not without dignity". An hour's argument ended in the nephew agreeing to repair the house, and in the uncle agreeing to live in it.

Much the most remarkable of my visitors was Nawab Sir Bahram Khan, acting Tumandar* of the Baluch Mazari Tribe. He came forty miles to greet me and described the life of his tribesmen—"just like Genesis, moving about from one spot to another with their families and their flocks". I shall have more to say about him later.

The Baluchis with their fine appearance and Old Testament ways were the most fascinating element in my kingdom. There was "one great moment" when four Baluch elders, "black-bearded and robed in white with long dark curls falling from their heads", strode into Court "with so splendid a carriage that infected with their dignity, I held my head higher". A dispute had been submitted to them for consideration under a special Regulation.† This allowed cases governed by Baluch custom to be referred to a Jirga or Council of Elders, in criminal cases for determining innocence or guilt, in civil suits for ascertaining the facts, and in both to recommend what action should be taken. More will be said about the system in a later chapter. Abduction cases were not uncommon in this tract and could be dealt with in this way. One such ended in my passing the following order: "As to the woman, it is impossible for her to live in future with her husband. The accused (who had abducted her) shall either pay him 500 rupees in cash or give him one girl." The cash payment—the equivalent of £33. 6*s.* 8*d.*—represented the market value of a marriageable girl and had "quite a legal smack about it".

In later days this system came under fire from legal purists. It was at least an improvement on trial by ordeal, which in pre-British days was not uncommon in doubtful cases. 'The accused was put into water; a man standing by shot an arrow from a bow. If the accused could keep his head under water until a friend could run and bring back the arrow, his innocence was established; if not, he was guilty.'‡

* Chieftain of a Baluch tribe.

† The Frontier Crimes Regulation of 1901.

‡ Extract from an unpublished note by Sir James Penny, K.C.I.E., C.S.I.

I had now the powers of a first-class Magistrate. The sword of justice did not rust in my hands. A single day saw one offender sentenced to six months, another with a previous conviction to eighteen months, and two more to twenty stripes. Another week my chief work was settling civil disputes, mainly between lender and borrower. They commonly ended in both parties saying—'Your Honour is our lord — what is pleasing to him must be pleasing to us.' So I would allow 15 or 16 per cent interest instead of the 37 per cent always claimed, add the cost of the suit and then fix dates for payment by instalments spread generally over three to six months. This was my first contact with the problem of rural indebtedness, which many years later led to the writing of my first book.

The end of my first week found me writing: "I cannot understand why I like Rajanpur so much." Several reasons are given. "I am glad to have got away from the artificialities and conventions of civilisation. It is something, too, to be able to sit down to dinner in tennis shirt, white flannel trousers and a pair of shoes—socks given up as clearly barbarous. I also vastly prefer a plain dinner, with a good book or the letters of my friends, to the more cumbrous appurtenances of the Club. But why I like the change best is that, though the work seems quite interminable, it is full of responsibility and it is your own."

"I know (continues the letter just quoted) that the first impulse on starting a thing of this kind is to dream all kinds of things possible only to find that you are lucky if you have kept everything up to the standard which you found. I know too that there is a certain excitement in getting face to face with what must tax one's whole energies and powers; and now I know, whatever illusions I had before, that I was born to work and that one cannot be really happy without it."

"I used to hanker after that office in Whitehall (says another letter of about the same date) and do so still in my less cheerful moments. But then there would always be the top hat and frock-coat, and these are far more demoralising, worn day by day, than dining as I have described." In short, in little more than a week Rajanpur had done more to reconcile me to life in India than Lahore in a year.

Domestically I did not take long to settle down. I had moved into a bungalow (rent £1. 7*s*. 6*d*. a month) "and now with my books and pictures my room is almost charming. I have a large compound too with two or three splendid trees." My fare was of the simplest as shown by a cook's account which has survived. It runs thus for one day:

> Soup 1½*d.*; Fowl (anonymous) 4*d.*; Cooking butter 1*d.*; Eggs 2¼*d.* He (the cook) tells me I had a six-egg rumble-tumble (scrambled eggs) for breakfast!
>
> 22 days have elapsed—total of kitchen bills £1. 1*s.* 0¼*d.* With European stores (from outside) total for month should be £4.

This was very different from Lahore, and I was soon making my first investment. It was only £27, but I had become a capitalist.

To ensure a steady supply of milk I bought a goat—"a fine black and white fellow"—hardly perhaps the way to write of a lady—for nine rupees (twelve shillings). "Her chief duty will be to give me as much milk as I want and, like Ruth, to follow me wherever I go." A boy was also engaged to look after her on two rupees a month. When he was not attending upon his mistress, he was to help the cook to wash up. The goat's milk proved so much to my taste that, having hated pure milk all my life, I drank hers with pleasure. She was a friendly creature and one night looked in to see me at dinner. After prowling about and eating some toast, "she made for my bedroom, but this seemed hardly *comme il faut*, and I ordered her instant ejection." She bleats in such forlorn tones that "I think she must once have had 'une affaire du cœur'."

With the arrival of the Deputy Commissioner on tour, and encouraged by a cellar which held one bottle each of brandy, cherry-brandy, whisky and port, I ventured on my first dinner-party. With the Deputy Commissioner came the Irrigation Executive Engineer and his wife, and Cooper made a fifth. It was not a success. My machine for making soda water produced water "as flat as a girl's complexion after an all-night dance". The mutton was tepid, the pudding most ordinary. Worst of all three of my guests hardly opened their mouths except to eat. The Engineer* aired his views on canals but the D.C. was too sleepy to listen to them. Cooper in the presence of his chief hardly dared say a word. Mrs E. and I had enough to say to each other, "but a duet is dispiriting when it should be a quintet".

* He died suddenly two months later.

M. L. Waring, the Deputy Commissioner, was a Civilian of about eleven years' service. He must therefore have been round about thirty. He was clean-shaven with full-blown cheeks matching a generous figure, and with a temper always sunny and cheerful and a fine sturdy sense of humour. Yet less than a year had passed since the earthquake at Dharmsala had robbed him of both wife and child. From his invariable cheerfulness and good temper no one would have guessed this. It was only later that occasionally I caught a glimpse of the void left within.

By this time I had served under three Deputy Commissioners: one had treated me almost as an enemy; the other two had been civil but aloof. Waring was very different. In spite of his seniority and position, he treated me as an equal, and it was only in our official relations that he was the D.C. and I the S.D.O. "He listens to any plan I may have and generally encourages me to go further than I had dared." He was full of kindness and commonsense, and a touch of irony running through it gave it a savour of its own. "After X. I was prepared to like anyone, but Waring I should have liked anyhow." He believed that for our work in India character was more important than intellect; and that you get the best work out of a man if you left him to do his job with as little interference as possible. Altogether my relationship with him was of the pleasantest, and all the pleasanter for being so novel.

Very different was my tie with Jhoda, aged perhaps six. "He met me in the bazaar today (says a letter) and clawed hold of my finger. I was reminded of a reckless promise that I would give him some sweets. I gave my chaprassi 4 annas and told him to see what could be done with that. When I came out after a meeting of the Municipal Committee, I received quite an ovation from a throng of children of all ages and sizes!" A rumour that sweets were to be had had evidently got about. They accompanied me to my gates, with Jhoda still clawing my little finger. I picked out all under ten and told the rest to go home. There were still quite a number left. These I took into my bungalow and there poured an extraordinarily rich four-pennyworth into their hands." This was the first of frequent encounters.

One day I was writing a letter when the gardener approached with his evening offering of flowers on a leaf. " 'Salaam, Ditta,' I said. 'Huzoor, salaam.' 'It is a kind act, Ditta.' 'It is the kindness of the Presence.' So we talked, and the formality is repeated word for word each time he comes. These are gentle folk (the letter continues). It is in their voices. They have a peculiar cadence rising a bar or two before the end, then dropping softly. It is almost cloying."

Touring was an essential part of every district officer's work, and during the cold weather one could hardly tour too much. It was the best, the only way to get any knowledge of the people in one's charge and any idea of what was going on in their minds, their villages and their fields. An eye had also to be kept on the large Land Revenue staff under one's control. At harvest-time this was doubly important here. Normally, the landowners—and with very small holdings they were legion—paid a fixed amount of land revenue each harvest short of some calamity such as hail or flood. But here, owing to the vagaries of the Indus, crops were so uncertain that a more flexible system was in force. The amount payable fluctuated with the condition of each man's crop. The crops had therefore to be appraised field by field. This was primarily the duty of the village patwari, but the system was open to obvious abuse and required close supervision. The patwari was supervised by the kanungo, the kanungo by the Tahsildar or his deputy, and both by the S.D.O. That is where I came in.

From what I have said of the landscape in the Sub-Division it might be supposed that this would not be a very long job. But until I went on tour I had not seen the Indus riverain. No barrenness there—the Indus with its summer floods saw to that; and when all went well, as on this occasion, a long green belt some miles wide ran along both banks of the river.

Accordingly, off I went on my first tour. "A great camel in the garden outside looms up in the dark against a jewelled sky. He is being loaded with my kit. All goes off except my bedding." I had now a retinue of seven servants, two chaprassis, a tent-pitcher, a police guard of four, and a goat. I also had two mounted orderlies to ride with me, one mounted on a camel, the other on a horse armed with a sword—a relic of the days when Rajanpur was a frontier outpost.

On arrival at my destination after one of my earlier marches, "the zaildar, a splendid-looking man, waited on me in my tent followed by retainers bearing offerings of almonds and raisins, sweetmeats and flowers, and last of all came a sheep with a retainer to itself. All this for the Presence! Words failed me. I rose from my chair—I bowed—I put my hand to my heart. Jupiter Ammon could hardly have had a more splendid sacrifice. This might have been enough to propitiate the Presence for one day. But no! Five minutes later I was the shepherd of another and yet more royal sheep. Both are with my cook. I cannot bring myself to enquire after them."

All this was in accordance with Baluch custom, and the beginning of what in time became a whole flock, also a problem. In one week I was given three—this when my retinue and I had already eaten as many. Three more had for a time escaped this fate. "One has too fine a coat; another too aquiline a nose, and a third was too lean." The flock went on growing and when it numbered well over twenty it was sold and with the proceeds every boarder in the school at Rajanpur was given a play-box for his possessions. In accepting these varied offerings I was only following traditional usage.

The work that I did at Rajanpur in kutcherry had now to be done in, or in front of, my tent (12 feet by 12). This had a semi-circular porch screened from the outer world by curtains of split bamboo, through which one could see without being seen. A chaprassi liveried in scarlet sat outside on a rug. I had only to murmur his name and I had what I wanted. Of the two chaprassis one was tall, the other a bare five feet. Ditta Khan, the tall one, had "a nose that Cyrano might have envied", but with it went a sleepy look about the eyes. Did he perhaps take opium?* The poppy was then a crop of some importance in my kingdom. "But he is a kind man and has the dignity which long service faithfully performed always gives."

Ghulan was the one I liked and have never forgotten. His service went back to the days of the mutiny. Despite his years any call to him would bring him instantly to his feet all eagerness to hear and obey—as if to serve you was his only purpose in life. It was a lesson to see him handle the men in Court—as kind and courteous to them as he was to me. Over fifty years have passed since then, but my heart still warms at the thought of that little figure in scarlet

* In May 1906, I reviewed Rountree's book *The Imperial Drug Trade* in the *Civil and Military Gazette*, Lahore. It was the first time I saw myself in print and it earned me £1. In the course of the review I wrote: "Everything points to the awakening of China. This must vitally affect Asiatic politics."

springing to his feet with an ever-cheerful 'Huzoor' and disarming any impatience by the sweetness of his temper.

One evening in Rajanpur I found him "standing motionless on the tennis court looking out towards the west, with not a hair stirring, not even in his beard. Suddenly he fell on his knees and that kind-hearted face was bowed to the ground. He was a Muslim and it was one of the Muslim's five hours for prayer."

On another occasion I found him sitting in my verandah with a large book wrapped in green baize on his knees. I was surprised: I did not know he could read. 'What are you reading, Ghulan?' 'It is the Holy Koran.' 'Can you read Arabic then?' 'Yes, I read it but I do not understand what it means.' 'Then why do you read it?' 'Because it is pleasing to God. He has ordered it and, just as I perform your orders, so I read this.' Reading the Koran in this way is based on the belief that it is literally God's word and that therefore its repetition must do one good.*

Ghulan was a keen sportsman and there I failed him. Of an evening I would go out with a gun and he would come with me to beat up any careless game-bird about. Some of the wheat was up to my chin. Ghulan's five feet liveried in red would disappear in it altogether, and a minute or two later there would reappear a fringe of white beard and the cheerfulest face in the world. One day, pointing to the sunset, I asked him, did it please him? 'What is pleasing to the Presence,' he replied, 'is pleasing to his humble servant.' On another occasion I asked him—'Do you understand English, Ghulan?' 'I cannot speak the Sahib's tongue,' he replied. 'Do you know what "fool" means, Ghulan?' 'No, Huzoor.' 'Do you know what "damned fool" means?' 'Ah!' he exclaimed, 'those are the Sahib's words.' "It is not always easy", I wrote, "to keep one's temper in the Indian climate, but there is one man with whom I can never be angry—the gentle-hearted Ghulan."

Another letter of this date suggests a subtler reason for the shortening of one's temper. While admitting the effect of the climate, it says it was due "chiefly, I think, to the enormous power we all have and power, Lord Acton says, corrupts all that have it".

Touring brought one into much friendlier touch with the people than was possible sitting in Court in Rajanpur. It also gave them the opportunity of ventilating a complaint or a wrong without having to go to Rajanpur. One day on the march I was waylaid

* Cf. the author's *Wisdom and Waste in the Punjab Village*, p. 60.

by a man whose house had been burnt down in the night. He was sleeping inside with his wife and ten goats, and woke up to find an enemy had set his thatched roof alight and locked him in. Fortunately neighbours heard his cries and broke the lock and he and his wife were saved, but not the goats. He was naturally in great distress and followed me some way. I could only promise him the fullest enquiry. Alas, when three weeks later I passed that way again, there was still no clue to the culprit. It looked as if the Lambardars* of the village had not done their best, as in duty bound, to help the police, for in an affair of this kind it was generally common knowledge in the village who the culprit was. So, to show my displeasure, I made them ride on with me into the night. The victim waylaid me again—"his face the very picture of a tragic mask with eyeballs starting from his head and a hunted glassy look, as Priam must have looked when his palace was set alight. There was something unearthly in his face: it haunts me." Unfortunately I have no record of the final issue. It was in any case a wretched business and threw a sinister light on village ways.

What I always enjoyed, and in later years never ceased to enjoy, was my chance meetings with peasants, mainly during my sunset stroll. One evening something shot into my eye. A peasant with a black beard going my way offered to take it out. He lifted two large fingers smelling of toil to my eyelids and in a moment I was free. We walked on in silence. The sun had just set behind the hills. From the distance came the tinkling of bells and the lowing of cattle. I made some remark about them, to which he gave the peasant's stock reply when something is not understood and a touch of flattery not unwise—'Your Honour is King'. We walked on. 'What is your name?' I asked. 'Ilahi Baksh.' 'Are you a good fellow?' 'That is as your Honour makes me.' A short pause, and then from him—'What is your Honour's name?' 'Darling Sahib.' 'Dalu Sahib?' 'No, Darling Sahib.' 'Da-Da-Darlin Sahib.' And there we parted.

Another evening I came to a general store, and a distribution of sweets followed amongst the children gathered round me. "Last of all a wizened old man held out his hand and I gave him some, remarking this was the biggest child of all." Result "laughter unquenchable". "I have at last found a corner where one may pass for a wit. I like these people: they crowd round me, yet no smell."

* Headmen.

At one encampment my visit coincided with a fair. A faqir had lived and died there in the odour of sanctity, and a shrine had been built and an annual pilgrimage organised in his honour. The natural consequence was a fair with its accompaniment of "merry-go-rounds, hawkers, wrestlers and prostitutes", the kind of thing described by Anatole France in *Thais*. "Yesterday afternoon my Munshi came to me and said—might the staff have leave to go to the fair that night?" 'What is it?' I asked, 'a tamasha (an entertainment)?' 'Yes,' he said and added with engaging candour—'prostitutes'. My visit to the fair was more formal. I rode there in state with my two chaprassis in front to clear the way and five or six officials behind me. The dense mass of spectators had formed themselves into a ring, those in front sitting on the ground, those behind standing, backed by black-bearded men on horseback, and towering over them mounted camels tossing their heads contemptuously at all below them. In the middle of the ring women in the gaudiest clothes moved round and round in a circle "raising their arms, waving their hands, snapping their fingers", the whole done "rhythmically and, I must say, with great grace" to the beat on a drum, but "monotonous and interminable".

My tent was pitched in very varying spots. The most attractive was one on a branch of the Indus, and so close to the river that, sitting at the tent door, "I could almost have pushed a pebble into it with my foot." Very delightful it was to sit out after dinner under the dome of stars and listen to the hungry voices of the river, to the gurgling of its eddies and to the mutterings of passing logs.

One evening with the smell of ripening corn in the air, I had tramped about with Ghulan, two beaters and a gun and seen nothing. "At last I heard a rustling in the bushes. I trod warily; my finger was on the trigger; I felt I could kill"; and there appeared an innocent little owlet perched on a branch "and eyeing me with an almost quizzical fearlessness". I sent gun and cartridges back and walked through the wheat fields to a hamlet of thatched huts, just rising above the sea of green wheat. Old and young came out to greet, or rather look at me. They stood round half wondering, half pleased. They were full of the wrong they had suffered from the men of Bahawalpur. Of that in the next chapter.

"This part of my life (I wrote) I like very much: it is human, and there is a grand simplicity about their lives. I know it is easy to idealise them: their children are dirty; they live in the middle of dung-heaps; not one of them can read or write. But the dignity of the older amongst them is most impressive: they have a look of self-possession, authority and wisdom uncommon in the West." They were, in fact, completely untouched by the self-consciousness of the modern age.

Returning to camp one evening early in May when the harvest had been gathered in and only stubble fields remained, "there came towards me a flock of sheep and goats, a dancing mass of white, brown and black, hurrying homewards over the golden earth with the night rushing on behind them. At their head, staff in hand and clad in white, with one black lock falling loosely on his shoulder, came their shepherd singing some Indian melody, which mingled plaintively with the tinkling bells of his flock." The scene was simple yet so captivating in its beauty that I have always remembered it.

CHAPTER 6

Rajanpur—The Hot Weather

I COME now to the trouble with Bahawalpur which had upset the hamlet just visited. Bahawalpur was an important Indian State 'about the size of Denmark' which lay across the Indus. News of what sounded like a big row between my villagers and theirs led to a sudden change of plan and a ride of forty miles. At Mithenkot, once a port for the Indus Steamship Flotilla, I changed horses and we sped on four miles to the Indus. This we crossed in a very mediaeval-looking boat high in the prow, even higher in the stern. It had a crew of four: two on either side darted up and down the gunwale on each side punting us along with poles "as big as Aaron's rod must have been when it had swallowed up the others". When it became too deep to punt, three of the four manipulated a long steering oar at the stern. The crossing of nearly half a mile took twenty minutes. On the farther bank "where I have a little territory", the local lambardar and zaildar were waiting to greet us. Remounting our horses "away we went at a tearing gallop, the natives sitting their steeds like horsemen of Panarhenaic fame—all except the zaildar, a deboshed old fish, who bit the dust".

Another four miles and we came to the frontier which divided my domain, indeed part of British India, from Bahawalpur. There we were met by State officials, including a Sub-Inspector of Police stiff with "the self-importance of an ante-diluvian mammoth". Our villagers and theirs had had a brush which had to be investigated and, if possible, settled before it developed into something worse. The Bahawalpur story was that fifty-four of our buffaloes had been found drinking in State territory at a forbidden spot, and had been seized and then rescued. Our villagers said it was all a lie.

We were now a cavalcade of twenty or more and careered from one spot to another looking for buffalo footprints. The stories of both parties were most circumstantial without one single fact in common. The State police demanded twenty-three of our men for trial, but that might have involved extradition proceedings and higher authority. To avoid this obvious complication, and prevent feeling getting out of hand, an early settlement was clearly desirable. It was therefore arranged that I should meet two State officials a day or two later. "A troublesome but interesting case", I noted. As to where the truth lay, a letter describing the affair said –"it is a case of G.K. as one doctor said to another when asked what his patient was suffering from–in other words, 'God knows' ".

Two days later at sunset I was just starting out with my gun when one of our villagers rushed up and said he had been beaten by Bahawalpuris, and baring a swarthy back, he showed me three weals. He was so excited that he could hardly make a statement. I was doubly glad therefore when the next day–Sunday–two State officials came to see me about the case. After two hours' discussion, it was agreed that they should choose someone from our side and we someone from theirs, and that the two should enquire into the whole affair. I reported what I had done to the Deputy Commissioner and, being still a tiro, awaited his verdict in some trepidation. In due course his approval arrived: he even 'commended my diplomacy'.

I had almost forgotten the whole affair when the peace of the border was threatened by another dispute, this time about a canal. It was considered of sufficient importance for a meeting to be arranged with the State's Minister of Irrigation. This was to take place in Bahawalpur territory at the unromantic townlet of Chachuran. It was now the 9th of May and the hot weather had us firmly in its grip.

I left Mithenkot, where I had spent the night, before six. As the crow flies, Chachuran was only six miles away, but in between lay the Indus swollen by the melting snows of the Himalayas far away to the north. Five side streams had to be forded, one with the water almost up to our saddle-flaps. The river itself was a mile broad, and in midstream there seemed to be nothing but water and sky. On stepping ashore I was met by a number of State officials and escorted to Chachuran, where I was put up in the smelliest of Rest Houses.

That evening the Minister sent me word that, if it were my pleasure, he would wait on me. I offered him immediate audience, and ten minutes later "I heard the clatter of hoofs, and a cavalcade of six rode into the compound. In a moment we were shaking each other effusively by the hand. Was my health good? Yes, as good as I trusted his was. And the Nawab Sahib's* health? Yes, that too was good." So we talked, warily for a time, until at last we came to the point of our meeting. "Till then he had been affability itself, protesting as much with his hands as with his lips. But now he changed: he shrank into mere politeness, drawing himself up and stopping the play of his hands, except in some deprecating though quite friendly gesture. However we are agreed on the general question, and tomorrow we go to the spot."

Before he left seven enormous trays loaded "with offerings to my Person—Our Person, I should almost say"—were laid at my feet: two trays of almonds, two more of raisins, one of oranges, another of bananas, and a seventh of mangoes. "With a wave of the hand I thanked him and gave him leave to retire. Again the clatter of hoofs, and he was gone." As if these offerings were not enough, two two-pound packets of sugar, which had apparently been forgotten, arrived the following morning. "I suggested to my bearer in a lordly way that gifts should be made from these stores to my retinue of orderlies and servants. I found that they had already dropped upon them like vultures but had put aside a portion for me."

At Chachuran I was the guest of the State. This led to a great moment—my first iced drink since leaving Lahore! And it had become hot enough for half a dozen each day.

"This morning", says a letter written that evening, "we were off on our ponies at 5.45 just as the sun stood poised on the edge of the plain." We were a large party—the Minister and his retinue, I and mine. We skirted along the Indus "cantering over cloth of gold, the gold of the stubble", and with a cool breeze from the river everything was as pleasant as possible. Seven miles of this brought us to where our villagers said some land of theirs had been taken by the State. We examined the spot, heard what each side had to say, "and in 10 minutes the business was settled". There had, in fact, been nothing to quarrel about.

But there was still the unsettled case of the fifty-four buffaloes. So little now did anyone seem to be in a hurry that the Commission agreed to on March 24 was not to meet until May 20. This seemed an opportunity to get also that hatchet buried. Accordingly, as we rode back, I asked the Minister on what terms the State would

* The Head of the State.

allow the matter to be amicably settled. He said that if our men apologised, he would see that the complaints against them were dropped, and such was his influence with His Highness the Nawab Sahib that this, he claimed, would certainly be done. I could not agree to an apology as it was very doubtful whether our fellows were in the wrong. He said he would call in the evening to discuss the matter further. So back we came with the water in the river "dancing madly in the sunlight".

At six o'clock he was announced. There followed an exciting evening. Throughout it "one continual struggle, chiefly of words; but words are important in the East". We began with the usual formal courtesies. Then to business. I suggested that bygones should be bygones and that he should be content with a pledge by my villagers to keep the peace in future and not to trespass on the State's canal-banks, which was the root of the trouble. "Forgetting about the apology, he whipped out of his breast-pocket a little red pocket-book, and out of it he unfolded a document—a draft of the conditions our fellows must accept. He read them out—a most one-sided affair. They would require modification, I said. This roused him: his eyes opened wide, his jaw dropped, he waved his arms, spoke very fast, tossed his head and ended dramatically by shutting the pocket-book with a snap and with the draft inside. 'Very well,' he exclaimed, 'let the Commission meet.' 'No, no, Minister Sahib,' I said in my most persuasive tones." I pointed out that we were really in entire agreement, that our only wish was for our two Governments and peoples to live together in amity and peace, and since that was so, it was as simple as possible. As I spoke, his hand stole back to the breast-pocket, his eyes closed a little, and the draft re-appeared. I then stated the kind of terms I would agree to, the chief of which, and the crux of the matter, was that spots should be fixed on the State canals where our fellows might water their cattle. In time we reached agreement and I called in two of my principal villagers to hear what they had to say about it. One of them seemed to be a *bête noire* of the Minister, and in five minutes he had flared up again with all the former effects on eyes, jaw and pocket-book. But before the pocket-book had quite reached the breast-pocket I had the fellow out of the room, and the storm subsided at once. By seven-thirty we were all agreed. It only remained to have the terms put into writing. The parties went out to do this and the Minister, a Muslim, to say his prayers. I went out too for a breath of fresh air. In the west daylight was fading in a last glow of yellow and green, and above shone the evening star. End of Act 1.

In a quarter of an hour all were back again with the agreement in duplicate. I was sitting in the verandah and as it was now dark and quite cool, I proposed that we should sit there, believing that we should be but a few minutes. We were nearly two hours. It was my first experience of the kind, and it was not long before I realised the perils of *al fresco* diplomacy. One is in the public eye and "it is difficult to walk backwards gracefully in public". It soon became clear that one of us would have to try and do this.

The agreement was read out. I found that it was in the form of a petition to the Minister and myself and begged that on certain conditions the complaints might be dropped. The wording was so deferential to the State that I feared, if I endorsed it, the Minister would parade it as an agreement between the British Government and the State. I refused therefore to have anything to do with it unless amended. We went through it clause by clause wrangling over this and that. The Minister again got excited. I called for cigarettes. "Would not the Minister Sahib have one." Common politeness—and he was certainly polite—demanded a reply. This turned his thoughts, and when in offering him a lighted match he burnt his fingers, the effect was complete. Cigarettes, as I noted, should always be handy on an occasion of this kind: they calm one and give one time to think. I do not know how many we smoked: on the Minister their effect was "instantaneous".

Still we fought, and still I refused to allow my name to appear on the petition. Instead, I suggested that as representatives of our two Governments we should draw up a formal agreement to waive all complaints. He agreed. "I thought this might be done in two lines, but *ma foi* he dictated eight whole paragraphs with the utmost fluency, reciting all the grievances between the two parties, the fear of mutual vengeance, the importance of friendly relations between the two peoples etc., etc. Even here there were things I could not allow. So the wrangle continued. At last, once more, we were agreed. I breathed a sigh of relief, offered him another cigarette, smoked my tenth and said it now only remained to strike out my name from the petition. He refused. I was almost angry: it showed what an old fox he was." He offered to amend the petition. I said I would do nothing to show that I approved of it. It looked now as if the whole thing must go, as he put it, "into water". We talked on. He was most voluble: I punctuated his remarks with cigarettes, and at last we agreed to an addition to the petition which made it clear that I did not necessarily agree to its contents, and it was of course open to these fellows to make any petition they pleased. "Now at last it was all settled and I told my Munshi to cut out my name from the petition. Would you believe it?" I wrote "The Minister refused to agree, and there we were at it again".

At last, at long last we compromised. My name was struck out, and I certified on the back of the petition that it had been presented to the Minister, and the petitioners had agreed to its contents—voluntarily. The battle was over: my point was gained, and the Minister's face was saved. It was half-past nine: we had been at it for three and a half hours. I duly reported what I had done and in answer came as brief and pleasant a letter as I ever had: 'Dear Darling—Capital—Yours sincerely, M. L. Waring.'

We were now, as I have said, in the full grip of the hot weather. As we were farther south with desert country round us, it began earlier than in Lahore. On April 8 I was already writing of its approach. "Nothing happens morning, noon, or night, except flies and sandstorms, and both are odious. Much must be forgiven people in this country for the shortness of their tempers. If I have killed one fly today, I have killed 200. Before sitting down to breakfast I strewed the table with 50 corpses, and still they came in their thousands—into the milk, into the jam, into the tea, foraging on your plate, settling on your nose, darting into your eyes. This is no exaggeration but a literal fact, and it goes on all day until dinner-time when most—thank goodness—are fast asleep. At night come the sandflies, tiny invisible insects which bite you and wake you up again and again with fearful words on your lips. Three nights running I had no peace. Last night I put on two pairs of socks—in this weather too!—and thought to sleep the sleep of the just, but a sandstorm came on and I had to sleep indoors with all the doors closed. Flies, sandflies and duststorms! three sure signs that the hot weather has begun."

The plague of flies passed, but with the growing heat the snakes began coming out of their holes. The very first night I moved into my bungalow a cobra was killed in the garden, and before April was out a second, five to six feet long, was spotted in the fireplace of my sitting-room and killed. I never left my shoes on the ground in case something unpleasant crept in.

A local proverb said 'God made Rajanpur, then why hell?' There were days when this seemed almost an understatement. "Ma foi!" says a letter written on tour. "Yesterday was a day. I doubt whether I should mind much about hell after that. I sat in a chair, I leant on a table, I lay on a bed; I ate nothing; I drank a lukewarm soda with visions of ice and fruit and dazzling drinks dancing before me. It is cruel this life without ice, when to lie on your bed is to feel yourself on the top of an oven. You put your hand to the back of your head to see if your hair is not singed. To-day, however, thunder and a dust-storm, and then, mercy of mercies the rain; only a shower, but I stood out in it and drenched myself with its coolness."

Fortunately few days in May were quite as overwhelming as this. More depressing, because more seemingly unending, was having to pass day after day between four walls with everything shut to keep out sunlight and heat. "Oh, those white blank walls" —exclaims a letter: "the spirit is imprisoned within them as Ariel in his tree."

If there were hours of loathing, there were also times of sheer delight. It was almost a case of '*od et amo*'—'I hate and I love'. There were, for example, the bathes in the swimming bath, and the nights sleeping under the stars touched by the bloom of the Milky Way. The stars never lost their loveliness, but I had to admit that, after waking three or four times in an hour, one turned more readily to the bottle of soda water cooling in a pitcher at one's side.

There was also one great moment every week when Ghulan would stagger in with an armful of letters, newspapers, and books. The English mail had arrived, and how romantic was its journeying! "Think (I wrote) of the slender rotundity of your pillar box, the mail cart tearing down the street, the train, the hold of a steamer, the heat of the Red Sea, the 1200 miles up country, the ferrying across the Indus (now in flood); then the tonga, and last of all (when I am on tour) the camel's back—surely a fine pennorth, and tonight it arrived in a whirlwind, on the very wings of the storm."

With no society books were my great stand-by. One must be mentioned: it was the arrival of E. M. Forster's first novel *Where Angels fear to Tread*, sent me by a friend. It took such hold over me that I started it one day and finished it before breakfast the next. In thanking A. C. I wrote "I agree with you that this is a very remarkable book; it is so simple and yet so subtle. I cannot believe that it is his first novel."

In hot weather the only variation in a normal day was whether one was at headquarters or on tour. "If I have to do a march, I am called before 5 and off very soon after. Otherwise I am called at 5.30. There is generally an hour's prowl in the city to look at something—the important thing in this country is not so much what you do, but to make everyone feel that you have your eye on them. At 7 or half past there is kutcherry with judicial work, criminal and civil. At 10 to 10.30 there is an hour's interval for the one meal that I sometimes welcome with an appetite; and so on until 2 or 2.30 when with luck my judicial business should be done. Tiffin takes another hour, not because of what I eat but I read, and then at 3.30 I call the punkah-cooly to the other room and I go to bed and doze for half an hour or more to make up the night's quota. At 4.30 I bath and in a quarter of an hour I am once more sitting in my office. There is generally enough miscellaneous work to keep me there till 7—a judgment to write, orders to be passed on the daily post, an important affair as this tells me of all the trivial happenings in my dominion. At 7, sometimes later, I am free and I sit in the glow of the sunset. Dinner is at 8, a simple affair of soup, meat, vegetables and bottled fruit. I have not the energy to mind the house-keeping, so it is always the same. Afterwards I write a letter, read a little and then at 10.30 I climb onto the roof to toss on my bed." Incidentally "we never get a half-holiday here, still less a whole. One Saturday the Court rose at 8.30 p.m."

In those days the British Empire was at the height of its prestige, and in India still unchallenged. On the 24th of May, Empire Day, its glory and beneficence were celebrated throughout the country. "It seems", says an irreverent letter, "that this is the day made sacred to the god Jingo in all parts of our Empire. At Rajanpur we showed a most proper frenzy." At 8.30 a.m. I rode to the school accompanied by a mounted orderly. As I entered the school hall, innumerable boys rose to their feet, each waving a paper flag. "There was quite a long walk down a narrow gangway to the head of the room, where were seated all the local notabilities. They too rose and I flatter myself that even King Edward appearing at the

Guildhall never showed a more profound sense of his own dignity. I did not scuttle to my seat like a nervous curate at his first service. I walked, or rather moved, slowly through the throng till I reached the throne—I mean the schoolroom chair", where stood "a menial to fan me". I gave the signal and the proceedings began.

To start with "two boys stood a few feet from me and shrieked most plaintively in my ears to the beat of a tom-tom. This lasted a long time and I had leisure to look around. Everyone was wearing either on his turban or pinned to his breast an emblem of his patriotism informing us that this was an empire upon which the sun never set, and reluctantly you admit it with the temperature at 110 degrees (in the shade) and only a menial to fan you behind." Above a central archway were more patriotic slogans "supported on either side by a kind of oriental heraldic god, with one arm black, one leg scarlet, the body a Cambridge blue", the head crowned in red tinsel, and the whole inscribed 'Vive le Roy'.

"But the singing is over: there is a stir on my left; the whole school rises: they salute—and what? A crude and lively-coloured Union Jack at the end of a 20 foot barge-pole." There followed a speech from the masters, and "the room was soon full of the incense burnt to the god Jingo". There was one dramatic moment when he called out in a loud voice—'Englistan! Where is this country?' And he pointed with a rod to that insignificant little island, which one can just make out on a large map of Europe. So it went on interminably, with another speech dwelling on the moral and intellectual feats of the Empire—here I felt the god Jingo give just the tiniest shake in his shoes. More singing to the tom-tom, 3 claps for the King-Emperor, and the National Anthem recited badly in prose (they do not know the tune). At last came the supreme moment when two gigantic trays of sweetmeats were carried in and the boys came up one by one and, as they received their share from the table just before me, each solemnly exclaimed 'Long live the King'. That I felt was genuine and I enjoyed "the look of honest glee that came into some of their faces as the little golden balls of *ladhu** were poured into the folds of their shirts. One little fellow came up in only a ragged shirt" and walked away all innocence and pride hugging his portion in its folds "and leaving bare the most charming little naked figure". It was now eleven o'clock and there were more cheers for the King-Emperor

* A sweetmeat made of lentils, sugar and clarified butter.

"and the usual noises for the Assistant Commissioner". I mounted my pony and rode away, "the fires of patriotism burning very low".

But that was not the end of the great do. "I was at dinner when I heard a clamour of voices coming up the drive. In a moment there were 50 heads peering through the open doors of the dining-room. The boys again! They had come to ask me to see the illuminations at the school. To such an invitation only one answer was possible. Ten minutes later saw me marching through the main bazaar at the head of 60 to 70 of these brats incessantly shouting 'Long live the King'—'God save the King' and sometimes breaking out into the moving chorus:

I love my wife
I love my friend
I love my children three.

varied by—

Twinkle, twinkle little star
How I wonder what you are.

All this in the most piercing tones. A whole mile I walked with this pack of yelling demons behind me." Not a second did they pause. At last we came to the school, and certainly it was prettily done, but I was too battered to linger. I walked quickly round and when I thought to escape, suddenly they all surrounded me shouting "Holiday". Where is the Headmaster? I asked. "Headmaster, give these boys a holiday." A deafening orgy of delight. "Boys, 3 cheers for the King-Emperor." Then I fled into the darkness. The day had been a lesson in synthetic patriotism.

In the Black Forest there used to be a dark vale called 'the Valley of Hell', leading direct to a more cheerful one called 'the Kingdom of Heaven'. It was now early in June and Rajanpur could well have been called the former, and Fort Munro the latter. This was a hill station where by Waring's kindness I could now take refuge from the heat. It was a formidable journey of over 130 miles by tonga and horse. I broke it at Dera Ghazi Khan. From there I went to Lahore for a brief week-end to see Wathen and buy "all those things which even at Rajanpur a man must have—wine, whisky, jam, silk pyjamas and shirts, shaving brush, vegetable dishes and curtains". The day I had intended leaving Lahore "a sudden chaos came into my most private life". My bearer, who had gone off on two days' leave to see his son, wired to say that he could not return because his son had almost died—more probably, because Rajanpur had proved too much for him. The next day produced another bearer, and back I went to Dera Ghazi. The Indus was now five to six miles wide and the bridge of boats of three months back had given way to a ferry steamer run by the Post Office for the mails. Hot as it was, who would not have enjoyed the crossing of that vast expanse of water with here and there one of the Indus' great barges sweeping majestically upstream under a single oblong sail swung across its mast, and in the distance only a fringe of land to divide the greyness of the water from the greyness of the sky?

Watered now by a canal fed from the swollen Indus, Dera Ghazi had turned from a camel brown to a spring green. But a mile or two out—I was back in a tonga heading for the Hills of Solomon—began a desert of grey sand. This had drifted like snow into hillocks tufted with scrub or into high banks lining the road, at some points almost burying the telegraph posts. The only water to be had was what was stored in shelters built by the Government for the storm-bound.

Happily that evening there was only a breeze, and a cool one, and a full moon gave mystery and beauty to the empty plain, with complete silence to deepen both. I enjoyed the thirty-mile drive "extraordinarily". The first hour there was just enough light to read the pile of letters from England which had met me at Dera Ghazi. Then I turned to the driver, a keen-witted, fiery Pathan, who answered my questions "with the lofty half-contemptuous assurance of a clever child. We discussed education. He had had none, but he gave a pithy definition of it—'Ilm Badshahi hai—Knowledge is Kingship'. Finally, for good measure, as we drove into Sakki Sarwar at the foot of the hills—it was close on eleven—I saw five Muslims absorbed in prayer, all robed in white and looking most ghostly in the moonlight. Two were kneeling, and three were standing motionless looking westwards towards the hills with hands clasped in front of them. It seemed to me the most perfect expression of prayer."

Next morning I was off again before six, this time on a Baluch pony with a tough Baluch saddle. For escort and guide I had one of the Border Mounted Police. With thirty miles to Fort Munro and a climb of 5,000 feet escort and pony had to be changed twice. The first ten miles took us across a waste of shingle and stone where Time, with rake instead of sickle, seemed to have gathered up all the rubbish of the plains. This led to treeless hills and up a valley as desolate as the Valley of the Dry Bones—but with one unforgettable moment. Rounding a sharp corner I suddenly heard the sound of running water, and looking down into the ravine below I saw a sparkling burn. I have always loved that sound, but none has stamped it so vividly on my memory as that obscure little stream. I had heard nothing like it for months, and those arid surroundings gave it an irresistible charm. The effect on my pony was also marked but different.

We followed its course for some way but it soon became a trickle and was heard no more. One of the three Baluchis who escorted me was a most pleasant companion, with laughing eyes and a healthy hatred of the town. God, he said, had made him a man of the country, and a week of Ghazi was more than he could stand.

It was one o'clock when I reached Fort Munro. The ride had taken seven hours, but I had gained my *Himmelreich*.

CHAPTER 7

Rajanpur – The Monsoon

ALL too soon came the day for my return to Rajanpur. My heavy kit went by camel and took a week. I as before went by horse and tonga, the tonga packed with miscellaneous impedimenta, and with myself squeezed into a corner. The first day I started at 4.30 a.m., reached Ghazi at 8.30, left it at six and arrived at Jampur at midnight to find the Rest House closed and the man in charge half asleep. I dined that night on biscuits and grapes. I was off again soon after five and arrived at Fazilpur twenty-five miles on at 9.30 in 'a muck of a sweat', though all I had done was to sit still in the tonga. Cooper happened to be there and gave me breakfast; then a nap and all the afternoon work till eight. Next morning I rode the remaining fifteen miles to Rajanpur. There it was so hot that, as I wrote, "every second line I mop: there is not a breath of air. I have just had a dip in the swimming bath, but the water was like the springs of Avernus. I came out at once and sat on the spring-board wrapped in a towel and read *Marius the Epicurean* till the sand-flies, mischievous imps of darkness, drove me back into my clothes."

Cases had piled up during my absence. This explains what I wrote the following evening. "The strenuous days have begun again. Out in the city at 6.30 inspecting the school – we have a new headmaster – then a murder case, adjourned at 3 for lunch and a nap, and from 5.30 till now (8.15) not a moment, winding up with an hour at Baluchi. One has little time to think of the heat. The mornings are cool enough, but in the evening when the wind drops, it really is the devil. I have just been for a short stroll with Walya Khan my Baluch pedagogue, of whom more anon. We went only 200 yards, I in pyjamas and slippers, the pyjamas pale blue with white stripes. How the passers-by stared and how I sweated! I sweat still even under the punkah" – the result of damp without rain. In Lahore, as I have noted, the monsoon would break early in July, but here we did not get a downpour until August 25, and it was the first since February. No wonder I could write in the middle of July: "The little energy that God spares you goes to send fellow-mortals to jail; and when that is done, there is nothing for it but to lie back and gasp."

There was one alleviation. "God be thanked for the wind" says a letter, "despite the chaos it brings to my papers (for coolness I was writing in the garden) and the dust it pours on everything I touch. It has blown merrily all this week till yesterday when it returned to 'the fields of sleep', and then the thermometer in my room shot up to 98 degrees." And there it was still when I went to bed at 10 o'clock.

Five days later I was writing: "It has been a scorching day without any wind and a hot grey mist lying low over the country." This went on for days and I lived in a breathless atmosphere of hot steam. I took scarcely any exercise, "now and then half an hour on my pony, but I come back in such a sweat and that sets up prickly heat. On Sunday I ran short of soda water and all yesterday I was drinking water with no ice. 'Tout cela ce n'est pas gai.' Yet there are things that relieve it. Grapes grown in the gardens here, are abundant, not with your Western flavour, yet moist and succulent. I devour large quantities. But here is my goatherd with a little snake he has slain: tuppence he gets as his reward."

Snakes began to creep uncomfortably into my domestic life. One day Cooper on leaving me killed one in the garden. Another was found in my bedroom. Then came an encounter with a four-foot cobra in the pantry. Two of my servants had spotted him there and given me the news. Armed with a cherrywood stick and escorted by them I went there, and there indeed he was, curled up under a chair. Seeing us, it slid into a corner and hid behind a large earthenware basin full of water in which my drinks were being kept cool. For a minute everything was quiet and we could see nothing. Suddenly it started scaling a stone pillar near the basin. One of the servants bravely hurled his shoe at it. It missed. Up went the hood with an angry hiss.

I took no part in the encounter which followed, leaving its despatch to braver and more experienced hands than mine. It was a lively affair: "with shoes and brickbats hurled at the unfortunate beast". Its hood opened and shut "with the quickness of an old umbrella in a gale", and a blood-stained mouth spat at us hiss upon hiss. Discretion prevailing over valour I left the field of action—the pantry was a small one—to those who needed all the space they could get for the combat and retired into the passage outside. In a last effort to escape the cobra shot out into the middle of the room and was finally despatched near the threshold. "During the fight I felt all the glee that a man may feel in attacking the arch enemy of his species, for there is something about snakes which forbids any sort of kindly feeling. I must however admit I have even less confidence in my valour than I had before."

With the great heat my dress became more and more unconventional. One evening when the thermometer on my table said ninety-nine, I inspected the jail in pale blue pyjamas. "Certainly they looked very bright against those lofty mud walls", and jailer and warder "stared rather. But there is a presence about Authority in this country which would check the most irrepressible laughter, and I looked a shade sterner than usual. Pyjamas (I added) are really the garb for this weather and a day or two ago I even went for a ride in them."

But pyjamas could obviously not be worn on all occasions. In such a climate too, European dress also had its limitations. Noticing that those around me let their shirts hang loosely to the knee, I did the same and this allowed any breeze, however light, to reach my body unimpeded. I must have looked odd to both Indian and European, for the European shirt is not designed for this airy traffic. Which explains what followed. On my way up to Fort Munro after the night's drive I was to spend the day in Waring's bungalow. As I entered his compound, I was suddenly seized with the Englishman's fear of the ludicrous and was on the point of tucking in my shirt when for once moral courage prevailed, and I sailed into the dining-room where Waring and the Superintendent of Police were at breakfast to be greeted with hoots of mocking but friendly laughter. It was the first step in what was called 'going native', a process which, if carried beyond a certain point, could lead to sudden transfer to more sophisticated surroundings.

One of the minor but daily hardships of life in Rajanpur was the lack of ice. I have already mentioned the "great moment" of my first iced drink in May. I had now arranged to have twenty pounds of ice sent me daily from Dera Ghazi seventy-two miles away. And that had first to come from Multan fifty miles by train and ten more across the Indus. Sometimes when it reached Rajanpur all that had survived the great heat was only enough for a single drink. Yet even so what music sweeter to the ear than the sound of clinking ice!

In one respect my state might well excite envy today. I had fourteen able-bodied men who had no other duty but to minister to my necessities. "Thank Heaven (I exclaim) five of them are paid by Government." But with servants quantity is no substitute for quality. The last chapter mentioned to what trouble I was put when a renegade bearer forced me to pick up anyone I could on a brief visit to Lahore. Here, on my return from Fort Munro, was the pick-up playing the same trick on me. I gave him leave to take back his family, who were ill, and "paid him handsomely to help him through". Two days later came a note–'please arrange other man'. "Fact is (I explain) they hate Rajanpur and its heat and mosquitoes, and he was a blubberer." All however was not lost. "My cook (I continue) has played up splendidly and is doing the work of two, and Ghulan calls me in the morning–the only time there is anything but the most devoted deference in his voice. 'Sa-hib–Sa-hib!' he says till I wake, and when I turn over and close my eyes, he adds–'the sun is rising–the Sahib should rise'. I love that man," I add. "And who would not with such deference, devotion and unfailing good-temper perfectly blended." Happily the bearer had second thoughts and some days later returned.

Fortunately, there was usually plenty of wind at night. It could also be cool enough for the doors to be kept open all day. And "after all", as I wrote to my mother who lived in London, "I have a better view than you have. One never tires of green trees and events are always happening beneath them: a bullock is brought out to graze, my goat seeks a shady corner, or two squirrels chase each other." At night too "the trees are full of noises, and the moon is very bright, throwing a blue light round my punkah-coolie", a dark shadowy figure who sits on a box in the verandah. "He matters most of all."*

I was alone as much as ever, and sometimes I was thankful to be so: I could dress as I liked and at meals I could read instead of struggling to be polite and 'cheery', word beloved of Anglo-India.

* The punkah was a long strip of cloth attached to a frame suspended from the ceiling. This the coolie swung to and fro over one's head to mitigate the heat by an artificial breeze. It was in common use until replaced by the far more efficient electric fan.

Except on Sundays there was little time to open a book between meals, "and in a small place like this one must read to keep the white ants from getting into the chambers of the mind". Moreover, I had with me some particularly good stuff, notably *Don Quixote* in Motteux's lively translation, which I had picked up in Lahore. My letters are full of the delight it gave me—"no better tonic for the heat" says one—"like champagne" says another. What I liked particularly was its open-air feeling: "you are hardly ever within four walls and these great white-washed bungalow walls make you feel the joy of that". Sancho was my favourite, and when I came to his island government I felt "I would give anything to have him here in Kutcherry".

All over India, wherever the British had their stations, there was a cemetery where they laid their dead, almost all struck down prematurely by the ravages of a climate then far more deadly to life than it is today thanks to medical research. In less than two years twelve persons known to me had died, none of them old and two of them from the small European circle at Dera Ghazi. They included two at the end of their service, three in their prime and three under twenty-eight, one of them a girl, another a friend who followed me to India from King's, and finally the wife of a colleague in childbirth. "My path (I wrote) seems strewn with corpses."

At Rajanpur the cemetery gave those that lay there a forgotten look. Its small walled enclosure was a mere dot on the plain which stretched away from it on three sides—"Within were a few shrubs and trees struggling also with death, and at their feet six or seven tombstones" with names that could still be read. The oldest was of an officer—a captain who died at thirty-three, and near him lay two subalterns who died at twenty-three and twenty-four. A former Sub-Divisional Officer had buried a daughter there in 1865, and two infants of five and seven months made up the tale. There were also some nameless and rather battered tombstones. When one thinks of the many alien countries over which our flag has flown, all dotted with the graves of those born and bred in a small distant island, one feels there was something not ignoble in a race willing to pay so big a price to uphold its power and prestige throughout the world.

Walya Khan, my Baluch pedagogue, had followed me into the cemetery. His reactions were naturally different: "he gurgled in his throat and spat and barbarically blew his nose". The time has come to introduce him more formally. He had a flowing beard dyed blue—"the blue of the ice cavern"—to hide the grey hairs of his growing age, and a bronzed wrinkled face but "a head oh so dense". He was however a merry fellow and went about with a staff as tall as himself. There was something about him which recalled the Wotan I had seen in the *Ring* at Covent Garden, and I christened him accordingly. The fact that he could neither read nor write did not perhaps weaken the parallel. I had engaged him to teach me Baluchi. This he did for a small remuneration—I forget how much—with a promise of 100 rupees if I passed the examination. This in time he won.

Baluchi is a language "so simple and crude that it is almost difficult". It has 'no written character and no literature'.* "Yesterday I watched two Baluchis meet. First a number of greetings as conventional as ours but far more elaborate, continuing a whole minute, shot out in short crisp sentences of 2 or 3 words. A's exactly fitting into B's, but never together. 'Is it well?' asks A. 'All is well' says B. 'Hale?' asks A. 'Hearty?' says B. 'Give your news' says one. 'You give yours' says the other. Then one speaks for 2 minutes without a pause—or interruption from the other: he tells all his news from when they last met, the earlier part naturally vague and, if necessary, leaping over big intervals, then gradually descending to detail till he comes to the day itself when every circumstance is told. At last he finishes, and away starts the other."

Thick-headed though he was, Wotan, as I shall now call him for short, was not insensitive to feminine beauty. One day after giving me a lesson a reproduction of Mona Lisa in my sitting-room caught his eyes.

'Who is that woman?' he asked. 'A woman of the West.' 'She is very beautiful. I could love that woman. Is she still living?'

'She *is* beautiful, but she is dead: she died four hundred years ago.'

'I shall not see her then'—this with a deep sigh.

'You may see her when you go to paradise.'

'What is her name?'

'Mona Lisa.' 'Monalissa' he echoed, and off he went. Her beauty had struck the "chord that is common to the most brutish amongst us,—the chord of Beauty felt through Woman".

* Ibbetson, *Punjab Castes*, 1916, p. 43.

Believing me to be twenty, Wotan could not understand why I did not marry and pointed out the charms of a certain young lady I had met at Fort Munro. I said I was too busy during the day for marriage. 'But the night (he urged) is the time for love." Later on, apropos of the examination before me, I said I would give more time to Baluchi when I returned to Fort Munro in September. "No (he said), that is impossible. Here you are old man, and there you are young man"—a remark followed by a guffaw straight, as it seemed, from Valhalla. He was apparently referring to my frivolous life up there.

Another time when I was on tour and we were walking our horses to spare them in the heat, we got on to marriage again but on less personal lines. They never saw their wives, he said, until they were betrothed—the case in those days throughout the Punjab; and when I suggested that our system might be better, he stoutly defended theirs and said—'if my wife turned out a failure, I would kill her'. 'In that case (I said) you would never get another woman to come and live with you.' 'Oh yes I would.' 'She would be a very foolish woman (I remarked) and not worth having.' At which he put his hand up to his mouth and guffawed a whole minute, exclaiming again and again '*Badshah! Badshah!*—a King! a King indeed!'

Wotan's 'I would kill her' was no laughing matter and was in full accord with Baluch custom. One morning there stood before me a tall black-bearded peasant who not twenty-four hours before had committed a double murder. He was clearing some jungle near his hovel with an axe when he came upon his wife and a man *flagrante delicto*. He slew them both before they could say a word. I had to take down his confession. It was weird hearing him tell his tale in the simplest, most natural way, without a trace of emotion, with hands quietly folded in front, and yet without the least hardness or bitterness in his voice. He did not seem dazed, his story was connected, and he had given himself up at once to the police. Perhaps there was just the slightest touch of pity for his wife.

That morning Wotan was riding with me on my way back to Rajanpur. "I asked him what he thought of the affair. 'He is a good man,' he said, 'he did well.' "

The case after being referred to a Jirga ended in a sentence of one year's imprisonment. 'Three days would have been enough,' said Wotan. It was indeed a case where English and Baluch ideas of crime and punishment clashed fundamentally. In obedience to all-powerful tribal custom the husband could hardly have acted otherwise. Was three days perhaps nearer the mark than twelve months? Not an easy question to answer, and I was glad that I had not to answer it.

Dera Ghazi Khan was, I think, the only district in the Punjab where the woman as well as the man could be punished for adultery—one reason was that it could lead, as we have just seen, to swift revenge. One of the women brought before me had a voice which recalled Sarah Bernhardt's. What, I wondered, was the proper punishment for her and others like her? I gave her two months' imprisonment as against the man's four. "You see," I wrote to my mother, "I am chivalrous even on the seat of judgment. My reason though is that a woman is more injured by imprisonment than a man, and certainly the man is most to blame. So much I will allow your sex."

'Whosoever lieth with a beast', says Moses,* 'shall surely be put to death.' The Indian Penal Code was a little more merciful and drew the line at transportation for life. I was puzzled how to regard it since it was as nearly self-regarding an act as was possible. On the other hand, it could be evidence of a nature completely debased. Acting very much in the dark, I gave the accused two years but spared him the period of solitary confinement usually included in a sentence of that length, it "would aggravate the disease", I thought. Today, I imagine, it would be regarded as a case for the psychiatrist.

A more normal case but one which made me wish for the wisdom of Solomon led to a woman appearing before me with two husbands. The first wanted to run her in for bigamy. She had, he said, been stolen from him in Bikanir and sold to the second for Rs. 150 (£10). Having discovered her whereabouts, he wanted her back, and she seemed eager to return to him. On the other hand, the second naturally wanted to keep what he had paid for. They asked me to decide between them. I ordered her to be restored to the first on payment of 50 rupees (£3 6*s.* 8*d.*). This I thought a fair ransom as the second had enjoyed her charms for a year or more. And so it seemed to be settled when the second came to me again with a petition saying that the woman was pregnant by him

* Exodus xxii. 19.

and that he should at least be allowed the child. That seemed fair, but first I ordered the woman to be medically examined.

Uneasy is the head that wears a crown, and my crown, I wrote, was "made of cactus leaves", an unlovely plant with innumerable tiny thorns. In Kutcherry work had to be done on three foreign languages, and I had no turn for any language. "A Tumandar comes to see me and I speak Balochi; my Munshi comes with the mail bag and we converse in Urdu. Then come the complainants, plaintiffs, defendants, witnesses—they all speak Jhatki, of which I have only a smattering. Now and then I relapse into good honest Anglo-Saxon." But the strain was sometimes almost unbearable.

With no one of one's own kind to talk to and with a thermometer oscillating day and night between 90 and 100 degrees in the shade, and with a dampness in the air which sucked away one's vitality, there was something contrary to nature in the life I was leading at twenty-five. Perhaps therefore there was some excuse for my moments of intense irritation when at work. "Some fools in Court to-day (says a letter) kept up an incessant chatter in that damnable brogue of theirs, one in a voice like the E string of a cracked violin, which tore through and through me. I could have planted my fist on his mouth and stretched him flat, and indeed in the mind's eye there he was flat on the ground before me—stunned"; or, as another letter says, "dead". Such moments, however, were rare and would give way at once to some human touch or to the sight of some lovely effect of colour and light. "Gad!" exclaims the letter writer on this occasion. "What a sky when I came out of court! What a foam of rose, amethyst and mauve! I went on to the jail—to those drear walls of grey mud shutting out the trees and the breeze. Yet over a corner of them was the Evening Star."

Amongst the twenty-five inmates were three women, two of them for adultery. They all seemed contented and were getting ready for the night with their coarse woollen blankets spread out in the open.

One could not be too watchful if scandal was to be prevented under one's very nose. "Under the lamp, darkness" says a Punjabi proverb. In the jail was a man whose release I had ordered six weeks earlier. A clerk had mislaid the order and never sent it to the jail, and for six hot weeks the wretch had "clanked about in irons". Good copy it would have made for the Indian press. There was some advantage, I thought, in being eighty miles from a railway.

That there had been knavery somewhere could scarcely be doubted, but hours of enquiry failed to track down the knave. One person I suspected and from him I extracted the most solemn oath he could take. With no holy book in his hand but a jug of water (probably from the sacred Ganges) on his head he swore he was innocent, and there I had to let the matter rest, but "it is uncomfortable to have dabbled in such a dung-heap without result". This was the first of many dung-heaps to follow during the coming years. Nothing in my work I detested more, and nothing could eat up more time, and when, as in this case, enquiry proved fruitless, one was inclined to agree with Sancho that "every stink is the worse for being turned".

In those days India had a salt tax which, many years later, led to a famous march by Mahatma Gandhi to the sea in protest. The tax was of the lightest and, falling indirectly upon all, was highly productive. But it led to what seemed to me in Rajanpur "a thoroughly iniquitous system of surveillance", for the soil was impregnated with salt and it was a temptation to many to dig it up—it might be in their compounds—and extract the salt from it. Three men had been caught doing this and were duly brought before me Two of them I fined Rs. 5 (*6s. 8d.*), but the third Rs. 50 plus a month's imprisonment, as it was his third offence. "I had to convict, but I hated it."

All sorts and conditions of men passed through the little room in which I held my court sitting at a table covered with green baize. One day they must have numbered over fifty. Amongst them was a member of a beggar caste as "happy, sunny and inconsequent" as one of Shakespeare's fools, his eyes "almost dancing with glee". He answered every question "as if he had a complete contempt for the world's affairs", as well he might seeing a young man of twenty-five from a country 6,000 miles away administering justice.

There was one Indian, and only one, who shared my interest in books and things in general. He was Dhalu Ram, the Municipal Committee's Hindu Secretary and Rajanpur's only pleader. After one of my first talks with him I wrote: "I learnt more from him about the present state of India in an hour than I have in the last 18 months." I described him then as "high-minded, warm-hearted, enthusiastic, and a philosopher with a touch of cynicism and a good deal of humour". But, I added, "I dare not see much of him or people will say he has my ear." There I came up against one of the barriers which made intimacy with Indians difficult for those of us in any authority. Indeed, after I had left Rajanpur, though our relationship had been cordial rather than intimate, I heard that I had been regarded there by the Muslims as pro-Hindu because I had seen so much of him. Unfortunately there was no comparable Muslim to balance him. Living alone and cut off from all European ties, eager too to learn about India, I naturally turned to the one educated Indian there. This seems to have been unusual, for he told me that only to one of my predecessors had he felt able to talk freely. The others had perhaps been more discreet.

A tiny fence between us was the Hindu taboo about food. Soon after my arrival in March he came to see me with Rajanpur's headmaster, a Muslim. I offered them both tea. The Muslim accepted, the Hindu refused. "He had no personal objection (he said), but it was against his customs." However, that did not prevent us discussing everything in heaven and earth.

One Sunday in May he came round to discuss my scheme for a slaughter house. "When we had done with that un-sabbatical subject, we went out into the garden and he talked of early Hinduism in the centuries before Christ and of how degraded it had become since." (This was of course nearly 60 years ago.) How, for example, in those days women went everywhere with their husbands unveiled. Passing on to the match-made marriages of the day, 80 per cent, he declared, were happy. Unlike many around him, he was emphatic that polygamy was bad. On this point he was ahead of his times.

Turning to politics, he agreed that in India they were inseparable from religion. He spoke too of the effect that Western thought was having on the Indian mind; how Indians had seized upon the idea of liberty as if Western thought contained nothing else. It seemed however to have loosened the shackles of superstition without undermining the faith in God. I was fascinated and only regretted that for so vast a subject the opportunities of discussion were so few. At the same time I noted how philosophic and speculative the educated Indian mind seemed to be; how ironic, too, it was that one could hardly find a body of educated men less given to philosophic thought than the class that ruled India—a typically youthful generalization, yet not without a grain of truth, and certainly applying to myself.

I lent Dhalu Ram Jowett's translation of *The Republic*. Having read the whole of it, he exclaimed: 'If only we had had a book like that in our course at College.' It was perhaps surprising to find a man of his education practising in a townlet like Rajanpur. He had one advantage there: he was the only pleader and so could take selected briefs and avoid having to plead for the side in the wrong. If, for example, he migrated to Dera Ghazi Khan, he would be forced by competition to accept briefs indiscriminately or give up the law altogether. He was already sufficiently uneasy about the honesty of his profession to be inclined to give it up. He had his full share of Indian sensitiveness. He came to me once in much agitation believing that the Drishak Chieftain had insulted him. He did not retort, he said, but retired in tears. He told me he regarded the incident as a visitation from Heaven for following what was not really an honest profession.

He had a remarkable father, who was still alive and lived at Dera Ghazi. Having launched his son into the world, true to ancient Hindu teaching, he renounced it and set up in Dera Ghazi a kind of almshouse where all who came in need were lodged and fed at his expense. Every morning he rose at three and meditated till six. He would then discourse with young students until nine. Rest and a meal followed. At three he would be ready to receive his friends and at five he walked till seven. In those days the Punjab was subject to periodic visitations of plague with a death-roll every year of many thousands. When it broke out in Dera Ghazi and all the Municipal Commissioners but one fled, every day he visited the plague-stricken and comforted the dying.

Renunciation of the world did not always follow these self-effacing lines. Years later when on tour I came to a rocky islet hill which had somehow managed to spring straight out of the Punjab plain. On its top was perched a shrine with a sadhu* in charge who ostensibly at least had renounced the world. With many others I climbed the rock's three or four hundred feet to see the shrine and pay my respects to the sadhu. On leaving I was asked to write a word in the visitors' book. Remembering one of Mahatma Gandhi's precepts, I wrote: 'Renounce the world and enjoy it.' I liked the apparent paradox but was a little taken aback when my stenographer, who had also climbed the hill and been shown the visitors' book, said with a sly look: 'Sahib, that was a

* Hindu ascetic.

true word you wrote in the sadhu's book: he greatly enjoys.' For the sadhu, as I discovered afterwards, there was no paradox.

But to return to Dhalu Ram. He had no illusions about human nature. 'Here (he once remarked) if anything bad is said of anybody, it is known everywhere almost before it is said. If it is anything good, you may hear it after five or six days.' One evening after discussing European and Indian politics, he turned again to our surroundings, and was even more critical. Dishonesty, he declared, was universal: there was hardly anyone under me who did not take bribes, and it was impossible to catch them out. I had already had to deal with two cases of dishonesty. But Dhalu Ram's wholesale condemnation was unexpected and, however instructive, very depressing. I took comfort in the thought that he at least was honest: "I pin my faith to that."

My trust was, I think, justified, for some thirty years later, when he had become a staunch supporter of Congress, he was jailed in some political crisis for acting on his convictions in defiance of authority. Hearing this, I wrote and asked him whether there was anything I could do for him—for instance, send him books. His answer was—'No, we are now in different camps.'

It was Rajanpur's Municipal Committee, of which he was secretary, that first brought me into contact with Dhalu Ram. I thought so well of his character and work that I planned to get him made secretary of the Mithenkot Committee as well and got the necessary resolutions passed. Apparently I should have consulted Waring first. The omission brought me the kindest of letters from him—"just a flick of the ear instead of the stinging rap on the knuckles which I should have had from X. at Lahore, and Waring's reminder—'festina lente'—was certainly not out of place." Actually a month later the scheme was sanctioned by the Commissioner without a word.

My Municipal work was too trivial and unromantic to figure much in my letters. There was much talk at our meetings but little opposition to the chair except on one point already mentioned—Rajanpur's need for a slaughter house. Education was the subject which interested me most, and at Mithenkot it certainly needed attention. "I started at six this morning (says a letter) with an inspection of the school. I found 20 little imps sitting on the floor of an ill-kept shanty. The Headmaster—Rs. 12 (fifteen shillings) a month is his princely salary—showed me his maps, which were in tatters." A new blackboard was also a necessity. But with both my Municipal Committees opposed to taxation how were needs like these to be supplied? A small sum could sometimes be provided out of the budget for a special purpose. For instance, I persuaded the Rajanpur Committee to spend £3 on a dozen cricket bats for the school plus a dozen cricket balls at a shilling each. The introduction of cricket into India was perhaps the least debatable of our services to the country.

Municipal work could be sordid as well as trivial. At Rajanpur a Municipal Commissioner had to be called upon to resign for getting a clerk to make bogus entries in the Municipal records, and at Mithenkot defalcations by the Octroi Superintendent led to a time-wasting enquiry. The Commissioners were apt to think that the Committee existed for themselves alone. They would pass a resolution ordering so and so to be prosecuted for evading the payment of octroi and then somehow get out of paying it themselves. Octroi was far from being an ideal tax, but at least it was not direct taxation, which the ordinary Indian abhorred. It led however to one great evil: it could be easily evaded, and to prevent this, most of the lanes leading into the town had to be blocked with mud-brick walls pierced by narrow doorways.

CHAPTER 8

The Monsoon, continued

'BIEN gouverner c'est peu gouverner' says Anatole France. At that time I was much under his influence and when I looked about me and saw how easy it was for a foreigner to go wrong, I was strongly inclined to agree with him. Yet like every young man who has something of the impatient idealist about him, I had my pet schemes for improving my surroundings. Small and unpretentious they were but at least they had the merit of variety. For Rajanpur itself there was to be a girls' school and a slaughter house; for the peasant, good seed and a co-operative society; for all, the shade of an avenue of trees along a mile of highway. They had one factor in common. I found it the hardest thing to persuade people to help themselves, "even to the lifting of a feather". All succumbed sooner or later to apathy or prejudice, the latter social or religious, or both. Finance, too, was a difficulty.

For the girls' school thirty girls were promised and Rs. 300 (£20) voted by the District Board. But where was a teacher to be found on a salary of 17*s.* 6*d.* a month, the sum available for the purpose? So that scheme had to be dropped. It was, in fact, far ahead of the times. In the village, it was difficult to get even the boys sent to school; in the town it was the same with the girls.

The slaughter house fared even worse. When the proposal came before the Municipal Committee, the opposition to it was so strong that it had to be dropped. "You would think from the way they talked that they expected to be the first victims!" Actually it was a case of innovation colliding with religion. Religion dictated that cattle should be slaughtered in one way for the Muslim, in another for the Sikh, and not at all for the Hindu. And so those who eat meat "are still killing their flocks as Jacob and Esau did, in their own houses".

The peasant's need for the good seed could hardly be questioned, but it was not till the thirties that the Punjab Government, in advance of most other Provincial governments, took it up for the Province as a whole. In 1906 both organisation and finance were lacking. This scheme, too, had therefore to be dropped.

I may perhaps be forgiven if I deal at somewhat greater length with the scheme for a co-operative society. For ten years later began a connexion with the co-operative movement in India, more especially in the Punjab, which in greater or less degree continued until my retirement in 1940, and even led after the last war to my returning to India and Pakistan more than once.

India was given her first Co-operative Societies Act in 1904, the year of my arrival there. In 1906 came the first society to be formed in the Punjab under the Act. How I came to be interested in the movement at that early stage I cannot recall. But here was I in July 1906 summoning all the zaildars* and more prominent landowners of the Sub-Division to a meeting to discuss a form of association, of the working of which I was almost as ignorant as they were. One thing which I did know, and they had no wish to know, was that an essential principle of the movement was self-help. "I have had long conversations today (I wrote) with those concerned and I find them sceptical and indifferent."

The following evening at six came the meeting. It was held in my garden. Sixty or seventy had come there in obedience to my summons. The occasion seemed to demand 'a few words' from the chair. I stood up, and as I did so all rose. I motioned them to be seated and "launched forth in crude and unintelligible Hindustani". Would not everyone benefit by Co-operation? Would not the people be helping themselves? was what I tried to din into their heads. When I sat down there was a hush and no one spoke—"just like the school debating society when opener and seconder had had their say". As a spur to discussion I called upon a prominent Hindu for his views. These I had already heard the night before, but that set others talking. The proposal was politely but unmistakably turned down. I learnt afterwards that many suspected it as a device on the part of Government to get hold of their lands. When nine years later I made my next effort to form a society—this time successfully—I came across the same suspicion. It was one which died hard, and it was eloquent of the deep distrust generated by a long succession of more or less predatory Governments.

That this did not kill my interest in Co-operation is suggested

* Headmen of groups of villages.

by the following incident. Every zaildar was obliged to keep a book in which touring officials could record their opinion of his character and public work. In due course I was transferred from Rajanpur, and it was not until over thirty years later that I re-visited it. On examining the book of the first zaildar to meet me—once more horse and rider had crossed the Indus—I came across a note I had written as S.D.O. that his father—the then zaildar—promised to start a co-operative society, 'and did he do so?' I asked. The son shook his head. 'And have *you* done so?' Another shake of the head. In later years we were often criticised for having developed an official rather than a popular movement. I have sometimes wondered whether without official encouragement there would have been any movement at all.

The one scheme which, for the time being at least, bore fruit was the one which made no demands on anyone but myself. This was the planting of roadside trees. The first steps were easy: the Garden Fund (with Waring's sanction) and later a grant of Rs. 120 (£8) from the District Board provided the means, and a dozen coolies dug the trench needed on either side of the road to bring water from the canal. Four hundred and fifty were quickly planted. Then came the difficulties. One Sunday morning I rode out to look at my nurselings: "like the dove when she took her first flight from the Ark, I found no green thing". A flood of water from the canal had drowned them. A much greater difficulty was to protect the young shoots from passing camel and goat. I re-mained in Rajapur far too short a time to nurse them to maturity; and whether any grew up may well be doubted. In my next Sub-Division I got 2,000 planted, but when two or three years later I was rash enough to revisit it, I found that only a bare 10 per cent had survived.

It was much the same with many a good scheme started by members of my Service. Few of us were left long enough in a district to see that they took root. Interest and activity could always be roused in favour of one sponsored by the head of the district as long as he was there, but with his departure it would melt into thin air. 'So it always is' said a Risaldar* to me in the early thirties. "There was B . . . : his passion was roads, nothing but roads: we all made roads. Much money was spent in collecting stones to make a big road. But he was transferred, and the metal

* A cavalry officer.

was auctioned for nothing, and no one thought any more about roads. When (continued the Risaldar) the Deputy Commissioner says a door must be opened, we all throw ourselves against it, because we want to please him; not because it is in our hearts to do this."* Fifty years ago change was not in their hearts. In the village 'new thing, bad thing' was a common saying, and with rare exceptions apathy was universal.

There was no escape from work on Sunday, but I tried to keep the pleasanter tasks for that day. One Sunday morning, therefore, accompanied by the Tahsildar I set out soon after five to inspect a well which had been sunk many years before by Government for travellers crossing the desert country lying between Rajanpur and the Hills of Solomon. It was a country to love or hate, or perhaps to love and hate at once. It had the fascination of something barely touched by man, but there was terror too, for it was dead: it had died of thirst though within a day or two's march of the Indus. The whole morning I saw but one bird. True there were stumps of trees, but each had had to fight for survival, isolated from its fellows. And yet how brilliant was the plain in the early morning sunshine with a surface as golden as a stubble field, for the thin grass that covered it had yellowed in its thirst for rain. But it was a beauty only of an hour. Suddenly we were caught in a gale of wind, and at once the earth was smoking with scurrying sand. Another mile and a large village rose from the plain compact with square-built walls yet half unreal in the clouding sand, and soundless too. Two children eyed us wonderingly from a roof, and a woman, on her way to the well with a pitcher on her head, seeing us, stopped dead and snatching at a corner of her red shawl to screen her face, she vanished within the walls. We had seen a quarter of the inhabitants. Once, as its houses showed, it had been a thriving village. Now four men, four women and a few children lived there. There had happened one of those mysterious climatic changes that mean so much to those who suffer from them and were then so little understood.

One tree still lingered, and within a stone's throw lay the well I had come to inspect. It was seventy feet deep and the only one for twenty miles of road in a country where a traveller on foot could die of thirst. It was now fast filling with sand. We entered the village. The wind blew harder and drove the sand stingingly

* See the author's *Wisdom and Waste in the Punjab Village* (1934), p. 39.

into our eyes. We were in the main street—the Bazaar—and there just ahead of us was a bank of sand as high as the houses on either side. We climbed over it and another bank blocked our way. Between stood the shops empty and silent. In some the doors were closed and half hidden by drifted sand. In others, they had been wrenched away and the sand had entered unbidden. In Solomon's village the sound of the grinding was low; here was no sound of grinding at all, only of scurrying sand. We climbed yet another bank, the highest of all, higher even than the house-tops. From its crest we looked down on a house with a courtyard cleared of the sand, which had been piled against the walls. It was the abode of the Lambardar, a Baluch, six foot three, black-bearded and, after Baluch fashion, long-haired. And here slowly vanishing before his eyes was the village where his clansmen had lived for 300 years raiding and raided till the English came and tied their hands. Though his neighbours had gone, he remained and proudly he bore himself as one still in authority. There we left him and the few who bore him company, and mounting our ponies we floundered away struggling with wind and sand.*

Not long after my visit I received a petition which contained the following:

'Respected Sir—Heard that your honour had come to Fatehpur and visited the well and city, but I was ill with fever, cannot come to resist you . . . Only I and two carpenters are yet sitting in the whole dissolated city. . . . As Fatehpur has been ruined I have nothing to live on so I most humbly beg that please to your honour award me 50 acres of land on which may live. I am a man of high respected family, but poverty has made me a beggar. I hope you shall consent to pay it please your honour.'

Not all the country I had crossed was desert. A canal which ran only when the Indus was in flood, irrigated a long strip ending near Rajanpur. A fortnight earlier when I was touring ten or twelve miles farther north the canal was dry, the monsoon had not yet given us any rain and the canal's head had silted up. The peasants, all tenants of a large Government estate for which I was responsible, were in despair. Their half-grown crops, sown in anticipation of a full canal, were beginning to rot and scores of

* This episode was the subject of an article entitled 'A Vanishing Village' which I wrote at the time and which appeared in the *Pioneer* of August 8, 1907.

idle bullocks were munching grass brought from a distance. I was met with cries of 'for God's sake give us water!' The next day I happened to meet Cooper. He told me a new head to the canal was being dug, but it would take time. I begged him to spare us a little water from a canal which was running brim-full not very far away, and got him to send a wire to his Chief to sanction this, after worrying him "like a gadfly" as he ate his breakfast.

Yet more scenes the third day and more reproaches. 'It is not my fault,' I said, 'I can do nothing.' 'Impossible,' they exclaimed. 'But I have no water to give you.' Still incredulity. At last I said—'It is the doing of God.' 'Ah, Ah, the doing of God.' Nothing can render that 'Ah' coming from all in one long-sustained note. Two days later came a telegram to Cooper sanctioning what we asked for, and then how pleasant it was to see the despairing faces of one day so happy the next.

The Indus was no respecter of persons and could be a source of trouble as much to the great as to the humble. One Sunday morning when I was hoping for a little respite from the daily grind, in came a brother of Nawab Bahram Khan, the Mazari Chieftain, with a pile of papers all in the vernacular "as big (I told my mother) as one of your drawing room cushions and far less ornamental". These he threw on to the floor at my feet 'for your kind perusal'. Amongst them I found a letter from Bahram Khan informing me that the Bahawalpur authorities had refused to build a temporary dam on a side-stream of the Indus, which would enable many acres of his land to be irrigated. His claim, he wrote, was based on an agreement of 1901.

I sent for my munshi to hunt for the agreement in the pile at my feet. As the river was falling, the dam to be of any use would have to be built within a few days. Bahram Khan, therefore, asked my permission to take the law into his own hands and build it himself. I was on the horns of a dilemma: I did not want further trouble with Bahawalpur, much less to upset the Bahram Khan, my most important 'subject'. On the other hand, I was completely in the dark: I had never seen the spot—very necessary in a case of this kind—as the whole question had been suddenly sprung upon me. Waring, too, was at Fort Munro, 130 miles away, and as he had heard nothing about it, it could obviously not be explained in a telegram and it would take two days for the papers to reach him. The brother thought that Bahram Khan could wait three days.

In that case, I told him, he must go to Fort Munro and get Waring's permission. I added, however, that if the Nawab chose to act at his own risk and trouble followed "I would support him to my utmost, but I could not assent officially. I told Waring what I had done, and he may perhaps think I went too far, but these Bahawalpur people are such rascals that I fancy the Nawab must be right." What the end of the affair was I cannot remember.

The Indus was now at the height of its summer flood. In May with the melting of the snows it awoke from its winter sleep, and with the monsoon deluging the Himalayas it took once more its place among the great rivers of the world. To a romantic young man this proved a marvellous antidote to the hardships of the climate. I sought its bracing companionship as often as I could. Once it even sought me. In winter twelve miles away from Rajanpur, it came at the height of its flood to within two miles. A light-hearted letter describes our meeting. "Have you ever heard of a 'King' (so the peasants dubbed even the youngest of us) who bathed on his own high road? Would Plato (I had been reading *The Republic*) have included that in the *βασιλικον ηθυζ*? Would he not have marked down such an one as unfit to govern? Well, well, he was never at Rajanpur, and no doubt the Ilyssus never flooded the high road to the Peiraeus." One morning at day-break, with the sun rising "in a cloud of pearly-grey", I had a most refreshing bathe, swimming down the road in water shoulder-deep, and "then over a hedge into a field with great gulls floating wonderingly overhead".

With the great, one should always keep one's distance. Those who did not do this and lived where a high flood could reach them sometimes found the Indus an embarrassing neighbour. One night on tour late in July I was sleeping on the roof of a Rest House "when I became aware of a strange white-robed ogre at my side"—I had been reading *Don Quixote*. I sat up, rubbed my eyes and there was Ghulan with a lantern and a long official envelope which had come from Rajanpur by special horseman with orders to give it to the Sahib awake or asleep. I tore it open, and by the flickering light of the lantern—there was a high wind—read that the Indus (at Attock) was fifty-eight feet above its normal level. Thirty feet was my last news, and its highest point ever, so I had been told, was fifty-four. Flood water took three days to reach us from Attock, so there was just time to warn all concerned. I ordered runners to be sent out at daybreak with the news to all riverain villages, and in the morning on my way back to headquarters I warned all I met of what was coming. A mile from Rajanpur the Tahsildar and others met me with faces as long as one of your drafts (I was writing to a lawyer). He, too, had sent out messengers with the news. Five minutes later I met Cooper to be told with a pleasant smile that he had just received a second telegram—'for 58 please read 33'! "So there was the whole subdivision as busy as Noah with his ark, all for an extra 3 feet of water!"

It was in August when the river was still in full flood that I wrote: "The last five days I have been living in an atmosphere almost overcharged with beauty—four evenings on the Indus, each in its way as wonderful as the last though quite different." One of the four, an all-night affair, I have never forgotten. Leaving Mithenkot at sunset I boarded a miniature ark, high in the stern, low in the prow, followed by my cook with for my further comfort a *chaise longue*, bed and bedding, a well-filled picnic basket and some soda water. Other dependants were preparing to follow me on board "but I said I would travel incognito and sent them all flying". Slowly we glided down a stream hardly wider than the Cam at King's, passing an unpretentious little village now a busy port with barge after barge moored to its banks; then out on to a wide lagoon of flooded fields all silver in the fading light. In the west the sun dipped in and out of fleecy clouds, scattering its light in pathways across the still lagoon. I too lay still in my chair on the prow, conscious only of repose and motion perfectly blended, and watched the clouds. The charm of looking at clouds, at least at clouds like these, "soft, delicate, exquisite beings, creatures of a hundred shapes, is that unbidden the most beautiful things in the world are wafted through the mind—the curve of an eyelash, a lock of hair, ripples of a sea just stirred by the breeze, the crest of a wave, the foam on a sandy shore, the shape and lines of a shell, all these and many others."

As we swept down stream—we had now entered a branch of the river, "I was astonished to find so many lovely things in a country one is apt to think of as empty and dull." The sight of so much flooded land was in itself exciting, and the water mingling with tree and bush added its own touch of beauty to the purple flowering of the tamarisk, and to the feathery pennons of the reeds, in their softness and whiteness outdoing even the clouds, and the call of the partridge sounded all the more melodious for the screeching of the gulls above us.

I lay there entranced, watching all this pass before me and listening to the birds and to the footfall of the barefooted boatmen as they went up and down plying their poles. When the current quickened even that ceased, and as the sun sank the voices of the birds died away and the bush became dark and lifeless. But colour stole into the western sky, and the evening star appeared and shot a golden spark into the water below. We glided on. And now, from far away down stream, came the moan of a Persian wheel, answered by the deep-toned '*La Illaha Illilla*—There is one god and no other god'—of a boatman at prayer on the stern. The moan seemed to express resignation to the burden of life in conflict with the struggle to escape from it. The prayer was its spiritual counterpart, breathed without passion but in deep awe of the Unseen—"the feeling that Moses must have had when he approached the Burning Bush".

When the moan had died away behind us, another sound broke the stillness, different from any before—"as mysterious but more insistent". As we drifted on, it became clearer, with the sound of a mill-race, then like the murmur of the sea heard inland. It was the Indus itself. A few minutes later, with its main stream just below us, we made ourselves fast to the bank.

"It was now dark—that early darkness of night which seems the darkest of all, but the stars were shining and there was a kind of reflected light from the water which showed a few shadowy forms of hovels that seemed to have lost all their squareness. I landed and hailed a sleeper spread out upon a wooden bed. It was a woman, and modestly I passed on." In my white shirt and trousers I was soon noticed by the villagers who came running towards me from unseen doors. They produced a charpoy (bedstead) for me to sit on "and they all sat round me squatting on their toes, 30 or 40 of them, thickly packed together, straining their eyes to make me out by the light of a lantern and its sleepy flame". We talked about the effect of the river on their land and crops. Were they under water? What had the river carried away? 'Twelve years ago (they said) our land was washed across to the other side, and now the men of Bahawalpur have it. Give it back to us: we are poor folk; you are our lord and king.'

After some talk about the local officials—were they liked? did they take bribes? and so forth—there was a pause and a man on my right edged a little closer to me, still squatting on his toes, and scanning my face asked "in a voice eager with hope" 'Has the Sahib had anything to eat?' When I said 'No', there was an 'Ah' of relief —'Then we may give him something to eat.' I thanked them warmly and said I had brought my 'bread' with me, and that what would really please me was that they should be happy. "This they took very well and only begged that they might bring me some milk, to which I graciously assented."

While it was being fetched, I asked them who was the oldest man there. They pointed to a man sitting in front of me. With the light of the lantern flickering through his beard, he told me he was born when the Sikhs were 'lords of the country'—that came to an end less than sixty years ago. 'Were those the good old days?' I asked. 'Or were things better now?' 'Yes (he said), they are better. There was then no peace in the land: everyone looted or was looted. The Baluchis fought together and raided each other ceaselessly.' A generation later when all this was forgotten, it was rare to hear any old peasant say that the present was better than the past.

They all followed me back to the boat, and when I went on board they squatted on the bank. A large earthenware vessel was brought me full of milk, "hot and frothy from the cow". I drank to them and then bade them go home, for the time had come for sleep. Only the village watchman remained to keep guard over us and the boat, and one villager to fan me as I sat on the prow and munched my sandwiches. Dinner cleared away, my bed was put out on the prow. Clad in my blue silk pyjamas I lay in it and looked up at the Milky Way arched over my head—was it ever more ethereal?—and listened to the murmur of the Indus. It had been hot, but now the softest, gentlest of breezes blew whisperingly over my face and caressingly in and out of my fingers. It was all glorious: in three short hours I seemed to have lived again "through all the most perfect things in my life, and so I slept".

"I slept the sleep of the profoundly happy. I woke once, and that was my only dream. I looked across the water, and there low in the east was the slender silver bow of the moon, drawing the finest of silver lines across the stream. It was only a moment for I slept again and perhaps I am like that fellow in Virgil—'aut videt aut vidisse putat per nubila lunam'."* I was called before daybreak when the east was still grey. The villagers were already flocking down to the bank doubtless to have a look at my person by daylight. "It is a question whether it was seen to the fullest advantage as I stood on the prow, still in pyjamas, sipping my early cup of cocoa."

Soon all was bustle. There was a fine breeze from the south, and the four boatmen set about harnessing the recumbent mast with rope and tackle to hoist it into place. This took time, but up at last it went and its flag, a little white rag which had been fluttering impatiently below, now danced as madly as the tail of a dog greeting his master. A minute or two later off we sped to a loud collective 'salaam Sahib'.

Now up went the sail to be swung across the mast. "It was grand to see it heave and swell with the wind, and then to feel the ship – for now it was a ship indeed – driven forward against the stream at 6 or 7 knots to the hour." To change course, a boatman had to jump overboard and pull us round. Once we grounded, then all four sprang overboard to set us afloat again. Sailing on flood water has a joy of its own. Your river is hemmed in between banks; the sea has no banks, nothing but water. But here land and water met in loving embrace round hedge or wood, in open field and winding lane, or in wide lagoon.

By nine we were back where we had started and there on the bank was the gentle-hearted Ghulan waiting to greet us.

A fortnight later I was off once more to Fort Munro.

* 'He either sees or thinks he saw the moon through the clouds' (*Aeneid*, Bk. 6).

CHAPTER 9

Fort Munro – The Baluchis of the Hills

THE last chapter left us on the banks of the Indus. A week later, on August 25, the monsoon reached us at last. It was not much—perhaps it rained an hour—but it left behind a sky alive with clouds—or as they seemed, towers, bastions, rolling breakers—and the Hills of Solomon, "hidden these last four months in mist and dust", swept once more into view all purple in the sunset. "Rain", I wrote, "is quite the most exciting thing there is in this part of the world." But even here there could be too much at one time. Some days later down it came torrentially, breaking up our roads and putting the mail cart service from Dera Ghazi, our life-line with the outer world, out of action. The relief was immediate but brief. The wind dropped, and back came "the bath of steam leaving us to sit and hear each other drip, with countless things that bite and bite till you spring from your bed with an ugly word".

"My head", says another letter of the same date (September 3), "has been in a sad state this last week. My complexion is still the finest within 50 miles, but these Sub-Divisions take it out of you—8 to 9 hours' work a day the average and Sundays never free, and of course Saturday is not a half-holiday. This last month I decided 65 cases—civil and criminal—and when you think of the Revenue and Executive work in addition besides the Baluchi and the people who come to see one, truly like the Policeman's the Civilian's life 'is not a happy one'. It is only because of the complete and utter lack of other distractions that one can get through it. And then think of having to work at this pressure in a climate where one hour's work is equal to at least 1½ elsewhere. I don't complain as long as the head is sound, but when it begins to spin, it's a nuisance. I am glad then that Fort Munro will give me a breath of fresh air." Apart from the heat I had a very personal reason for getting there: two months had passed since my last hair-cut, "and the nearest barber who can be trusted with that operation is at Fort Munro. As it is, I am growing like a Baluchi." The ever-considerate Waring said I might 'make a bolt' on the 1st of September, and two or three days later I did so. The 130-mile drive and ride to get there had already been described, but not what I found there. For that we must go back to June.

Fort Munro was part of our Indian Empire but outside British India, which meant that it was free from all the complexities of our Revenue and Judicial systems with no taxes or formal Police, but with a Force recruited locally to maintain order and the *Pax Britannica*. With that side of its life I had no concern. As a hill station it surpassed all expectation. I had been given to expect bare rock with not a shrub. Even had this been so, after the heat and monotony of the plains there would have been a sense of new life, charm too in the broad back of a hill. But there was much more than that. Fort Munro itself was an acropolis set amongst unpeopled valleys and silent ravines. Crowning it were three or four grey stone bungalows and a little church with squat buttresses; and by them stood a stone tower "very like a Norman keep" dating back to the days when Fort Munro was indeed a fort and an outpost of dominion.

Compared with Dalhousie there was a difference of heaven and earth. In Dalhousie one was on a saddle-back rising so steeply "that you hardly dare move off it". Here after breakfast or lunch one could plunge into a ravine, climb the opposite hill and dive into the valley beyond and yet be back for dinner. Socially too it was very different. Apart from children we numbered only sixteen or seventeen, five of us (when the Commissioner of Multan was up) members of the Punjab Commission. We lived together "in complete peace and amity" and pleasantly free from conventionality.

I lived with Waring and found him as before "the soul of cheerful good-nature". He was also that *rara avis* in Anglo-India, a lover of books. Far from dressing for dinner, which in those days many thought essential to self-respect, we dined in dressing-gown and pyjamas. At the very start of my first visit he did me a characteristically good turn. I got a wire to say that a riot was imminent on my Bahawalpur border. I prepared to go back at once but Waring, as philosophic as he was kind, said—'Let them break each other's heads.' So all I did was to wire back that I would hold the Lambardar of the village concerned personally responsible if anything occurred. And nothing did.

Much of the pleasure of life lies in its contrasts, and after Rajanpur and its gruelling grind Fort Munro was a delightful interlude—

"a life of what clothes you please, of simple amusements, simple fare and simple people, with not too much to do—not too much you can do—and with plenty of God's air". For exercise we played tennis and in the valley below a small lake, shaded by poplar and willow, had cool deep water for the bather and canoes for the idler.

Our greatest excitement in June was a moonlight picnic by the lake. Waring wired to Lahore for a ham. The reply was unexpected: "Your wire 'please send pam' not understood. Perhaps you mean commode pan? If so, please give measure and we will despatch." In due course explanation brought the ham, and the picnic took place. The party of eight included Waring our host, a subaltern, a captain, a missionary doctor, a girl of nineteen "fragile as china but very deaf", and the two daughters, eighteen and twenty-four, of an old missionary padre who believed that reading only teaches you "a pack of lies". I was placed between Waring and the girl of eighteen. She had become engaged at fifteen, broken it off at seventeen and was still "unbelievably empty-headed". During most of dinner she did nothing but spin little tops made out of her bread: Her sister, a good-humoured creature, laughed without ceasing, even when no one was speaking. As to the deaf girl of nineteen, the doctor who sat beside her, to avoid what might have been a painful distinction between his right and his left, ignored both. Dinner therefore was a little frosty, but a game of hide-and-seek amongst the poplars woke us all up, and when it had got us into "the proper state of heat and excitement", we launched the canoes and paddled across the moonlit water to where the willows made a perfect bower. There the croaking would have put even Aristophanes' frogs to shame. It was now approaching midnight and we were beginning to feel with Comus—'what hath night to do with sleep?' when Papa padre appeared coming down the hill with a lantern to fetch his daughters home. There conventionality still bound us, as too in another respect for male and female were allotted alternate days for bathing in the lake.

For me Fort Munro had a special interest. Down below I had met the Baluch of the plains, but here in what was virtually a part of Baluchistan was the true Baluch—the Baluch in his native fastnesses untouched by the sophistication of modern life. With his almost Biblical appearance and customs he was an interesting study. In June I had hardly been in Fort Munro a day before I witnessed an intriguing example of this.

Rain was badly needed, and in such a case men's imaginations have devised various attempts at drawing it from unwilling skies. Elsewhere I have described how an Indian official of position allowed himself to be soused by village women with twenty buckets of water for the purpose.* Here the Baluchis, with a shrewd eye for gain whatever the issue, declared that if they were given sheep to roast and eat, the higher powers would be appeased and rain would follow. Custom was on their side and a grant was made from Political funds to cover the cost. But before the sacrificial feast could take place, down came the rain. The feast now seemed superfluous. Not so to the meat-loving Baluchis—was it not a necessary thank-offering? One evening therefore the hillside smoked with the roasting of two dozen sheep. When we approached the thanksgivers they were already gnawing away at flesh and bone and far too absorbed to take any notice of us. Arranged in white and wreathed in the blue smoke of the wood fires, they were a picturesque sight. But with the entrails of the slaughtered sheep lying about and their stomachs being used as pans to catch the dripping fat, the scene had about it a smack of the slaughter house.

During my long service in India I never liked a people better. They were not adventurous like their neighbours, the Pathans, but clung with their sheep to the stony hillsides. They had however both dignity and charm, and an independence without a touch of subservience, and would respond warmly to any kindness however slight. One day, for instance, one of their chieftains, who was both old and blind, came to see me. Touched by my speaking to him in Baluchi, he "held my hand for 2 minutes and when I helped him out of the room he was nearly overcome".

Their customs, of which I have already given some examples, suggested a close affinity with the Mosaic law, and even their features made one wonder whether they were not the descendants of the lost ten tribes. They had their weaknesses of course. Of one I was specially conscious in September; this was their disinclination to wash when it was cold. Even so, their strong sense of humour made them the most genial of companions out-of-doors.

I had many talks with them. "This morning (says a letter) you would have found me seated against a cairn with 3 Baluchis sitting round me on the ground—like all Baluchis, white-robed, white-

* See *The Punjab Peasant in Prosperity and Debt*, 4th edition, p. 79.

turbaned and dark-bearded with flowing locks. You would have heard, as you climbed the hill, peals of laughter, and as you rounded the top you would have caught, had you understood them, scraps of the most Rabelasian talk." One of the three, a fellow with long bedraggled hair, finding that I was not married plunged into an eloquent account of the charms of married life summed up in the remark—'to the unmarried the night is dark'. He had a wonderful flow of language and for five minutes hardly paused. Asked why I was still unmarried, I said my work gave me as much worry as I could stand. At that they burst into loud laughter which echoed down the valley. 'Your heart is a stone,' exclaimed one of them. 'Though it may be as stone towards women (I replied) it is soft as butter towards my People.'

The one with the bedraggled hair was a victim of the vendetta system. The Baluch, like the Pathan, looked upon 'the exaction of blood for blood as the first duty of man'.* This meant that if a quarrel between two families ended in murder, to settle accounts the murderer or a near relation must be murdered, unless the injured party would accept compensation in cash or otherwise. In this case my companion had avenged the murder of a nephew and to escape the inevitable counter-stroke, like Moses when he killed the Egyptian, he fled and took refuge with the Mazaris and was given land by their Chieftain.†

On one of my walks I came upon an old man—'the oldest man he seemed that ever wore grey hairs'. Sitting on the ground at the entrance to his hut, he was kneading dough for the evening meal. I sat down beside him and pulled out a pipe. Yes, he smoked. I offered him my pouch and he emptied its contents into a corner of his turban, knotting it tightly, and then returned to the dough. With a domed forehead and flowing beard he was strangely impressive as he sat there on the harsh hillside bowed with age. He regretted the days before the English came. So much, he said, was theirs elsewhere: it was hard that they should want these hills too. Relapsing into silence, he took a smooth round stone which

* Ibbetson, *Punjab Castes*, 1916, p. 42.

† When I visited Baluchistan in 1953, I was told that the Jirga compensation rates for injuries inflicted were as follows:

Murder of a male Rs. 2,500: of a female, R. 1,250.
Cutting off the nose, Rs. 1,000; the ear, Rs. 600.
Knocking out a tooth, Rs. 50.
Castration, Rs. 1,500.

had been warming by a fire crackling at my feet and slipped it deftly into the heart of the dough, and with long bony fingers shaped the dough this way and that. Placed on hot ash by the fire, it was left there to bake while he watched it in silence. When this had been done to his satisfaction he struck it against a rock and the stone dropped out. Then breaking the loaf in two, one half he gave me and the other he munched in silence. The sun had now almost sunk behind the hills. I made this my excuse to leave him the whole of my half except a token fragment which I broke off and ate. If St Martin was generous in giving half his cloak to a beggar, doubly so was this simple shepherd, for what he had given me was half his evening meal, and his morning meal had been the same. Overwhelming can be the hospitality of the poor.

On another walk I fell in with the Baluch who looked after the canoes on our miniature lake. He was on his way to see a sick wife who lived on a hill across the valley. Talk led to my asking—could he sing? To encourage him, I filled my lungs; he filled his too and out came a prodigious 'Ah' which echoed down the valley. He was a good deal pleased with his effort and repeated it but could not be persuaded to do anything more elaborate. One of his 'Ah's' was answered above us, and down came two of his kith and kin. Our talk now took us back to the days twenty to thirty years before when each man lived by his own right hand. One had killed a Pathan when the Pathans swooped down to lift their cattle. Twice they had fought at a spot close by. Another had killed four. Scars were shown with almost a note of pity for the one who was too young to remember those days. But they were careful to profess "a firm love for the Pax Britannica". Questions were put about England: for instance—had we fruit there? The relative merits of their clothing and mine were also discussed: they thought mine the best because they were warmer; also, I suspect, because they were too polite to think otherwise. Every now and then we broke into loud laughter over nothing in particular. They laughed because I was strange to them, and I laughed because they were strange to me—perhaps too because I was happy and showed it. With the simple, laughter is a real tie. "They went down the hill and I climbed to its top, and as I reached it, the sun was just dipping into a sea of cloud and a last shiver passed through the grass before the light upon it had gone."

Again and again as I talked to these hillmen, their voices

would drop almost to a whisper, and their notes of exclamation and surprise had a peculiar musical softness, almost a dreaminess which fascinated me. I had never seen such striking-looking men, and never men who in some respects so much resembled women.

Most striking were they when gathered together under their *Tumandars* or Chieftains.* Such an occasion was the September meeting of the District Board–the District's County Council. Waring was in the chair with Nicolas, now Political Assistant, and myself seated a little behind to mark his greater dignity. Everyone else sat on the floor, the Tumandars with a rug and a bolster in deference to their consequence. They were a remarkable assemblage, all robed and turbaned in white, with dark shining ringlets, full beards, and ruggedly lined foreheads.

I came in late and to my deserved embarrassment all rose from the floor and in deep measured tones came the word 'Salaam'. With a quick comprehensive bow I made for my seat. For nearly two hours we talked about dispensaries, wells, schools and trees. As each proposal came up, Waring never asked whether it was approved, but when the two or three who had anything to say had finished, in his quiet, good-humoured way he said 'all right' and down went the word 'sanctioned'–democracy in its embryonic form, and well suited to time and place. Nothing could have been better for my own proposals: they were all approved *nem. con.*–Rs. 300 to start a girls' school in Rajanpur, Rs. 550 to enlarge its boys' school, and Rs. 120 for planting trees.

The Jirga system, under which cases affecting Baluch custom could be referred to a Jirga or Council of Elders, has already been mentioned.† Provided the Elders were chosen with care, there was much to be said for the system where tribal ties were strong and custom omnipotent. The delays and niceties of our Courts were avoided and, subject to ratification by higher authority, penalties in accord with tribal custom could be imposed. In short the truth

* 'When the tribes were independent the Tumandar was monarch, chief judge and leader in war, to whom every tribesman was bound to render military service, but . . . he was expected to consult his muqaddims (heads of sections) on all matters of importance, nor would the muqaddims give advice without consulting the elders of their sections. Under us the Tumandars retained much of their authority.' Sir James Penny, *op. cit.*

† p. 50.

could be more easily ascertained and justice more speedily and truly done.

In September the twelve Tumandars of the district met together at Fort Munro in a Shahi or Royal Jirga to deal with inter-tribal and other important disputes. Curious to see how the system worked, Waring and I one day attended one of their sessions. As we entered the hall where they were meeting, all rose and chairs were fetched for us—there were none in the hall, for as usual all were sitting on the floor, the four leading Tumandars on a rug each with a bolster to support him. The others formed three sides of a square, with the clerks in front to record the little that was written. The proceedings were public and onlookers filled the body of the hall.

A civil suit about land was in progress between a Tumandar and his brother. The reading of some documents led to a violent altercation with five or six all speaking at once, not just to express an odd thought but in a continuous flow regardless of equally fluent and determined speakers. Amongst them was Nawab Bahram Khan, Head of the Mazaris. He outspoke them all and, more important, outclassed them—a good example of *primus inter pares* (first amongst equals). With a nose "as hooked as a pastoral staff" he might almost have passed for a Jew. Moses himself could hardly have been a more dominating figure: as point after point came up, while others were making up their minds, he was ready with his opinion. It was he too who examined the witnesses and dictated all that had to be written, including the final finding.

The proceedings could hardly have been less formal. A witness hobbles in and squats on the floor in front of the Tumandars. Having sworn to tell the truth, he is asked—does he know anything about the ownership of the land in dispute? His evidence is not recorded: the Tumandars somehow keep it in their heads. This was too much for one of them, the portliest of them all. He slowly sank between the Mazari Tumandar and the well until his head had almost disappeared. He had some excuse, for the session lasted all day.

Returning from tennis one evening, Waring and I came upon two long lines of spitted joints roasting on the hillside in front of log fires entrenched between them. The Tumandar of the Bozdars was ill and sheep had been slain that heaven might be appeased and his recovery hastened. 'Salaam, Sahib! Salaam, Sahib!' came the general greeting as Waring was recognised, and "30 or 40 hands touched 30 or 40 foreheads". A charpoy* was produced and we sat round a fire of spluttering olive logs with a dozen loaves baking in the hot ash. Quickly the news spread that 'the Big Sahib' (the Deputy Commissioner) had come to the feast. Around us the ranks thickened with tall, bearded, white-clad forms—sixty or seventy of them—some standing some squatting, all seemingly intent on our faces while the light from the fires played magically over theirs.

As the joints sizzled and the sparks flew upwards, a minstrel played to us on an instrument of olive wood, strong even rich in tone, with over a dozen strings across which he plied his bow like a 'cellist. Tall and black-bearded, he wore a padded red cap with flaps to guard his ears against the cold September air. With perfect ease and a touch that never faltered he slipped from one melody to another, ever returning to a lovely theme "of half-subdued melancholy". So must Demodocus have played to the Phaeacians. I could have listened to him all night, yet he was but an ordinary hillman. Waring said he had never heard anything so good in India. All this under a sky with "the Milky Way catching the stars in its shimmering spray".

There came a pause, and we were asked: "would we share their fare?" Would we not! A Baluch came forward with a loaf which had been baked round a hot stone and broke it in pieces "smiting it with his hand". Another followed with a dish of steaming meat. After prodding it all round with his fingers to make sure it was tender enough for the Sahib, he took a knife from the folds of his dress, cleaned it on his hand, and having sharpened it against a stone chopped up the meat and presented it to Waring with a hunk of bread. Waring cautiously chose the smallest piece. I came next. The hunks were impossibly large. I took the knife and dug it into a vast kind of chop. It stuck and I could do nothing. But the Baluch severed a portion and gave it me with his hand. "I started chewing it—but what can 20th century teeth do with sheep bred for 100 years on these rugged hills! I thought I should never get my teeth out, so fast were they stuck, and there were all those fellows round laughing at my helplessness with their white teeth shining in the dark." The juice from the meat was delicious but the stuff itself was all muscle and gristle. I was then offered a slice

* A wooden bedstead.

from the tail. 'This the Sahib must eat: it is the choicest morsel of all.' I could but accept, and in my hand it became a mass of soft steamy suet. "These sacrificial feasts (I wrote) are beyond me. They want some Homeric hero who will eat for 9 days and 9 nights to do them justice." Indeed the whole affair had a Homeric flavour, not least the minstrel when he went on to sing of the exploits of the Bozdars in the past.

At this point "an old tottering figure appeared wrapped up in clothing and scarves. It was the Tumandar himself. He had heard that 'the Big and the Small Sahib' were taking part in the feast and he had risen from the bed of sickness to welcome us among his own people." It was a touching mark of Oriental courtesy and the climax of a fascinating experience. "Think of it! (I wrote) I have only to walk 100 yards down the hill and I am among the people of Homer."

The last event of the Fort Munro 'season', and for the hill Baluch the great event of the year, was the annual race up and down 1,000 feet of steep hillside. This took us down into the valley below and there set out in the shade of a Rest House garden we found a table loaded with cakes from Lahore and giant melons from Quetta ordered by the Tumandar for our delectation. Leaving us to regale ourselves, our hosts withdrew to a respectful distance and squatting in a circle on the ground exploded bottles of soda water to quench their thirst.

We were next taken to an old fort built on a hillock to guard the valley against marauders. Though now only a police station, with its grey walls glowing in the evening sunlight and with turbaned heads looking over the parapets, it still had a touch of romance. Below us the hillside was alive with Baluchis, as ever white-robed and black-bearded, all expectation for the coming race. The sixteen competitors, their swarthy bodies clad in little more than a ribbon, were now receiving their last instructions. A handkerchief dropped and away they bounded at what seemed a furious pace for so steep a climb. All eyes were upon them, many shaded with a hand against the setting sun, and in the Fort even the old craned their necks over the parapet as eager as any to watch the runners, now mere specks as they climbed higher and higher. When the first was seen coming down the hill leaping from rock to rock with another close behind him, excitement became intense; for not only was the prize a whole sheep but tribal pride was at stake. It was still impossible to see who was who, and the whole hillside buzzed with speculation. Even the prize sheep "seemed to catch a little of the general feverishness". The winner, whoever he was, came in looking as fresh as if he had never run.

The oddest race of the day was for the minstrels across a ploughed field with each playing his instrument as he ran. This produced much mirth, also a touch of pathos, for "far behind the others one old, old man, wizened and white-bearded, struggled on still thrumming his guitar".

As the moon rose behind the hills the day ended with a hillside feast. Huge morsels of mutton roasted as already described were set before us on chairs. We were each given a plate but only one knife for the twelve of us. Not that that mattered. In such company nothing mattered, not even that the meat was tough and our hands sticky. To eat with Baluchis in this way is "the most sacred of guest rites and a pledge of eternal friendship". Since then nearly sixty years have passed and I still value the bond.

The return to the plains followed almost immediately. I never saw Fort Munro again, but I have never forgotten the deep content which its hills and hillmen gave me after the rigours of Rajanpur.

CHAPTER 10

Rajanpur in the Cold Weather

FOR the stranger the Punjab of those days suffered from one great disadvantage: it had no literature to which he could turn for an intimate picture of the life around him. No novelist had written of its peasants as Tolstoy and others had written of the Russian peasant. No poet had sung of its rivers and plains, of the lowing of its cattle and the echo of their bells; still less of the glow of its sunsets behind the hills and of its nights under the stars. The fascination of all this, and much more, despite the hardships of exile and great heat, I had felt to the full, and when in July I was told I must shortly make way for a senior colleague, I exclaimed in dismay—'Now that I am to be deposed, I love every sod.'

Happily, two months later came a reprieve, and I was left to enjoy the delights of the cold weather in my kingdom. These led to a lyrical letter. "Think of the freshness of the air as you hoist yourself into the saddle, of the glow of orange and crimson in the east where the sun is yet to come. Think, too, of the still evenings with the calm glory of the west; and when the lamp is lit and the breeze dies in the topmost branches, you find your chair: a moment's hesitation before you sit down as to which book it shall be. Or you are too tired to read and you watch the trees sparkling with mimic stars where the moonlight pierces through."

Continuing a little more soberly—"I would rather be here than in any other place in India. I have work which grows less and less difficult, also more interesting. The natives I like, and sometimes I hope that a few are accustoming themselves to me. It is exciting now going from place to place, exploring the kingdom. The smallest things have their interest. One evening I strolled into a village near which I was camping. I stopped by a shop with some trivial question and the usual crowd gathered round me headed by the Lambardars. Knowing that the latter had a bad reputation, I gave them some commonplace advice about how leaders should behave. Curiously, it seemed to have some effect as if for a moment the fear of God had suddenly descended upon them. I am afraid (I add) that we rule them too much from the desk, too much by files, regulations and circulars."

If that could be said in 1906, how much more so in later years as Government grew more and more complex. The remedy was constant touring with the ear open to all and sundry. In a Sub-Division it could be more intensively applied than in a district with its much larger area and greater responsibilities. But even in a Sub-Division much had to be left to subordinates, and all one could do was to see that they did it. This involved much inspection with an occasional surprise visit to prevent any tidying up before one came.

One evening, before going to bed, I decided to have a look at the jail. As I approached it, the sentry was taking it easy on a bench. Spotting me, he seized his rifle and began marching up and down with that air of portentous solemnity dear to sentries and butlers. Inside it was worse. I went straight to the watch tower and though we were now a large party and clattered noisily up the stone steps, there was the sentry fast asleep on the floor "as snug as a dormouse" with his rifle against the wall. Having handed this to one of those with me, I addressed him "in stentorian tones". He moved a little and slept on. Others shouted to him and "slowly he raised his head and looked round with a vacuous stare". 'Where is your rifle?' I asked. Another look round and suddenly the truth dawned on him. Away went his hand to his waist: 'my stomach, my stomach! (he cried) I was ill and fell asleep'. I took him straight to the doctor, who pronounced him normal. The next morning I 'paraded' the guard—a head constable and 7 constables. "I felt like Caesar when he addressed the 10th Legion after it had mutinied." I had some reason for concern, for the sleeper was the third since August to be caught sleeping at his post.

In Rajanpur the surprise visit was comparatively easy, but in camp with a baggage train of fifteen camels and with one's every movement watched it required a special effort. This I made once. I was twenty miles away from Rajanpur and without a word to anyone slipped away at crack of dawn. Midway I changed from horse to bicycle—the latter I had left at a Rest House—and rode into Rajanpur at nine. This time the sentry was actually on his feet, but the Jador was not there, and a warder on duty I found struggling into his uniform. There were other petty irregularities but I took no official notice of them: "it would hardly be playing the game" since I had never done this before when on tour; but I warned all concerned that next time it would be very different.

As against the easy-going ways at the jail, the man who was guarding my bungalow was actually there, and the new trees were also being watered. In short, not much of a bag for my forty-mile ride. But at least it showed that no one within twenty miles of my camp could feel entirely secure.

Content as I was in Rajanpur with my 300 books around me, I was even more content in camp. As dawn broke over the world with the fiery glow of a pomegranate, the divine freshness of the air made one feel like "the man 'in populous city pent' who 'forth issuing . . .'

> . . . from each thing met conceives delight;
> The smell of grain, of tended grass, or kine,

Gad! each furrow, each dipping bird, and far away the lapping tongues of bells—all make you vow that it is a most glorious earth. It is the furnace heat behind you that gives the zest; the skies of brass that make these look so soft." And when the day's work is done, it is to see crimson clouds puffed through skies of liquid green over a world folded in autumn mist. "And finally comes sleep under the open sky, and if you wake, a glimpse of the Great Bear reaching from earth to heaven."

Some of my encampments had a special charm. Four days I lived on the very bank of the Indus, and when I supped at my tent door, the river was so near that I could almost have poured a libation into it as I sat. The Indus affected me almost as strongly as the Himalayas had done at Dalhousie. One evening I came upon it suddenly: it seemed so noble, the sweep of its waters so measureless and the harmony of its colours so exquisite that I felt I could worship it. The sky was cloudless, the shore on either side low and treeless and, as the river swept swiftly by, one heard the laughter of breaking eddies, the mutterings of drifting logs and tiny gobbling noises as it nibbled at the bank and now and then a distant boom where the bank had plunged.

The autumn harvest was now ripening and, as with the harvest in spring,* I had to see that it had been properly appraised, field by field, for the payment of land revenue. This often meant three hours' tramping before breakfast. With such familiar crops as

* See p. 54.

wheat and barley appraisement had not been entirely guess-work. Now I had to deal with the unfamiliar millets and cotton. "The mockery of it (I wrote)! I go round pretending I can discern good cotton from bad. I finger the bushes, feel the stalk, dissect good cotton, cast an eye this way and that; and then oracularly—'this field is altogether bad'." The millets too were difficult to judge: often they were so tall that it was impossible to see into the heart of a large crop—very symbolic in a way of the foreign ruler's difficulties in India.

I was riding back from one of these inspections when I came upon a four-post bed drawn across my path with a Baluch Lambardar standing beside it. Whisking away an ill-looking cloth from the bed, he revealed the carcase of a sheep cut up into portions roasted whole with kidneys, liver and tail.

'Would the Sahib eat?'

'The Sahib was not hungry.'

'But it is a Baluch custom. They are his guest rights'—meaning that it was his right to entertain anyone in authority passing through his own sphere of authority. I dismounted and sat on the bed with the severed portions beside me. A pocket knife was produced and a moment later I had in one hand a piece of liver, in the other a kidney.

'Would the Sahib not have more?'

'No, he must be going.'

'Then it would be sent to the Sahib's house (6 miles away).'

'The Sahib was grateful but he already had thirteen sheep.' So the argument went on. At last I had to give in and soon after I arrived in came it all.

In this remote area with the Sub-Divisional Officer constantly changed, very little attention had been paid to the education of the peasant. Even where there was a school, the school building was often in a state of decay. One I saw was nothing but a small square room with a low doorway and no window, and its only furniture two blackboards with a coil of rope on the floor. The forty-six boys worked all the year round under a tree. When I passed by they were not working at all as their one and only master was down with malaria. This was a yearly scourge after the monsoon and laid low, at a guess, nearly 30 per cent of the population. Out of twenty-four boys on the roll of another school a dozen were down with it. The school building there had two rooms, but the walls were badly cracked and "the beams looked as if they would snap like thread". The school's one asset was a master who seemed to feel the dignity of his work. In another case the beams *had* collapsed. There too the master was absent—gone to Rajanpur, it was said. The only education being given in the village that day was by a mullah seated on a mat under a tree. He was teaching four boys to read the Koran in Arabic, not one word of which could either master or pupil understand—yet, according to the orthodox, better read so than not at all.*

In those days the crucial difficulty in bringing education to the village was not so much lack of funds as the ordinary peasant's refusal to send his boys to school. It was not till at least twenty years later that his attitude on the subject began to change on any scale in the Punjab, and then only for boys. He wanted them at home to take the cattle out to graze, to help in the harvest, at the right age to learn to plough, and in general to harden them while still young for work often to be done under a scorching sun. He knew, too, that if their schooling went much beyond the primary stage, they would become not only too soft but also too proud for manual work.

Living amongst peasants, I only once had the luck at Rajanpur to be accompanied on a march by anyone with even a touch of modern education. On that occasion my companion, a young Muslim of twenty-five, was an odd product of the latter. After tea and biscuits at his house we rode on together at a walk with a half moon overhead and the plain around us glimmering with stray lights and fires. His father had been Chief Minister of an Indian State and had left him some 20,000 acres; also several lakhs of rupees hidden, it was said, under the floor of the room where we had tea. I thought I had an orthodox Muslim at my side, but the talk which followed revealed a mind steeped in the scepticism of the West. He had been educated at Lahore and spoke throughout in English, often of a curious type.

The conversation opened with some remark of mine about Ramzan, the month during which the orthodox Muslim is forbidden either to eat or drink between sunrise and sunset. It had just begun. He himself saw no need to fast: the Prophet had enjoined it, he thought, to counteract the heavy eating of his day. Nor did he pray the prescribed five times a day: it took up too

* See the author's *Wisdom and Waste in the Punjab Village*, 1934, p. 60.

much time. He prayed once a day, and with its bowings and bendings that was good for health.

Asked whether he believed that Mahomet had had a special revelation, he said: 'No, and this I must humbly beg to request, my kind Sir, he was as you and I, only very pious.' He did not believe in the seven paradises, nor even in immortality: 'We die (he said) and we are dead: we shall not meet again.' He did however believe in God. The root idea in his mind seemed to be: God has given us life; He is therefore responsible for us, and it is to his interest that this life should be good.

From theology we passed on to ethics. Did he think it wrong to commit adultery? 'Yes, certainly; it would insult the grace of the woman, and the beauty of her body.' The same applied even more to prostitution. This insulted the body of both man and woman. He then came out with the sweeping statement—'Although this is not the etiquette, I most humbly request, my kind Sir, there is not a single highborn Indian family (presumably in his *milieux*) in which the wife has not a paramour, often several, because her husband does not satisfy her. And in England, my kind Sir, are the girls in the schools much addicted to adultery and debauchery?'

He was anxious to come to England 'to see the Lords and Commons', but in such a way 'that I may appear amongst them with veneration'. He said that a Canal Officer had given him a list of English papers to read. He had forgotten all their names except one—*The Forget-Me-Not*! Not a paper I had ever heard of, or have since been able to trace. I found the talk so absorbing "that I almost forgot about dinner though it was 9.30 when I arrived".

For Muslims who fasted during Ramzan—in those days the large majority—a great moment was the sight of the new moon which brought the fast to an end. "I was walking through the city this evening (says a letter) after the sun had set and was surprised to see the house-tops crowded with anxious groups peering westwards to the golden glow behind the Hills; old men with grey beards as excited as their grandchildren, and tall women in red shawls and flowing skirts of russet brown. Suddenly there came a voice through the still evening air—'I have seen it', and 'Ah! Ah!' was muttered from a hundred lips. It was the moon that proclaimed the end of the fast, a slender silver bow floating in a mist of mauve."

Early in November I paid my first visit to the domain of the

Mazari Nawab Sir Bahram Khan. It was a ceremonious affair. One of his officials met me on the border, and a mile from where I was to camp the Nawab himself was waiting with a retinue of tribesmen, all in white and armed with swords. The Nawab was on foot. I did not dismount—such was our local protocol—but leaning forwards shook him by the hand. There followed the usual Baluch greetings—'Are you come in safety? Are you well? Are you pleased? Is it peace?' When we had satisfied each other on these important points, I bade him mount, and a magnificent black charger was led forward. We rode the last mile side by side with the retinue hard on our heels. At my tent door we parted "with a long and almost affectionate shake of the hand". We had met frequently before.

After breakfast he paid me a state visit, and in his wake came two sheep, and on a tray four tins of biscuits, a box of chocolate biscuits, another of mixed chocolates, yet another of preserved fruits, and finally two tins of sardines. He had already sent me two dozen apples, a dozen pomegranates and twelve pounds of grapes. By a curious coincidence that morning I had read in Samuel an allusion to this very custom: when Saul was made king 'the children of Belial brought him no presents. And Saul held his peace.' Certainly I had no cause to hold my peace and thanked him warmly. But at dinner that night, thinking I should like a chocolate biscuit, I opened the box and in a moment the tables was crawling with little black insects. I then tried the chocolates: they tasted of musty hay. The grapes were nearly all bad, but the pomegranates were worthy of their fiery red.

On the morrow the Nawab paid me a second visit. We talked for over an hour of our joint affairs, and very instructive it was to discuss them with so remarkable a personality; and yet how ludicrous that all that capacity and experience should be even nominally under oneself. A hooked nose dominated his face and gave it a masterful look. Yet there could come into his eyes, especially when speaking of his English friends, the softest of expressions. He returned in the evening and we sat on a rug outside my tent in front of a log fire; and beyond it, where its light faded into darkness, two minstrels sang Baluch ballads. When I bade him farewell, holding my hand he bowed low with a respect which was dignity itself.

I was off in the saddle before sunrise with the headmen of three of the Mazaris' four clans as my escort—"one of them a massive old warrior in a pea-green padded coat with the kindliest look in his face". They told me that the men of the Tuman numbered 12,000,* which again recalled Samuel—'and the men of Judah were 30,000'. The first figure was undoubtedly swollen by tribal pride, and was not also the second?

The visit to the Tumandar of the Mazaris had to be balanced by one to the Tumandar of the Drishaks. This led to a further addition to my flock, and each evening "all the more important sections of a sheep" were borne into my tent on a charger by the Tumandar's brother, Mureed Khan. The first evening when he appeared, I was undressing, and, as I hid my bare legs behind a newspaper I had by me, he dropped gracefully on to one knee and laid the charger at my feet.

In one respect the visit differed from the earlier one: 'Would I shoot?' asked Mureed Khan. 'Yes, indeed, but what?' 'Hog-deer and pig.' As must be clear by now, I was no sportsman, and so the event proved; but it gave me a pleasant afternoon and one lovely sight. For the shoot Ghulan was naturally in attendance, and very odd he looked dressed to his knees in a khaki coat and on his head a saffron-coloured helmet. As we crouched together behind a screen of tamarisk, from far away came the sound of the beaters, breaking as they drew nearer into a peculiar mixture of surprisingly musical notes and cries—whua! whua!—ho-ho-ho-ho—shabash—shabash. Before speech was invented, when men hunted in packs, such must have been their common cries. Fox after fox appeared, but nothing else until out came the beaters themselves, greybeards and striplings armed with sticks, and following the hounds which ran barking towards us. All very lively and stirring.

It was decided to draw another jungle of bush near the Indus. I mounted Mureed's camel and away we went jogging across the fields with great gobbles of protest from the camel at the double burden. Then came the lovely sight. 'Look!' exclaimed Mureed pointing upwards. And there high above the Indus was a host of pelicans wheeling this way and that, wreathing and unwreathing, and as their white wings caught the sunlight, it seemed as if huge snowflakes were showering down from a cloudless sky in all the

* See Ibbetson, *op. cit.*, p. 47: 'Our returns show only 9,000 souls in the Province and there are very few beyond our border.'

warmth and splendour of a summer's afternoon. Then with a flash the white turned to black, the black of their underwings. There were now three great flights. Two drew slowly towards each other until the white seemed to thread the black, while the third lay strung across the horizon like a necklace of pearls.

It was about this time that the sound of a bugle echoed once more through Rajanpur and its deserted cantonment. Two squadrons of Indian Cavalry were on their way to Ambala. In the evening the Colonel and his two British officers came to dinner. "The Colonel, a short dark man with bushy eyebrows, would probably have passed elsewhere for an earnest-minded bore. But in Rajanpur—la! it was good to hear him tell how he had done 10 years here and seven years there, and what a remarkable thing this was, and how he had marched one day with all his men etc., etc." He was more than polite in his appreciation of his rustic entertainment. 'Oh, Colonel, I am awfully sorry but you see I have no fish knives.' And a little later: 'By the way, Colonel, no bread has come today; I hope you don't mind these husks.' The one dish served with pride was a plum-pudding which had come 7,000 miles.

"After dinner we discussed Indian politics, warmly but with complete good temper. I find myself opposed to everyone I meet, and as they always insist upon their experience I can say nothing, though in fact I do say a great deal! You can't trust the native, they say, as if you could trust nine Englishmen out of ten. Then there is the 'sedition' and the 'disloyalty': and finally 'they want to shoulder us out'."

There, so far as the towns were concerned, he was right. School and college were growing fast and they had in them the germ of a momentous change—the birth of a national feeling, "very weak at present" says a letter of July (1906), "still it is there." England had now a Liberal Government and with Morley at the helm for Indian affairs 'Reforms' were in the air at Westminster. "He has caught (I wrote) an echo of the new spirit that is bringing the educated classes at least all over India to act together." On the other hand, "the official mind here is as hard set as a rock and it will need an almost superhuman force to shift it". The memory of the mutiny still lingered—"a kind of phantom standing behind official chairs".

"The next 20 or 30 years," says another letter of July, "will be very critical in India's history." Public opinion was "just in the making" and this, the letter points out, was an important point, for it was doubtful whether public spirit, of which there was all too little at the moment, could thrive without it "since men will only sacrifice their immediate interests if there are others to applaud them".

A letter of November is more explicit. "Nothing (it says) can stop the change now, and no one knows yet whether it will break with soft fertilising showers or with swirling rain and hail, destroying everything in its path. All agree that things are not as they were: the relations between East and West, it is said, were never so strained since '57. This is probably true of the educated, but not of the millions."

The position of the educated, the letter continued, was as difficult as could be imagined. Nurtured on the British tradition of Liberty, Liberty was denied them. At their best they were perhaps a match for England's best. And yet what could they aspire to? If they felt the thrill of patriotism, how could they not but wish to govern where at most they were asked only to advise? "It is bad, very bad, for a country to be governed from outside, for in time rulers and ruled must be opposed, and power is the hardest thing to give up. What Englishman (exclaims the letter) really looks to the time when we shall leave India to itself? Yet that is the only seal of success." This, I added, was "all vague talk". Nevertheless, these were questions that all thoughtful Indians were asking themselves "and if I were one of them, I know how I should answer them".

Here the letter broke off for dinner. Continued later, in spite of a draught of Hochheimer, its tone is a little more dispassionate. After emphasising the difficulty as well as the importance of the problem, it points out that on the one side there are "the conservative English officials, at their best profoundly conscientious and hardworking, but not imaginative, clinging to their prejudices as the ivy to the oak; on the other, a subject people young, passionate, inexperienced, thinking all things possible, and claiming all. They too are prejudiced."

My ideas (I admitted) on what should be done were not at all clear. "The Indians are clamouring for power, and power we must give them or shut up our schools. We can enlarge the Legislative and Executive Councils; we can give them more time to discuss the Budget; but in a few years they will seek to control it. Once let them control the purse, they will attack the Army, and then Imperialism and Nationalism will clash."

A change that all demanded was that the examinations for the I.C.S. should take place simultaneously in England and in India, and not in England alone, an obvious handicap to the Indian. What would that mean? I asked. The answer pointed to a cloud then no bigger than a man's hand but destined to overcast India's whole sky. "Hindus (the letter said) will be reigning over Muslims and vice versa. Government may become impossible. Only the other day when the Lieutenant-Governor visited a district with a Hindu Deputy Commissioner, the Muslims placarded the station with 'Deliver us from native rule'. The feeling between the two religions is becoming increasingly acute. This may make it worse. There are great difficulties as you see. Yet we cannot stand still. In short we must go forward."

These views, expressed no doubt with all the assurance of youth, were not popular with Anglo-India. My Commissioner—a soldier-civilian—thought me 'a red-hot Radical' because I suggested the possibility of self-government for India. Others would remind me that it was impossible to know anything in two years. Even so, I wondered why people looked so contemptuous when I said I took in *The Tribune*, an Indian newspaper published in English—"as high-minded a paper as I have seen anywhere". Anglo-Indians regarded it as 'seditious' and spoke of it as die-hard Tories of those days spoke of *The Daily News*.

I never felt completely at home with Anglo-Indians in general. With individuals it was different, and even in this early critical stage I realised what sterling qualities they had at their best. A letter of June (1906) describes them as robust, always practical, free and easy with each other, typically English in their love of activity and common sense, with a keen interest in the visible but with little or no imagination for what lay outside their surroundings. Independent, resourceful and capable of great endurance, they developed the qualities which the exacting daily Indian round required. But, says the letter, "the softer virtues are needed too—now more than ever", by which I meant the qualities which, to quote Delphi's tribute to the Athenians, 'made gentle the life of the world'.* Indeed they recalled Sparta rather than Athens.

* Quoted by Gilbert Murray in *The Rise of the Greek Epic*, 4th edition, p. 2.

Although I saw the need for the gentler virtues, I could lay no claim to them. I was still "furieusement jeune" and all too liable to be swept by sudden gusts of feeling far from gentle in their effects. Both emotionally and mentally, too, I was still without a fixed anchorage. A process which began in the all-questioning atmosphere of King's had by now completely undermined the highly orthodox faith in which I had been brought up as the son of a clergyman who held firmly to the tenets of the Church of England. The result was agnosticism—not the more arrogant atheism, yet not much less destructive in its effect on faith and its conventional values.

'Every life', wrote Bishop Creighton, 'has to be built upon something.' The question now was what? "Forty years back", says a letter (March 1906), "men followed Tennyson or Browning, Ruskin or Carlyle, according to their bent. Now we are all adrift. A few follow George Meredith, two or three Tolstoy, but goodness only knows what the rest of us do. Some with a faculty for jumping over the centuries go back to the Greek, but most of us drift. We live, as Creighton said, on our emotions. In the middle of these perplexities Goethe's words sometimes come to my mind—'do that duty which lies nearest to your hands'—" No better advice for one drawn this way and that.

"I do not think", says another letter (June 1906), "I was ever depressed till I came to this country and began to grapple with things that were too strong for me." Occasional depression was inevitable in so unnatural a life as mine at Rajanpur. I was isolated not only from kith and kin but also from all that Europe then stood for in the eyes of avid youth. A letter written in August is full of the emotional discord this produced. One evening going straight from Court to my lesson in Baluchi, "I caught myself addressing 'Wotan' in an operatic Baluchi recitative, which I must say sounded uncommonly well, though Wotan replied only with a half guffaw out of the pit of his stomach. Ah, it is hard to let off steam in a strange land when you are alone and everyone around you is as it were your subject; and at 25 the world should be a bit larger than Rajanpur." "I have (I continue) a most unwholesome craving for *la vie*. I want to know my fellow-creatures—men and women (chiefly the latter, I admit, they are so much more interesting): I want the colour and the glitter of life: I want to be mad and foolish, and I am bound in by a river and a chain of hills with the dry plain in between and not one living soul that understands me."

A. C. had recently introduced me to Plato (in translation). This explains what follows. "Plato is very soothing, not because he drives away that instinct for life, but because he shows me in a way that I cannot dispute that all that is wrong—unhealthy, disorderly, discordant. And so I am really content—especially when the day's work is done and I climb onto the roof and sit in my long armchair and watch the moon break from the cloud in the east and Venus glittering in the west, with the last cries of the birds, the hum of the town close by and every kind of thought crowding confusedly in my head. I am never dull then, never when left to myself with a good day's work behind."

CHAPTER 11

Rajanpur in the Cold Weather, continued

My thirty-five years' service in India gave me many delightful experiences, but few so novel and so satisfying as a voyage of some days down the Indus. This was now to come, and what led to it was the marriage of the Mazari Tumandar's daughter to her first cousin at Rojhan, in the far south of the Sub-Division. Waring and I were both bidden to the wedding, and as he was coming by boat, he said he would pick me up near Mithenkot—at Mithenkot itself it was no longer possible, for the Indus had withdrawn into its winter bed six miles away.

I set out at nightfall under a starlit sky domed as is only possible over sea or plain. As we approached the river and its ferry, the flames of a large bonfire made by the ferrymen leapt fluttering into the darkness. Lesser lights shone from the farther shore where a phantom ship, actually Waring's boat, lay moored. As we crossed towards it, Orion appeared on the horizon and around us the stars shot flickering lights into the stream. Leaning out of his cabin, Waring gave me his usual cheerful welcome. He was in his dressing-gown and with him at dinner was the District Superintendent of Police. Joining them, I found myself on an ordinary Indus barge transformed into a house-boat with two cabins made of bamboo and thatch, one the dining-room, the other Waring's bedroom. After dinner as the moon rose, "lovely as only India and the Indus can make her", I retired to another boat, also with two cabins, the larger with table and bed and a rug to cover the floor of straw; the smaller, my bathroom; and there in the morning I found my goat.

At 4 a.m. with the plash of an oar we pushed off, and how pleasant to turn over with that sound in the ear and sleep again. For breakfast, and for all our meals, a third boat containing our kitchen came alongside the dining-room and, as we drifted on together, dishes were handed in from the kitchen steaming hot. After breakfast Waring and I were lying on the roof of the dining-room in the sunshine when he suddenly exclaimed—'Look—on the bank there—a crocodile.' He fired but still it slept. He fired again and this time it turned over and slithered into the river. Farther on we saw another, a smooth dark green, lying on a sand-bank seventy yards away. I fired, and with a lashing of an angry tail he toppled in. The tail reappeared still lashing, and then his nose just above the water. He had been hit but not killed outright, as must be done if he is to be secured.

We were lunching when our boat was boarded by a black-bearded Baluch armed with a sword. The Tumandar, Nawab Bahram Khan, had sent him to greet us where first we touched his domain. All we could offer him was a seat on a box. After a question or two from Waring followed by a long silent pause, he asked leave to present the customary Baluch offering. Waring having graciously assented, a henchman in white, also girt with a sword, appeared in the doorway and, bowing low, presented the usual four quarters of a sheep spitted and roasted.

As we drifted on, the sun set in a ball of fire, and night swept over us from the east—"not the ink-stained night of your brutal winter (says a letter) but in a cloud of azure into which all merged. We landed and in the light of a blazing bonfire were greeted by the Nawab and those in authority under him. With princely courtesy, and apparent sincerity, he briefly expressed how greatly he and his tribe felt the honour of our visit. His leading tribesmen—heads of sections and village headmen—all girt with sword and scabbard, were then presented and 'Salaam, Sahib—Salaam, Sahib' echoed through the half-darkness. Waring gave them all a genial smile and being English said little."

Next morning, mounted on a black charger, he made his state entry into Rojhan, the Mazari capital. The District Superintendent of Police and I rode behind him, and behind us came a troop of Baluchis, all mounted and robed in white, some with scarves of red and gold thrown lightly over the shoulder. As we neared the capital, cannon crashers exploded, schoolchildren clapped and cheered, and two concertinas and a mouth-organ added their welcome. Our horses curvetted and reared, and the Superintendent of Police narrowly escaped impalement on the pegs of our tents.

After lunch came the Nawab's official visit to the head of the District and, as custom prescribed, he did not come empty-handed. The wedding of his daughter made it a very special occasion. The result was prodigious. The wine alone included

Bordeaux, sherry, whisky, liqueurs and six bottles each of champagne and hock. Not content with this impressive libation to the English godlings, the Nawab sent his brother round to me with the more traditional offering of five sheep and three trays of apples, pomegranates and grapes. The sheep were added to my flock and brought the number given me since October up to twenty. Their fate has already been related.*

In rural India the test of propriety was custom. So, after formal remonstrance, all was accepted and the giving of offence avoided. In later years, with the growth of prosperity, the custom in the Punjab came to be abused and acceptance of any kind of offering or gift from an Indian was strictly forbidden. Almost too strictly, for there were many occasions when custom and ban clashed and refusal was not understood. The niceties of propriety do not, in fact, lend themselves easily to Government regulation. In the case of sheep custom had now to be satisfied by a touch of the hand on the victim's head. Yet even as late as 1953, when I was on tour in Baluchistan, I had some difficulty in getting the change accepted.

The Baluch is noted for his hospitality, and on this occasion it was on a royal scale. Not only were our complete establishments the Nawab's guests—mine alone with clerks, orderlies and servants came to twenty-four—but every Mazari who came to do him honour and see the fun was also entertained by him. One afternoon I was taken to an open square thronged with men and women; 100 cows and 500 sheep had just been slaughtered for one evening meal, and men by the score were chopping up the carcases. It was not all butchery. I came upon a group of women sitting on a heap of dung, which their hands were moulding into singular shapes and, as they did so, I heard infant cries. Looking closer I saw the fat blubbering face of a babe. My first feeling was one of disgust, but curiosity prevailed. I then learnt that on great occasions like the present, children who were bruised internally or diseased were immersed in dung until only mouth, nose and eyes could be seen. To clinch the cure a slice of raw flesh, still bleeding, was placed on the forehead. The child was then left to sleep and an hour later, so they claimed, it was cured. It was, in fact, today's mud bath in its most primitive form.

From there I was taken to the kitchens—"large, open courts, where stood giant caldrons seething with the Nwab's bounty and

* pp. 54–55.

men shovelling out the food, chiefly rice, into sacks for the tribesmen to take away home. A fellow would present a slip of paper entitling him to a meal scaled to the number of his family, and he would be served accordingly." In another court were long trenches filled with burning faggots supporting rows of red earthenware jars sizzling with a brew of meat and red pepper. At the far end were two bakeries where 4,500 pounds of flour had been made into bread. "Today (I wrote) the Nawab can be feeding at least 6,000. It is royal, royal and altogether a splendid thing."

The morning was devoted to a tribal Durbar in honour of the occasion. It was my first sight of Waring in a collar, and long since I had worn one myself. We drove to the Durbar hall along a street lined with thick-bearded tribesmen, as ever armed with swords and dressed in white. As Waring passed up the hall from every side came the familiar 'Salaam, Sahib' and hands were respectfully raised to shade the eyes from 'the Presence'. The Nawab was in plain white, but his brother, who read the address of welcome, wore a pale blue turban and a dress shimmering with gold. The address ended with a call for three cheers for each of us in turn—the Superintendent of Police was also there—and hands were suitably clapped. A huge bundle of draperies then appeared and 'robes of honour' were presented by Waring as tribal protocol dictated. "I felt", he said later, "as if I were serving behind the counter." I was still young enough to enjoy what was to me so novel and Eastern a sight.

I was delighted to see 'Wotan' amongst the honoured shuffling up in a red quilt. He certainly deserved recognition: Had he not got me through my examination in Baluchi? There were tears of joy in his eyes when he stalked into my tent to collect the promised 100 rupees.

Next morning—my twenty-sixth birthday—I was lying in bed musing on Dewas and Destiny—of Dewas later—when a message came that the 'nikah', the marriage contract which made a couple man and wife, would be 'read' as soon as I could attend. Half an hour later I was ushered into the room where the ceremony was to take place. The room was crowded, with a clear space in the centre, and there I sat, the only European present, hedged in by black beards.

The bridegroom appeared a little later. To look at, he was not a match for those around him. Opposite him sat a Maulvi* with the

* One learned in the Muhammadan Scriptures.

two formal witnesses to the marriage. Turning to the bridegroom —the bride did not appear at all—and swaying gently backwards and forwards, the Maulvi recited the Nikah, and as he did so the furrows on his forehead deepened and his thin tapering fingers dwelt "with a strange impetuous beauty" on some word or passage he wished to stress. When he finished, oil seed mixed with sugar was poured into a large cloth. The bridegroom was the first to taste it. The Nawab then rose from the floor on which he was sitting and sprinkled a pinch of it on my hand. 'It is our custom (he said) that the guests should eat it.' I ate and was sorry it was only a pinch. From every side now came 'Mubarik! Mubarik'—'Congratulations, congratulations' addressed to the bridegroom. I shook him warmly by the hand, and when I did the same to the Nawab, raising his other hand with a dignity all his own he shaded his face and said what honour I had conferred on his House and Tribe by my presence.

All this before breakfast. Later came the races. "I love an Eastern crowd, and here were horses and camels, men riding bare-back, a whirl of legs, a cloud of dust and the noise of a hundred hoofs on the bare ground"; and finally a camel race, a case of dignity taking to its heels.

From Rojhan Waring and I rode on to the borders of Sind, accompanied by the Nawab on his coal-black charger. We were marching through his country, and everywhere people came forward and touched his feet. The more I saw of him, the more I admired his mixture of kindliness and strength. His father, Sir Imam Baksh Khan (died 1903), was also a remarkable man: even when he became blind he continued to ride about his Tuman.* We had our usual retinue of Baluchis. "Amongst them was 'Wotan' with a great stack of blankets and coats behind his saddle to keep that well-nourished body of his warm at night."

Waring was down with a sharp liver attack and at first he had to be carried on an upturned charpoy. This left the Nawab and myself to ride along together. He was full of talk, explaining why the new Frontier Province (recently severed from the Punjab) was discontented, wondering whether the Marri tribe would come to blows with the Bugtis—they were at loggerheads—and

* Under them 'the Tuman was something of an *imperium in imperio*, British Indian in form but Baloch in sentiment, and in effect a benevolent patriarchial despotism'. Penny *op. cit.*

deploring that the younger officials toured less than the older—a change which with the arrival of the car became more and more marked.

In spite of the liver attack, the most depressing of minor complaints, Waring radiated good humour. One would never have guessed that there was anything wrong with him; much less that since last year's earthquake wiped out his family, there was nothing he really cared about except perhaps a good book. The better I knew him, the more I liked him. In appearance he had the genial outdoor look of an English squire, but his dark eyes he owed to a Spanish mother; perhaps, too, his philosophical outlook on life. He was always courteous to Indians and never interfered in their concerns. He may have carried *laisser faire* a shade too far, but what was more important, he was "a perfect gentleman (in those days a term of high praise) and that counts for much in ruling".

He was a complete contrast to my first Deputy Commissioner. The latter had now become Excise Commissioner, and that brought him and his wife to Ranjanpur for a night. They came to tea "which sets me almost even with him in hospitality". When next day I went to see him off, I saw him knock off his sice's turban and kick him "on the buttocks" in the presence of half a dozen subordinate officials.

To return to our tour: one day we went out hawking. A partridge is put up, the hawk set free and in a flash it has pinned down its prey. Or if the partridge has sufficient start, we would gallop after hawk and prey and perhaps arrive in time to see the huntsman draw them apart and slice the bird's neck with the hawk still plucking at its feathers. In those mediaeval surroundings it all seemed natural enough and the hawk itself, feathered in the softest grey, was a most gentlemanly-looking bird—until you looked into one of its eyes—"like the eye of Fate," said Waring, who knew Fate's look all too well.

A less exciting but more genial experience was breakfast on the march spread out on a village charpoy in the shade of a tree. The whole village came out to watch us, and our escort stood around with their ponies necklaced in shells which glistened in the sunlight. "God! Waring," I exclaimed, "this is better than Whitehall." "Yes (he said) and now we should be on our way there in the Underground." For the six months of the cold weather we certainly had the best of it, and in December how easy to forget the heat of June!

Christmas was now approaching and I was due to spend it with my brother at Benares and there meet my mother, who had just arrived from England on a visit to us both. On December 16 I was on the borders of Sind, and before I could set out for Benares I had to attend an official function at Dera Ghazi, return to Rajanpur and deal with my arrears of cases. Only then could I start off on a journey of well over 1,000 miles, the first eighty of which had to be done by horse, bicycle and tonga. My time-table is perhaps worth recording:

Tuesday (Dec. 18)—arrived Dera Ghazi from the borders of Sind at 2 p.m.
Wednesday—back to Ranjanpur by tonga, 72 miles.
Thursday—started work at 8.30 a.m.; last judgment delivered at 11.30 p.m. (highly unorthodox); to bed at 2.30.
Friday—at 8 a.m. left Ranjanpur on horseback because the tonga did not turn up: after 6 miles changed on to a bicycle; arrived Jampur (42 miles) at 3 p.m.
Saturday—arrived Dera Ghazi at 10; off at mid-day;
Sunday—arrived Lahore 6 a.m.; off at 1 p.m.;
Monday—Dec. 24—arrived Benares 3 p.m.—"a rag but happy".

There followed "three great days when time seemed of no account and the last two years as if they had never been".

Of Benares I wrote with all the romantic enthusiasm of youth. "It is certainly the finest thing I have seen in India, always excepting a sunset in the rains at Dalhousie." With its bastioned palaces, "more magnificent and impressive than those of the Grand Canal", and all the life and colour of the pilgrims "bathing and splashing and laughing and praying", it was beyond anything I had ever imagined. "By moonlight, too, with the ringing of temple bells and the chanting of the Brahmins echoing through the night and here and there a column of smoke and flame marking a funeral pyre, it was incomparably mysterious and lovely." It was my first contact with the mysticism of the East and superficial though it was, it fascinated me. It was perhaps as well that my brother, who had to deal with the problems of a famous pilgrim city, was there to draw my attention to the drains, the fountains and the police stations.

Lahore, and its government house, where on the way back to Rajanpur my mother and I stayed, were a complete contrast. The camel carriage (last met in Jhang), with two postillions and three orderlies in scarlet, met us at the station, and a vast mansion housed us with countless servants in red and gold and with sentinels shouldering arms whenever we went in or out of the garden. Lady Rivaz, fragile as porcelain, was, as usual, all kindness. Sir Charles was obviously bored by his large Christmas house-party: after over forty years in India he was "in a hurry to hand over the reins". One incident of our visit is stamped on my memory and also recorded in a letter.

Congress had just held its annual meeting at Calcutta and for the first time it had declared its aim to be self-government. One evening after dinner, as we were sitting round the fire, someone asked Sir Charles what he thought of this. One word was the answer—"bunkum"—and it was greeted with a titter of deferential laughter. "Bunkum it may be (I comment); I think much of it is, but when you see a spark near gunpowder, it is better to take the thing seriously. That is the English fault—a defect of the imagination"—a defect that was to mislead us again and again during the next thirty years. Even as late as 1940 when I ventured to urge on L. S. Amery, who had just become Secretary of State for India, the need, as a pledge of our sincerity, to fix the latest date—one or two years after the end of the war, I suggested—for our leaving India, he refused even to discuss it.

At Dera Ghazi we embarked in two barges, as before fitted up with cabins and a kitchen. Delightful were the four days we spent winding our way down the Indus to Mithenkot. It was a happy interlude. "There is nothing to do (I wrote) yet the day has slipped away 'between a blush and a flame'." The early mornings were sharp with frost and later the sun was too warm. With the unceasing plash of the great oars the sound of water was always in the ear, and mingling with it, as one fringed a bank, came the tinkling of bells where cattle grazed unseen. For the eye there were crocodiles and pelicans, flocks of geese and duck all basking in the sunshine, and an occasional horseman pricking across the plain towards a ferry; and at sunset, such "marvellous melodies of colour" that "as with Philip in Forster's novel* they were apt to make one late for dinner".

* *Where Angels Fear to Tread.*

A stirring moment was when we came to where the Indus swallowed up the accumulated waters of the five rivers which gave the Punjab its famous name. Four of them—Jhelum, Ravi, Sutlej and Beas—had already been gobbled up by the Chenab, and now the Chenab itself was to suffer absorption. Divided at the last by a mere spit of land green with tamarisk, the two rivers finally "met with hardly a murmur of greeting". Both were in their winter sleep.

The voyage was not all play. On the third day when we entered my domain I found some seventy complainants and petitioners waiting for me on the bank. After dealing with them, with the sun sinking behind the Hills of Solomon, I rode off to a village three or four miles away to choose a site for a school. There was much wrangling over where it should be and it was past eight when I was back on board.

My mother's visit was a complete success. She was fifty-seven and almost everyone at home advised her against it. A. C. was one of the few who encouraged her to come and to him she wrote: 'I can never express how happy I am and how thoroughly I enjoy this delightful unconventional life in a country unknown to Cook and globe-trotters.' She accompanied me everywhere, in Rajanpur even to the jail, where she "implored" me to let all the prisoners out! On tour she sat the liveliest pony "as straight as a girl of 18". I confess that at first I was doubtful whether she would be happy on a horse, especially on one not too well trained, as she had not ridden since she rode through Palestine in 1899. But horsemanship, to which she had been bred, once learnt is never forgotten, as her first ride showed. When I appeared she was already in the saddle: she had mounted by standing on the trunk of a tree. "Malcolm was dreadfully nervous (she wrote) and would hold the reins one side, while the sice followed suit the other, till I rebelled and said I was not a baby. I was only allowed to walk! At last I got into a trot. Seeing that I could keep my seat I finally had a canter, which I much enjoyed. The sice came up beaming with delight. Malcolm even yet is not satisfied and said: 'what would you do if he (the horse) kicked?' 'Stick on', I replied." Stick on she always did, and only once did she give me any cause for alarm, and that was my fault.

What happened was this. An early-morning ride took us out into the desert towards the hills. Through some misunderstanding on my part we got separated. 'Here was I alone (writes my mother) in the vast plain of caked mud, only relieved by scrub in patches. I looked at the range of hills far away and knew that Rajanpur must be in the opposite direction, but how to get there I did not know; so I thought I had better let my Baluchi horse follow his bent. It was wonderful being alone in such an expanse, not a creature or a hut in sight, quite thrilling. The horse was very clever threading his way in and out of the scrub. . . . At last we came to an *impasse* and I wondered how I should ever be discovered entangled in the scrub. My horse paused for a moment, as if thinking and then made up his mind to climb a canal embankment. Up he got, and I found myself riding along the top of a high bank of earth about 2½ feet wide, and very steep on each side. To my joy I saw some cattle about a quarter of a mile away crossing a bridge over the canal, so I knew the high road must be there. I was glad to reach it. I said to the herdsmen – Rajanpur? – pointing and they signified that was the way.' And so she got back. Meanwhile having returned to Rajanpur and not finding her there I had gone off to look for her, and now people were sent off to look for me. After a ride of 20 miles I got back and at about one o'clock we thankfully sat down to breakfast.

One day we paid a surprise visit to a small hamlet lying in a sea of young wheat. While I talked to the men, she somehow managed to draw all the children round her, and with the women passing by with pitchers on their heads, she "found a language which is known the whole world over". They touched her familiarly on the arm, and one offered her a slice of turnip which she proceeded to peel and nibble. Another, old, sallow and wrinkled, sitting in her courtyard by the children's swing, showed us how she span. And, as she did so, another came up and displaying two lean hands "as dry as old parchment" asked for medicine. With our nearest doctor over seventy miles away, my mother had brought out a number of medicines for herself – phenacetin, quinine, mustard leaves, chlorodyne and lozenges. Fortunately she did not need them and the peasants did; so to them they went.

For one accustomed to the comforts of the West life in Rajanpur was not without its hardships. Our bread had to come from Dera Ghazi seventy-two miles away, and once there was a gap of four or five days. The scones made in its place were 'like bricks' and the chappatis 'like bad dough'. My mother had brought out a cake from Buzzard. 'How I longed (she wrote) to turn it into thin bread and butter.' The cook, too, fell ill and the soup became 'uneatable'. My furniture also was very different from hers. 'If I move a little table, the top comes off and the trestles collapse. If I sit on certain chairs, they begin to slide or an arm gives way.' In spite of these minor discomforts my mother enjoyed Rajanpur "as it can never have been enjoyed before".

But a momentous change was impending. In mid-November my peace of mind was rudely disturbed by a letter from the Chief Secretary to the Punjab Government, which ran as follows:

'The Foreign Office (of the Government of India) have written to say that they wish to obtain the services of a young Punjab Civilian as Tutor and Guardian to the Raja of Dewas (Senior Branch) and that the officer selected will probably, if found suitable, be admitted to the Political Department.' After stating the terms—Rs. 700 p.m. with free furnished house and carriage, etc.—the letter continued: 'It is considered advisable that the Raja who is 19 years of age and has finished his studies at the Mayo College, Ajmer, should live with the officer selected to be his tutor. The Lieutenant-Governor desires me to enquire whether you would care to be recommended for the post.'

A later letter from Government said: 'The Raja has actually completed his literary education and the object of the Tutor would now be to teach him the principles of administration preparatory to his being granted ruling powers, which would probably be in about 2 years' time. Whoever is appointed should be prepared to stay for that period at any rate and should not take leave (ugh!) unless compelled to do so. . . . The Raja is of good character and reputation; he is very intelligent and our object in appointing a Tutor is simply to assist him in guiding this intelligence in the right direction, etc. etc.'

The offer threw me into a state of complete indecision. On the whole I enjoyed my life at Rajanpur with its independence and taste of responsibility and power; and I liked the people, especially the Baluchis with whom I was now able to converse in their own tongue. The work was heavy but varied and first-rate training for the future—unless I went into the Political, a doubtful bait. It was little too I knew of the Raja. What if I disliked him, or got bored by the half idleness? I had to sign on for two years. That meant no leave home till 1909. Could I bear that? On the other hand, Waring strongly advised acceptance and others thought it "a good thing to get out of the ruck as soon as possible".

In the end I accepted "less with a smile than a grin". A letter gives my reasons in brief:

"It would be a novel experience and I hankered after all experience."

"It would give me an insight into Native Rule."

I should see another part of India, perhaps even see India as a whole, which was impossible from the Punjab. "There is no such thing as India say some, but it is coming. It is the most interesting movement of the day. I shall be in the middle of it." (That was optimistic.)

I had had nearly a year of Rajanpur, and when one is young, one should regard one's work not as an end in itself, but as a preparation for the work to be done in one's maturity; and for that the broader the basis the better.

I had had nine months of living alone. I liked it, and that was a danger. The life was unnatural and some knowledge of the world is necessary if you wish for power—dangerous word as later I realised.

Ever since August I had been suffering from repeated headaches due to some kind of sunstroke. This was an opportunity to repair the damage.

Finally, "I thought I should despise myself if I feared to plunge. It is a plunge—into Cimmerian darkness—and so why reason? I admit I was guided by instinct, as I was when I chose King's, rejecting Oxford, and when I chose India, rejecting its Office. I regret neither. There is luck in 3 and this will be the 3rd throw," and so it proved.

Part III

HIS HIGHNESS

CHAPTER 12

Dewas – First Impressions

FROM Rajanpur to Dewas, from the banks of the Indus to the uplands of Central India, was to pass from the domination of Islam to the heart of Hinduism, of India herself. I had gone through an agony of indecision before taking the plunge. Now the question was – what was I in for?

First of all, a journey of 1,300 miles – over 100 by road – had to be negotiated with all one's kit and in sufficient comfort to make it possible for my mother. On leaving Dera Ghazi Khan, owing to being held up at the Bridge of Boats across the Indus, we reached the railhead with only five minutes to spare, and then to discover all our kit – boxes, portmanteaus, trunks, cases, bicycle and guns – piled on a bullock cart left in a siding. "For 15 minutes the station was in a most terrible uproar. Every coolie was driven to the work; porters weighed it, clerks drew appalling bills – 960 lbs I must pay for, they said. The guard shouted – 'either you leave luggage or miss train'. 'I shall do neither' I said." At last all thirty-five pieces were stowed away. It was then my turn to stamp with impatience; the guard had threatened that I should miss my connexion at Multan for Lahore – "and there he was at the door of my compartment meekly asking – 'may the train start now, sir?' "

Next day we entered Hindu India with a typical scene at Mathure of clamour, clatter and colour. As we came to a stop, the crowd on the platform broke into a rush for seats with rolls of bedding, striped blankets, and metal portmanteaus bobbing up and down on their heads. Amongst them but less hurried was a copper-coloured fellow hawking oranges; another shouting 'water – water' offering it to the thirsty from a leather skin; a railway official scratching a coffee-coloured nose with his whistle, and just as the train was about to start, a man rushed by with tea spurting out of his teapot.

At Agra we were back in the days of the Moguls and properly affected by the Taj, which we visited four times in less than twenty-four hours. "I could not look at it long: it made me feel the burden of my body—of the earth earthy." At Jhansi where our train stopped for dinner we ran into "a fellow called Marten" who had taught me history so stimulatingly at Eton that at Cambridge I discarded the Classics and read History instead. Much later he became Eton's Provost. He was globe-trotting and we had hoped to meet at Rajanpur, and here we were suddenly face to face in a railway refreshment room with "a bare 20 minutes to discuss Eton, India and the world and scramble through a six-course dinner", before parting, he to Bombay and England, I to Indore.

At Indore we were hospitably received at the Residency by Major (later Sir Hugh) Daly, Agent to the Governor-General for the States in Central India, and there at last I heard at first hand about my ward, Tukoji Rao Puar, a Hindu Prince. "He is really His Highness (says a letter) and at first I am to slip it in now and again *par politesse*, though Raja Sahib will usually be sufficient.* He is clever, remarkably sharp, and Ajmere, where he was at the Chiefs' College, used to parade him as their show boy. Better still (continues the letter) he is a thoroughly nice fellow, brought up on English lines, accustomed to liberty and unmarried. This took me by surprise: I expected having to call him out every morning from his harem!" I gathered that my predecessor had done "something foolish" and was then "moved on". What this was I never learnt, and it was characteristic of the Raja that he always spoke of him with liking and regard. Whatever it was, it probably explains why Reynolds, Major Daly's 'First Assistant', told me that I was in for "a very difficult job which will require all your tact and patience." 'Make a friend of him if you can,' said Major Daly, and that, thanks to his lovable nature, I had no difficulty in doing.

On February 6, 1907, after a three-hour carriage drive of twenty-two miles, we finally reached Dewas. The country we crossed was flat with hills in the distance and much of it looked black, due to a soil famous for its cotton but with spongy holes highly treacherous to the rider, as I was soon to discover. At one point we crossed "a lovely little rock-strewn stream" called the Sipra, just large enough to harbour crocodiles and separate the States of Indore and Dewas. Another seven miles and we were skirting the Hill of Devi—the Hill of the Goddess— immortalised by E. M. Forster. It towered sharply above us like an acropolis,

* In 1912 he was given the title of Maharaja.

very brown for lack of rain, but at its summit curiously black, "as if Providence had upset a sack of coals upon it".

The Raja came round to see us as soon as we had breakfasted and talk followed in the verandah of the State Guest House, where we were lodged. Reynolds had a good deal to say to the Raja and since I had no part in this I was able to have a good look at him. This, I think, he envied, for every now and then he shot little nervous glances at me. In a letter I described him as "short and slim, a mere boy in build, but a thick black moustache makes him look much older than he is (19 on Jany. 1st last). His mouth is large, especially the underlip, which he can purse up, or relax into a generous smile. His eyes are as unfathomable to me as all Eastern eyes, but I have seen them dance half closed with good spirits. He is certainly high-spirited and alert. He has, too, a most engaging manner. I like him and I think we are almost certain to get on together." And most happily we did.

My mother expressed herself more vividly. "I quite fell in love with him. He is a charming boy of 19 with long eyelashes and a pleasant expression, always full of fun."

That afternoon we were driven to the local tennis club, where later I spent many pleasant hours of talk and play. A tournament had just concluded and after my mother had given away the prizes, we were introduced to "the flower of Dewas aristocracy". The club pavilion was adorned with portraits in green frames of Kipling and Tennyson. "Great awe when I said I knew Tennyson's grandson. The Raja made a neat little speech; my mother beamed, everyone beamed and a State band played (ye gods!) and we went home." In the evening the Raja dined with us dressed in pale blue satin and wearing a coral-red turban. 'Take Mrs Darling into dinner,' said Reynolds. 'He laughed (she writes): he did not know how and held my hand and I led him in.' And so ended our first day in Dewas.

My mother was exhausted by the long trek from Rajanpur. Since she landed in mid-December, she had travelled about 3,000 miles, with in the last week three nights in the train. 'The dust was appalling,' she wrote: 'I don't think I ever felt so miserably dirty; and the vibration made my body ache as riding never did.' For this our new quarters provided the right restorative. The Guest House stood at some distance from the town on an artificial lake with, in front of it, a small garden full of roses. In a hot country a lake of any kind is a refreshment to the eye. In this case a wooded islet or two and a cluster of palm trees on the far bank gave it a special charm, and the activities of washermen and cattle around it gave it life; for background, too, it had the Hill of Devi.

The Guest House itself was a solid comfortable-looking building coloured a rich maroon picked out in white. Its round-arched verandah and massive porch gave it a certain dignity, which went well with its surroundings and purpose. Inside, the ground floor gave us ample accommodation "with furniture of varying ugliness and discomfort, but after Rajanpur it all seems regal". For my mother, too, after her months of travel, it seemed the acme of comfort. 'Imagine (she exclaims) the luxury of arranging my clothes after living in my trunks since October.' But one luxury was denied her: 'I long for a big bath. My last was at Government House (Lahore) and even there no hot water was laid on.' It was long before the zinc tub was replaced in private bungalows by the porcelain bath. The upper floor of the Guest House was kept for State guests, happily so infrequent that when the hot weather set in, I was generally able to sleep on the roof of the porch under the stars.

That my mother was with me for the first four or five weeks at Dewas was the beginning of my good fortune there. Her delight in the Raja's company, her eager interest in his way of life and her obvious sincerity did much to smooth the way to the happy relationship which soon developed between my charge and myself. Of an evening he would take her for a drive in his dog-cart and she would ply him with questions about himself and his views on life. 'I like hearing him talk,' she wrote. 'I go alone with him, then tell Malcolm the stories of his life and what he believes; so by degrees M. will get to understand his mode of thought.' And a week later she adds: 'I like the Raja increasingly, we have very intimate talks while driving and I get an insight into his way of thinking.' She did not suppose for a moment that she understood the working of his mind; she wrote indeed: 'It seems almost impossible to bridge the gulf between East and West: one can but show one's sympathy.' There she hit upon the master-key to understanding.

That the Raja felt at home with her is suggested by an incident on one of her drives with him when she had charge of the reins. 'May I tuck up my leg?' he asked. 'Certainly, both if you like.' 'I can't do both as my trousers are too tight: this does very well, thank you.' And as he said this, he tucked his right leg under his left on the seat of the dog-cart. Conversation then turned on the use of poison. Once he had been very ill after a meal due, he thought, to poison. Since then he always had his food first tested on a pye-dog, and once, he declared, the dog died in ten minutes. When dining too with the Rani, his mother by adoption, before trying any dish he always offered it to her first, and if she refused it, he would not touch it.

Another talk a few days later points to the same easy relationship between him and my mother. This time their drive took them through the town. 'That,' said the Raja, pointing to a house, 'is where my father's mistress lived: he built it for her.' This in a most matter-of-fact tone. 'But you (said my mother) would surely never do such a thing?'

'Oh no, but all the Chiefs do it, some on the sly. Baroda is the only one who does not. I never shall.' This he added so confidently that it led my mother to quote the well-known text—'He that thinketh he standeth take heed lest he falleth.' The Raja seemed struck but turned from himself to others. 'You know that man whose puggaree you admired last night (at an Indian dinner to be described later) has a mistress, but he is old-fashioned.'

'But do the others we saw do it too?' asked my mother.

'No, they are more up to date.' Some might have questioned this tribute to modernity. The Raja went on to tell her he had vowed before God to have only one wife, but if at forty she had not borne him a son, he would marry again, and then only if his brother had died. But this was to speak with the easy idealism of youth.

The only order I ever gave the Raja was four days after my arrival. But for my mother's soothing presence and the Raja's good sense it might well have started us on the wrong foot. The occasion was a courtesy call I had to pay the late Raja's widow, who for want of an heir had adopted her husband's nephew. That was how the Raja had come to succeed his uncle. Discovering that it was long since he had seen her I suggested that he should come with me. When he objected, I said he *must* come, and he came but with not too good a grace. Later I learnt he had good reason for not wishing to see her; and it was only when our friendship was firmly established, that he told me his coming with me had been touch and go.

The visit, which fortunately passed off without incident, gave me my first experience of an interview with an Indian lady in purdah. We had tea under mango trees in the Rani's garden to the pleasant sound of four bullocks drawing water from a well. To do us honour, or more probably just to impress us, an enormous green plush carpet embroidered with gold had been spread out in front of "a kind of Punch and Judy box" curtained in white muslin with a screen of split bamboo through which anyone inside could see without being seen. Caged within was the Rani herself, a woman of about twenty-six, who was said to be pretty and was certainly not over-austere in her ways. Conversation with her was of the simplest character. 'What a charming garden you have, Rani Sahib,' I said. 'I hear you are a great botanist.' 'Yes,' and a long simper. 'I see you have mangoes,' I continued. 'Yes,' and a still longer simper. And so on until somehow we got on to the subject of nationality. The Rani said she would like to be an English lady and hoped that God would make her one in her next incarnation. 'She is a perfect child,' said her English companion, Miss M. As I peered through the bamboo screen, all I caught was a glimpse of a moon-shaped face with large dark eyes.

At Rajanpur the silent Cooper was my only fellow-European, if one who had never been to Europe could be called that. Here the only one was Miss M., who talked often amusingly but without ceasing. She was a quarter French and well past her youth, and a convent education had turned her into a strong Protestant. With her long thin nose "sharp as a razor" and a prodigious interest in herself, she was not without personality. She declared she was never dull and that she loved Dewas, her three dogs and the Rani.

Our next State call was upon the Maharani Sahiba, the Raja's grandmother, who for some years during his minority had been Regent of the State. She lived in a dirty house in the middle of the town. A narrow mud-plastered staircase led to a room cut in two by another bamboo screen. My mother had the questionable privilege of being allowed to talk to her face to face. She was so 'uncomfortable' afterwards – one can guess why – that she vowed she would never do it again. The Maharani was a remarkable woman. On the one hand, during her Regency she had hanged seven men, one for attacking a noble with a sword without hurting him, so it was said. On the other hand, she had sold her jewels to build a hospital, and in those days a normal Indian lady would almost sooner have parted with her eyes than with her jewels. And for her to build a hospital was in itself almost an eccentricity.

Calls had also to be paid in Indore. This gave me my first drive in a car. In the India of 1907 cars were both a novelty and a luxury, and up country with no tarmac, they could be very expensive in tyres. The Raja's small De Dion was also expensive in time: it was constantly breaking down, and the chauffeurs of those days were not the efficient motor mechanics of today. It was in this that I set out one morning for Indore, twenty-two miles away. I got as far as the Residency without mishap, but there at the front entrance the car stopped dead "travailing with titanic pangs, and with the sentinel at attention". The remaining calls had to be paid on foot. When I returned, the car was still blocking the entrance, but now at least silent. For half an hour I stood there watching the chauffeur, an Indian in a green coat, struggling with screws, pistons and valves and trying to coax life into its motionless body. "Elisha stretched on the body of the Shinamite's son could not have laboured more devotedly." But in this case all was in vain.

When however I came back after lunch, he had triumphed, and we started back to Dewas. With only two enforced stops, we sped along at a fearful pace setting horses rearing, riders clutching saddles, cattle flinging up heels, goats scampering to the four winds, bullock-carts plunging into the fields on either side, and peasants rushing from the fields to see the latest miracle from the West; all to be swallowed up a moment later in a cloud of dust thicker than a London fog.

One day we climbed the Hill of Devi. It is said to be a mere 350 feet high; but some hills are to be judged less by their measurement than by their effect upon the imagination. Isolation and sanctity can both add to their stature. Devi not only rose up straight from a flat earth but with her cave-shrines and phallic symbols attracted pilgrims. The pilgrim made the ascent barefoot. For my mother the Raja ordered a palanquin with eight men to carry it, four at a time; but we had almost reached the top before it appeared. Not that that signified, for my mother had decided in any case to walk up. This she did to the surprise of our guide, the Raja's Private Secretary, who said he had never known anyone of her age do this before. Over 100 steps brought us to a small temple. 'It might easily have been a Roman Catholic chapel (wrote my mother) and the goddess in the apse could with very little trouble have been turned into a B.V.M.' Farther on, after passing the abode of a Sadhu and scrambling over black rocks, we reached the top.

Here a flag was flying at half-mast, in whose honour, I wondered —to be told that it did no more than mark the division of the hill between Dewas Senior and Dewas Junior. For Dewas was the capital of two States, each with a fifteen-gun-salute Raja at its head, and each with its own territory and administration. Each too had its own temple on Devi. Mast and flag, on the other hand, were held in common; hence the curious position of the flag to mark the fact.* School, hospital and Guest House were also joint; so much so that at the Guest House we were guarded by each State month by month in turn. In keeping with all this was a carriage which had been specially built for State occasions. That Government might treat the two Rajas with the minimum of discrimination it had been made wide enough for the two Rajas to sit facing the horses with the Agent to the Governor-General tucked in between them. Fortunately for all three parties Major Daly was of slender build.

Each State had its own army, and never were armies less militant in their purposes. The Senior Branch had a muster-roll of 70 foot and 80 horse with a bodyguard of 14, plus 60 irregulars and 14 guns, two of them in actual use for firing the indispensable salutes. In the mornings the air is full of drums and tramplings for the Army drills. In the evenings the band plays. It numbers at least 10. It is therefore an important part of the State Forces!

S.B.'s territory measured only 442 square miles, "which makes me sniff a little after Rajanpur, but Providence has packed over 60,000 inhabitants into it". In the capital the High Street made a neat if unusual boundary between the two States. To add to the freak set-up, which went back to the year 1818, each State was split into 4 districts each enmeshed in the network of the larger States around them. Altogether, as I wrote to E. M. Forster in May, Dewas is "the oddest corner of the world outside Alice in Wonderland".

One morning we drove to the Treasury to see the 'Crown Jewels'. The State's annual revenue was no more than £50,000,

* Later in the year it was replaced by a red banner ending in two streamers.

but the jewellery was worth, it was said, £60,000. A tray "large enough to hold tea for six" was set before us laden with bracelets and bangles, necklaces, anklets and rings for nose and ear. We fingered them gingerly eyed by a Committee of six who had to be present when they were viewed. Five more trays appeared with ropes of pearls, each about four feet long. At Curzon's Delhi Durbar one of them got caught in the Raja's diamond-studded sword and broke. After the Durbar pearls were shaken out of his dress, but a number were lost, for the Durbar was hardly the moment to hunt for them. As tray followed tray, I 'sickened' at the sight of so much 'barbaric pearl and gold'. The pearls too had lost their lustre and the diamonds looked like glass. "Give me rather," I wrote, "a flight of pelicans over the Indus or the stars as they are tonight."

His Highness—or H.H. as I shall now call him for short—had dined with us: it was now our turn to dine with him, and it was to be an Indian dinner in every respect. A question which troubled me was whether my mother should follow Indian custom and dispense with table and chair. For myself I was in no doubt, but at her age I thought there might be difficulties. She brushed them aside and said she had no intention of being made peculiar by sitting differently to the other guests. And of course she was right, and right again in declaring that she must also take off her shoes. That I should have suggested the contrary shows how little I had been able to learn of Indian social etiquette in the two years I had been in India. This was indeed my first chance of having an Indian dinner.

We were received by H.H. dressed in a pink satin coat and pale blue turban. His fifteen Indian guests had already arrived and were standing in a solemn semicircle visibly shrinking against the wall. A little later Miss M. rustled in, talking without stop. We sat down, the Indian guests "silent as the senators sat when the Gauls were sacking Rome". H.H. was restless because dinner was not ready. In and out he went, and each time he rose we all rose, and each time he sat we all sat. At last, when even Miss M. had stopped talking, dinner was announced. We all took off our shoes, Miss M. explaining to H.H. that she had not expected this and so he must not be shocked if he saw a hole in her stockings. In a pair of shot-silk socks fresh from the Burlington Arcade I had no fears. H.H.'s Court-Room was our Banqueting Hall and its space was fully needed, for we were seated in separate groups according to caste and race. At our head, under an oleograph portrait of Queen Victoria, there was a silver-plated stool with a shell-like back raised only a few inches from the ground. Here sat H.H. beaming upon us all, his feet tucked away under his pink coat. The Indian guests were on mats, but we were given cushions, and on these we squatted "with our knees almost knocking against our chins". In front of each guest was a low stool stencilled round with a cunning pattern in blue and white chalk; and upon each of our stools thirty-five bowls, and in each bowl a different dish.

"Lud! how I stared at my dishes (I wrote) and wondered where I should begin, for the Brahmins had chanted grace, a few Sanskrit words, and all were setting to as silently as they had sat before. We laughed from pleasure, and H.H. laughed to see us dipping our fingers gingerly into a bowl of rice. I had started greedily with two hands, but I discovered that this was not etiquette (another example of my gross ignorance of Indian ways) and for the rest of dinner I managed somehow with one, though it is a most difficult thing to break off a morsel from a well-cooked rissole or chop with only one hand."

Into which of the thirty-five bowls should one dip one's fingers next? There was no fixed order but every now and then H.H. would consult the menu— a large sheet of paper at his side—and call out—'try so-and-so'. But which was so-and-so? Was it the little fish, or the green sauce, or the silver-papered sweetmeat? The sweetest things jostled against the most fiery. My mother was in despair. "I tried one thing (she exclaimed) and that was too hot; I tried another and that was still hotter; then a third and I felt like Dives calling for a drop of water." I went boldly like a bee from bowl to bowl, from rice to pastry, sweetmeat to omelette, from omelette to that fearful green sauce, and managed to make quite a meal, though once or twice I thought it would all come up again. Meanwhile the room echoed with H.H.'s spirits and even the Brahmins smiled to see us eat.

At a dinner like this it was apparently the custom for each guest to sing in turn, and one by one they did so, 'except a few old ravens'. I was then called upon to do so too. Yielding to pressure, I said I would try if H.H. would give us something first. This he did very pleasantly, ending up just as I had filled my mouth with my twenty-fifth dish. When this had been disposed of, I gave them the first verse of the *Eton Boating Song*, and complying with a polite encore I gave them two more.

Dinner was now over and from one or two corners of the room I was reminded of that pleasant heading to the 45th Psalm—'*Eructavit cor meum*'. To the sound of a gramophone playing Indian music a servant went round with silver basin and ewer and poured water over sticky fingers through the head of a lion. Each guest was also given a tiny scented wad of cotton to slip into the upper fold of his ear 'that the scent might be prolonged' it was said. This gracious service H.H. did for me himself.

He also explained some points which had puzzled me. Why, for instance, so many dishes—actually thirty-seven, for two had no bowls? The answer was simple: it was the limit of the cook's inventiveness. When the Maharaja of Kolhapur, the Raja's father-in-law to be, came here on a visit, he was given fifty dishes, but all the master-cooks of Dewas had to be summoned for the purpose. For a dinner with no guests six or seven dishes sufficed, and for a formal dinner-party twenty-five. Only a special occasion demanded as many as thirty-seven; and that we were given this within fifteen days of our arrival was H.H.'s characteristic response to my mother's warm-hearted interest in him.

For the orthodox an Indian dinner-party was a complicated affair in more ways than one. In this case the Indian guests represented four different caste-groups, and in a sense we Europeans made a fifth. Two were of Brahmins, one hailing from the Deccan, the other from Malwa, the plateau on which Dewas stood. These two could eat together if, as on this occasion, the cooking was done with milk and not with the less purifying water. The rest of us had to eat separately group by group.

There were other taboos touching propinquity and food, and they did not make social intercourse between Indian and European any easier. Over twenty years later, when attending a conference at Lyallpur, I and some others were invited by the Chairman, Sir John Maynard, to lunch. In telling his wife that he would do this he suggested that it should be a cold lunch as it was uncertain when the session would end. For this, ham and cold beef seemed the very thing, and Lady Maynard ordered lunch accordingly. But Sir John had omitted to tell her that some of the guests might be Indian. What was her concern therefore when he returned with both Hindu and Muslim guests. The Hindus ruled out the beef, the Muslims the ham. An uneasy half-hour passed before a new lunch could appear. Matters became even more complicated with the emergence of Indian ladies from purdah. I was once ticked off by my Hindu host for shaking hands with his wife—here the taboo was touch—instead of saluting her with both hands raised palm to palm. Similarly I got into trouble with a Muslim friend when absentmindedly I did this to his wife instead of salaaming her.

On their side, Indians who adapted themselves to our ways could run into far greater troubles. H.H. had narrowly escaped the Hindu equivalent of excommunication for dining with Europeans, and for some time many Indians had refused to dine with him. The tiniest incident too might lead to difficulties with the orthodox, then an overwhelming majority: as occurred one evening at the club when only one unused tumbler was available to quench our thirst after tennis, and H.H. and I both drank out of it in turn, H.H. insisting that I should drink first. With him friendship brushed away all petty scruples.

H.H.'s position in these matters was complicated by the intrigues surrounding his adoption as successor to his uncle, the late Chief. Those who had opposed it seized on any excuse for getting him into trouble. I was concerned one day to find that he had not been to see his mother for six days though she was ill. He explained that he saw her as little as possible, otherwise the Rani, his adoptive mother, would put it about that his real mother was getting him into her hands. In the past the mischief-makers had made things so difficult for him that he actually wrote to my predecessor that he wished to abdicate. To me, too, he said, no doubt with the exaggeration of strong feeling, that he had never had a happy day in Dewas since he was twelve; and even now, he added, he was pestered with pin-pricks, which evidently touched his highly sensitive nature to the quick.

During my first month in Dewas there occurred two annual celebrations, one of importance to the Shia branch of Islam, the other to the Hindus. Muharram, as the former was called, came first. Its object was to mourn the martyrdom of Ali, the son-in-law of the Prophet, and his two sons, Hassan and Husain. The celebrations lasted several days, and they brought us one evening to Dewas' main bazaar. With its tiled houses, shadowing eaves and purely Indian atmosphere, Dewas by day was always a pleasant sight. But at night, and as now under a half moon, with scattered lamps throwing an uncertain light upon the houses and upon the turbaned heads passing to and fro, its charm was irresistible. We had come to see the customary procession. The sound of drums and the flare of torches announced its approach. At its head came one of the State's two 'serviceable' guns drawn by a pair of phlegmatic bullocks. The State infantry followed with glittering sabres and behind them came H.H. in brilliant yellow silk with the dashing Maratha puggaree on his head.

We entered his carriage and a group of excited processionists rapidly formed round us—men wrestling dagger in hand; tumblers rolling on the ground or leaping into the air with jugglers slicing potatoes under a man's chin as he lay prone. Standing on a wicker chair and towering above them all was the Court Jester in a green coat and a red-peaked cap three to four feet long. He was a State servant and drew the princely salary of Rs. 6/8 (about 9 shillings) a month. At the moment it was only through him that religion got a word in. 'Yad Allah—Yad Allah—Remember God, Remember God,' he cried. The crowd's response was a burst of laughter as torch-bearers tried to set his cap on fire. With that the procession moved on, and I went home with his cry echoing in my ears.

A significant feature of this Muslim celebration was H.H.'s participation in it though a Hindu. It was a happy way of showing his Muslim subjects that as Ruler he did not distinguish between them and his own community. In British India we did our best to treat both communities equally but as we belonged to neither it had not the same effect.

What I saw that evening might well leave a stranger wondering whether he was witnessing an occasion of sorrow or rejoicing. He could be in no such doubt about the Hindu celebration of Holi, which took place a little later. This was the great festival of the Sudras, the lowest and far the largest of India's four major caste-groups. For six days Dewas gave itself over to a Saturnalia, with all social barriers swept away so completely that H.H. had to walk through the town and be roundly abused by someone told off for the purpose. As with the younger of us on April Fools' Day, there was much fooling of the same kind but by no means confined to the young. H.H., for instance, was given a costly-looking parcel to find that it contained nothing but mud. On his side—he ever loved a practical joke—he offered his entourage cigarettes with horsehair sandwiched between tobacco at both ends. That, however, was nothing to Holi's central feature—a promiscuous pelting of each other in the streets with a lurid red liquid to the singing of songs, mainly obscene, in the riotous but good-tempered spirit of the day.

On the sixth and last day a durbar, attended by the nobles and officials of the State, was held to mark, as it were officially, the climax of the festival. For good reason, as will appear, it was held, not in the durbar hall, but in front of the palace. H.H. was in white with ropes of pearls about his neck and a jewelled sword in his hand. All rose and bowed low as he came down the Palace steps and took his seat on an improvised gadi.*

The durbar opened with music and song, the music from four minstrels and the song from three gaudily dressed dancing girls, all seven, like the Court Jester, State servants on Rs. 6/8 a month. So far, it might have been any ordinary durbar. But now H.H. was handed a squirt and the proceedings took a livelier turn. The squirt was filled with a fluid made from crystals with the curious trade mark 'Magenta—1 A (A 1?) Crystals—Hoechst on Main, Germany'. Magenta-coloured indeed was the fluid which came out as H.H. squirted each noble and official in turn. With him went the Hereditary Controller of the Treasury, basin in hand to keep the squirt well primed, and with the rough humour of the day he would suddenly find the squirt turned upon himself full-face. Last of all H.H. himself was squirted. For full measure a red powder was then thrown about leaving nothing white behind it but teeth grinning with good humour.

The Durbar had been marked by a certain formality, even restraint. Now that it was over, the real fun was to begin. Seeing two water-carts approaching and two hoses being prepared for action, we thought it prudent to leave, doubting whether our grins would be equal to what might be in store for us if we stayed. And wise indeed we were judging by what H.H. told me later.

Two sides were formed, the officials on one side, the nobles on the other headed by H.H. Each side was given a hose with a water-cart to feed it, and every hose-bearer a large round shield to parry attack. Each side's aim was to force the other back; and the best way to do this, said H.H., was to ply the hose straight at your opponent's face. After a time—an hour or so, it was said—

* Cushioned throne.

a truce was called, and a procession formed to march through the town and fight the burghers, who were given one of the hoses for defence. And so another hour passed.

The Rani was not to be kept out of the fun. At the very outset of Holi she had shown her appreciation of its spirit: a noble sent by H.H. one evening with the compliments of the season had found her dancing with her maid-servants all dressed in male attire, or as the Raja put it, 'like the public women'. She now announced the wish to spray the leading personages of Dewas. As she was in purdah and up a flight of stairs, she plied the hose upon them from above. H.H. and the few allowed to see her she squirted in the presence of her maids and for much longer than she would allow herself to be squirted.

After a good wash H.H. dined with her but he would only eat what she ate, partly, he said, from friendliness, partly also on account of 'something else'—an oblique reference to what he had already told us. After dinner she pressed him to stay and hear her maids sing, but the hour was late—they had not dined until eleven—and he refused. She cried. He declared he had work to do for me. She pretended to vomit. She was, he said, no longer sober. So the not too sober Saturnalia ended.

What perhaps surprised me most in my new life was the spy system around me. The Rani employed a spy to keep an eye on H.H.'s doings, and H.H. did the same by her. The Rani had used my predecessor's scullery boy (now mine) to spy on him, and no doubt continued to do so to spy on me. Miss M. had very recently begged for a guard. H.H. gladly complied with her request and sent a man who now acts as his spy on her. As he told me this "he slapped his thigh with delight". "I must say (I add) a month at a native Court throws a new light upon existence." And yet is the gossip that goes on in any small community so very different?

One day in Holi week when all were at leisure a carriage drove up to the Guest House and, headed by H.H., out came the Superintendent of Education, the Hereditary Controller of the Treasury, the Commander-in-Chief, and a Magistrate, the last with a portable harmonium. They came at one o'clock, and in the cheerful spirit of the festival they thought to divert us with an impromptu concert of Indian music.

The magistrate was given a chair for himself and a table for the harmonium. The others, with H.H. amongst them, sat in a row on a sofa; and a pleasant sight it was to see them grouped together in their different coloured turbans—red, yellow, green and rose—ready to start at H.H.'s signal. The Commander-in-Chief led the singing in a high falsetto voice, to the accompaniment of the harmonium, and H.H.'s beat; and after each song the Superintendent of Education told us what it was about. The first was a hymn to "God, boundless as the Ocean". The second warned us to lay up treasure in Heaven, for youth and wealth, eating and drinking, all passed away, even sleep. Then came an extract from a new musical play in Marathi ridiculing incongruous marriages between old and young with the heroine complaining that she was to be betrothed to a man with many wrinkles. This, we were told, was 'literature' and was aimed at a Raja who had recently married a girl in his old age. The attack might have passed unnoticed had not the theatrical company decided to hold their *première* in the Raja's own capital. This brought him down to the theatre in a rage with a threat to have it set on fire and so, we were told, he did to a corner of the building when they persisted. "You see, said H.H., he was old-fashioned." It was anyhow an unusual musical *ensemble*.

On March 6, exactly four weeks after our arrival in Dewas, my mother took her last drive with H.H. "The conversation (says a letter of the same date) turned upon his bride-elect, a girl of 13, the daughter of the Maharaja of Kolhapur. 'I mean to be obeyed when I am married. I shall make her fear me. At first I shall talk to her very little, and she will never talk to me unless I talk to her. My father-in-law says that if she is disobedient, I am to beat her with a shoe and that the shoe shall have nails.' A cry from my mother! 'But I shall not do this. If she is disobedient I shall send her back to Kolhapur and the Maharaja can beat her. He beat her once.'

" 'But she will be your slave then,' said my mother.

" 'Yes, she will be my slave; and I shall make her do some of my *Puja** for me. She is very fond of this and does *Puja* now for 3 or 4 hours a day. We shall not sleep in the same room, but I shall sometimes go to her, and when she likes she may come to me. So our rooms will be close by. I want 2 sons. If I have a daughter, I will not look at her.' And so on."

"Most curious things he told my mother (says the letter). He is

* A Hindu's devotions.

great friends with the Maharaja of Kolhapur, and sometimes when they travel together, they share the same bed. The Maharaja is in the habit of putting one leg in his sleep across his (H.H.'s) and he has to remain quite still or he would wake him. So now he puts his leg out first across the Maharaja's to keep it still." That he should have talked so intimately to my mother shows, I think, that he had become genuinely fond of her, and this proved of great service to me.

'I have had a glorious time in India,' she wrote; and 'a glorious time' she deserved, for at fifty-seven she had set out in uncertain health and in the face, at her end, of almost universal discouragement. 'I was mad to go to Rajanpur,' said one friend, 'and Rajanpur cured me!' And doubtless remembering her visit to Khartoum in 1900 and her ride the year before from Jerusalem to Damascus, she added: 'I am not a novice in travelling. If I followed everyone's advice, I should have had a very dull life.' She now proposed to see southern Spain on her way home.

CHAPTER 13

Personalities

AT Bombay, after seeing my mother off, I drove to Phipson's, India's most famous wine-merchant. As a complete ignoramus about wines I had hoped to discuss my very modest needs with some underling in the firm. What was my concern therefore when I was taken up a flight of stairs and ushered into what looked more like a library than an office! At a table bearing many books and a bottle or two sat a middle-aged figure whose well-bred manner and bearing suggested that he must be Mr Phipson himself. 'Perhaps you have a wine-list,' I said rather nervously as he motioned me to a chair. I knew what I wanted, but should I have the courage to stick to that? It was so little, and here everything was by the dozen and the surroundings such that "like Wordsworth in our chapel at King's, I felt it was a case when 'high Heaven rejects the lore of nicely calculated less or more'."

The price list was handed me and I hoped that with the opportunity for a little reflection behind its pink pages I should recover my sangfroid. But as I turned them over, the different wines and vintages danced before me in such a Bacchanalian rout that I knew I must do something foolish. Happily I was saved by Mr Phipson himself. I was prudent enough to consult him, and he not only singled out the cheaper wines but even advised me not to buy much at a time. 'You see, sir' (the way he said 'sir' was enough to undo the most confirmed teetotaller), 'wine will not stand the climate. I think you will be wise to buy frequently but in small quantities.' I was saved: I felt now he would not scorn me if I ventured upon a modest order of the cheaper wines. "Once I thought I should be caught: he was so insinuating, so polished. 'If, Sir, (he said) you want a Hock of special quality (I shivered), we have just got a new stock—not yet down on the list—with a strong flavour of muscatel, and only 54/–.' I felt I was done for, when he added—'the ladies like it especially'. I breathed again. 'But I have no Ladies'. 'Oh, I did not mean that, of course not, but entertaining.' 'But I have no one to entertain.' " With that

I wrote my order, and it was the first of innumerable orders given to the firm during the following thirty-three years.

Soon after my return to Dewas the prospect of a visit from His Highness Sayaji Rao Gaikwar of Baroda set us all agog with excitement. The Gaikwar was one of India's premier Ruling Princes nearly related to H.H. He was due to come with his wife and daughter and a retinue of three nobles and seventeen servants. It was decided that we should meet him not on the border of the State as would have been appropriate to a Ruling Prince of his importance, but at the entrance to the capital—H.H.'s retort for not being met at the station when he went to Baroda. The Gaikwar must have got wind of this, for when we reached the appointed spot he had come and gone, and we had to follow him a little sheepishly to where he was staying.

The visit was ostensibly one of courtesy, but its real object was to induce H.H. to marry his daughter, Princess Indra Bai, who had now reached an age (sixteen) at which it was a slur to be unmarried. But as already related, H.H. was engaged to the daughter of the Maharaja of Kolhapur, far and away the Deccan's most important State. There the Gaikwar's visit was viewed with some alarm, which explained the sudden arrival of a chauffeur from Kolhapur, sent by the Maharaja on the pretext that for so important a guest H.H. would need an experienced driver.

The Gaikwar was so worried about his daughter being still unmarried that he told H.H. one day he wished she had never been born. He even suggested that he should take her as his second wife. H.H. was too shrewd to agree to this though by no means insensitive to the Princess's charms. It seemed to me that he was playing a little with fire, and seeing that their combined ages were only thirty-five, this was not surprising. I felt therefore that something should be said, and I reminded him of the story he had told me of a Raja who, though already married, had felt obliged from a sense of chivalry to marry a girl who had taken a vow not to marry anyone else. On his side it was at most 'the perfume and dalliance of a moment' for he never wavered in his allegiance to the Kolhapur Princess.

He was not the only one to be touched by the Baroda Princess's attractions. His Highness of the Junior Branch—J.B. for short—felt them so strongly that he suddenly decided to accompany the Gaikwar back to Baroda and at such short notice that he took no spare clothes with him and even had to borrow a handkerchief from H.H. on the railway platform. The Gaikwar was taken by surprise, but in India the word 'No' is a particularly difficult word to say to a would-be guest. What he did was to leave an A.D.C. behind to find out all he could about the Raja.

To me the Gaikwar was much more interesting than his daughter. He was one of India's leading political figures and his State probably the most advanced in India. In the eyes of Anglo-India his loyalty was open to question, and when four years later at the Delhi Durbar (at which I was present) he paid his homage to the King and Queen with what looked more like a jerk of the head than a bow, he was angrily denounced as having deliberately insulted Their Majesties. In the two long talks I had with him at Dewas there was no hint of disloyalty and I should guess that the abruptness of his bow was more likely due to a determination to avoid any touch of the obsequiousness which marked the obeisance of some of his peers, and that pride carried him too far in the opposite direction.

In appearance he was an insignificant little man, with a head "like a cannon ball" and lower down the same suggestion on a larger scale. A double chin, a short thick nose and a complexion "bad even for the East" did not add to his attraction, and but for his eyes and a royal affability of manner, he would have looked completely undistinguished. But there was, however, no doubt about his mental capacity. He talked very fast and in fluent English, and he gave one the impression of a man who thought things out for himself.

An essay by H.H. on Patriotism, which he thought good, led to our discussing how a young Chief should be educated. He himself had read authors like Maine, Leslie Stephen and Bentham, and he still kept an hour or two a day for reading. I suggested that people in India would be better equipped for dealing with the questions of the day if they read more. That brought us to politics. Were English and Indian, I asked, more estranged from each other than thirty years ago? No, he said; but the dawn of self-consciousness had led Indians to clamour for more equal treatment. Would they then be satisfied with admission to the higher offices of State? He thought not: they must have some control over the Government itself. I then suggested India's 600 Ruling Princes should elect representatives to sit with representatives of the eight Provinces of British India, and that a certain measure of control might then be given them. He said he had already urged the setting up of a Council of Princes, but so far without result. Many years later this was done.

In his own State he had shown the same progressive outlook. He had done his best to revive the Village Council, rightly believing that a democratic system of government required to be built from the village upwards and not contrariwise. But he admitted that the Councils required much supervision and that power tended still to remain with the local official—a difficulty not yet overcome with the official spread of the system all over the India of today.

He had also raised the age of consent to fourteen, but confessed that it affected the poor rather than the prosperous, who could afford to pay the fine for non-compliance. Then, too, he had introduced compulsory education; successfully, he claimed, but it was expensive and it was difficult to keep the number in a class under forty. In all three measures he showed himself ahead of British India.

"How he talked! It was difficult to get a word in, he darted so swiftly from sentence to sentence." Apropos of the way things were going in India, I managed to slip in the question—how would it all end? He was definite that India must follow Europe. She would become less spiritual, but it was in the West that "the great sane minds of the world" were to be found.

Part of the fascination of India, especially for one who had 'read' History at Cambridge, was the sharpness of its contrasts in time. Here was a country where almost every phase in man's development from the dawn of civilisation could be witnessed. If the Gaikwar was one of the most modern of India's Ruling Princes, the Maharaja of Orcha was certainly one of the most mediaeval.

H.H. and I were on a visit to Indore and encamped in tents when one day I found him at his tent door in conversation with this Maharaja, who had come to call on him. Boasting a lineage "coeval with the great Himalayan streams", he suggested an old deodar on a mountainside. He wore a long saffron robe and looked about sixty. His sword lay across his knee and his feet were in pumps! But it required an effort to notice these trivialities. It was his head which drew the eye—massive and hairy "with a nose like Hercules' club", and with the ends of a long beard caught up on either side and a look on his face which said – 'I fear neither God nor man'. H.H. said he would stick at nothing for his ends, and that for marrying without his leave he had banished his son for twelve years. For Englishmen he had unmitigated contempt.

Talk was staccato and almost monosyllabic. In the world in which he lived conversation had hardly been invented. When something occurred to him he would say it; then silence, until some fresh thought struck him. 'Was I a European?' he asked H.H. And as he did so, "he gave the meanest of God's creatures in white flannel trousers a look of Olympian scorn". Two gun-men stood behind him to guard his person. Another retainer carried his hookah. When he rose to go, he deigned to give me his hand. H.H. he embraced, folding him in his arms against each shoulder in turn.

Very different from both the Gaikwar and the Maharaja of Orcha was the Muslim Ruler of Bhopal. No mere man here but a woman generally known as the Begum of Bhopal. She was by no means unique for her mother and grandmother had each ruled in turn.

On a visit to Bhopal with an English friend the two of us were privileged to be received by her. After climbing the narrow staircase so common in Indian house and palace, we were ushered into a simply furnished room divided from another by a screen of split bamboo. 'Salaam, Sahib' came from behind it in a clear cheerful voice. 'Salaam, Your Highness' we replied, and with that conversation began, in Urdu. She had a soft musical voice, with a note of helplessness in it as she spoke of the plague. This scourge had just returned to Bhopal, and she told us of all she was doing to fight it. In those days it was sweeping its victims away by the hundred thousand, notably in the Punjab. She had had her whole army inoculated against it and had virtually compelled the school-children to be done too, but her subjects as a whole were against it. She also deplored their lack of enthusiasm for education. She was building a High School and hoped that it would enable her to recruit some at least of her officials from within the State. At present, she said, they came from other parts of India.

The Begum was not only an enlightened ruler but also a hard-working one. Nothing was too trivial for her attention and when she was on tour she would sometimes work till three o'clock in the morning. With her youngest son of fourteen in the care of an

English tutor, whom she described as 'Oxford-Pass', she characteristically asked me many questions about what I was teaching H.H. When we came away, I assured her of our deepest respect in a courtly Persian phrase which flashed across my mind, and she laughed unseen. It had been a delightful half-hour. She spoke so unaffectedly and showed such longing to do good but felt the powerlessness of her womanhood or perhaps of her humanity.

I must now return to Dewas and say a word about H.H.'s entourage. Closest to him was his brother,* known to me as 'Bhau Sahib'. Small in build and impassive in manner, with a sharp nose and secretive eyes, he had the gift of silence. His self-effacing reserve concealed an affectionate sensitive nature which showed itself in his relations with H.H. Though only a year or two younger, he always treated him with the respect due to the Head of the State. He never went to him unless summoned and invariably addressed him as 'Your Highness'. He kept firmly aloof, too, from the intrigues which inevitably gather round those with power. But that is perhaps to look ahead, for at the moment he was only seventeen and an inmate of the Chiefs' College at Indore.

Wamand Rao, Hereditary Controller of the Treasury, I have already had occasion to mention. With over-ripe lips, puffy cheeks and pock-marked face, he was no Adonis; and a portentous solemnity, broken only by great guffaws over the simplest jests, made him the target for unceasing teasing.† This he bore with unfailing good humour.

As different as stork from goose was Rajaramji Deokar, the Hereditary Commander-in-Chief. He was a child of nature, eager, impulsive and gay, with a most infectious laugh, and an English all his own. Describing his first dinner-party at which English ladies were present, he said: 'I had a lady by my side. Parts of her body were bare and that was very strange to me: it was so cold, I had put many things on my shoulders. I was very sorry for her. Now I am habituated to it, but then I did not look at her. I did not eat—she talked and I looked down and down; then I was afraid, and I ran away.'

Rajaramji was a mighty hunter. Hearing one day in Dewas that a panther was troubling a village six miles away, he rushed off there with only a shotgun—a rifle would have been dangerous to

* Shrimant Jagdevrao Puar Vishwasrao.

† See p. 148.

the villagers at work in their fields. At a critical moment it misfired. 'I was very much displeased (he said). The panther ran after me and the villagers who had promised to help me disappeared. Oh, it was very laughable—very laughable. Then the panther began to grumble'—and so on until at last he shot it dead at close range. I remember the glee with which he described the arrival at that moment of J.B.'s brother with a whole battery of huntsmen and guns to find he had polished off the panther with only a shotgun and unaided. No climbing of trees for him.

Finally, there was Pundit Narayan Prasad, a Malwa Brahmin, then generally known as 'Master Sahib', because he had once been H.H.'s tutor. He was now his Private Secretary. He was an Indian of unimpeachable honesty, who never stooped to the petty arts of flattery, who could show respect without subservience, and who would give H.H. his opinion fearlessly yet deferentially. H.H. owed more to him than to anyone else about his person.

After twenty years' service in the State Master Sahib's pay was only Rs. 200 a month. On this, as head of a family which shared a common purse, he had to support eight persons in addition to himself—his wife, two young daughters, an infant son, a brother and three nephews. A small piece of land brought in Rs. 300 a year. That he gave his brother. In spite of these obligations, thanks to simple tastes, he had saved Rs. 2,000 when, in deference to all-powerful custom, he had to spend Rs. 1,800 on a nephew's marriage which included a dinner to 100 of us in his village. In India, he said, it was almost impossible to save—there were so many ceremonies to be performed and paid for. As H.H. put it, 'religion permeates the pettiest details of our social life'.

CHAPTER 14

A Visit to Kolhapur

MAY had come and with it the hot weather. A change to a cooler climate would obviously be pleasant. That could be had at Kolhapur in the uplands of the Deccan, but the expected invitation from the Maharaja had not come. Clearly a reminder was necessary, but nothing that looked like one. To H.H. this presented no difficulty. He wired the Maharaja that we were thinking of going to Uticamund (a famous hill station in southern India), and would he let his two sons come with us? Back by wire came the desired invitation. This put H.H. into a state of great excitement; now he would be near his beloved Princess and might even hope for some stolen glimpses of her. The Court Astrologer was summoned and asked how soon the stars would allow us to leave Dewas. He pulled a paper book out of his pocket, fingered the pages till he he came upon the one he wanted, made a few calculations, then said we might go on the 14th or the 15th, but the 14th was the more auspicious of the two. So on the 14th we left.

H.H. was putting a finishing touch to his moustache when we steamed into a station carpeted in red and thronged with the élite of the Kolhapur Court. The State band struck up, a guard of honour presented arms—to the wrong compartment—and H.H. stepped down from his and touched the feet of a colossal figure, whom mace-bearers proclaimed to be 'His Highness the Chhatrapati Maharaja of Kolhapur and Emperor of Hindustan'. Garlands and introductions followed, the band struck up again, and H.H. drove away with ten Lancers clattering behind him.

I followed in a second carriage with two Lancers and was driven to a palatial Guest House, where my every possible need, even scissors and stamps, had been anticipated. Red-coated orderlies (I write) "sit outside on the verandah, and a clerk hovers about to wait upon my slightest whim. Whenever I go out, I have to run the gauntlet of the guard, who tumble out to salute me." Inside "I sit on yellow satin cushions whether I write, shave or brush my hair". At sunset "23 lamps are lit that darkness may not cover me. The meals are sumptuous—six courses for dinner, four for breakfast. I have had to insist that the cook shall not run riot in future."

Not content with a courtesy call on the day of my arrival, the Maharaja some days later paid me a visit of three hours. Two evenings before I had dined with the Resident and it soon became evident that the Maharaja was aware of all we had talked about. I knew he would have spies everywhere but I had not realised the efficiency of the system. Happily everything I had said about H.H. was to his credit. Later I asked him: 'Is the clerk who hovers round me the Maharaja's spy?' 'Oh, Sahib, how can you ask me such a question?' In other words, he was. The Maharaja knew all my doings, even that I had charged the cook to be "more merciful". Then came another indiscreet question: had not the Maharaja called upon me twice to flatter me into helping him in some way? 'I tell you, Sahib,' and leaning back in his chair and rocking with laughter, he repeated, 'I tell you, Sahib, you should never have asked me that.' 'Oh, it's the marriage then,' I exclaimed. He nodded assent and said he had told the Maharaja he should not have done what he did: 'the Sahib with his clever head will see through your plot'. Not much cleverness needed for that.

What the Maharaja wanted of me was support for his daughter's early marriage with H.H. The Gaikwar's counter-approach had alarmed him. He feared also the opposition of Government. The year before they had opposed it on account of the Princess's age. Now however, like Juliet, she was thirteen, and as I learnt later, they opposed it no longer. For the Maharaja the added year was of special importance. According to Hindu custom, in those days almost universally observed, a daughter should not remain unmarried after reaching the age of puberty; delay might 'cast a slur on the family'.* In this case there was a special reason for not delaying: during the coming Hindu year which began in April, owing to the stars and their courses no Hindu marriage could safely take place. It was agreed therefore that the marriage should take place in March. Even that seemed too distant for the lovesick Raja. 'All other women,' he said, 'leave me cold.'

One afternoon the Princess was brought to see me by her uncle, the Chief of Kagal, with Kolhapur's Chief Minister in attendance. It was a stonily formal affair. We sat round a table, for a time in

* See the author's *Rusticus Loquitur*, p. 40.

complete silence. Tea was brought but they would not touch it. I had heard that when roused the Princess would 'flash fire'; but all I saw was a slender figure in a crimson sari embroidered with gold and a face with a pleasant smile, for me a little spoilt by a nose-ring. I tried for a word or two with her through her uncle but in vain, and I had to be content with stolen glances, which found her doing the same by me.

When I was in France sixty years ago, I was told that an engaged couple would not be left alone together for long 'en cas d'accidents'. In Hindu India restriction went very much farther: they might not see each other until the actual moment of marriage. This was more than H.H. could bear. On an earlier visit his patience gave way. He would be sent out riding in one direction and the Princess in another. One morning he said he felt too unwell to ride. The Princess had no sooner gone off than he galloped after her and rode with her for five minutes. She turned her head away and said not a word; but it was enough, he told me, to make him feel certain he would like her. Her mother took it very ill, but the Maharaja saw no harm in it 'just for once'.

The five minutes were not without their effect on the Princess. She was at a window when we arrived, and a day or two later H.H. caught her looking down at him from the top of a staircase in the palace. Great was his delight when the Maharaja allowed them twenty minutes together. Entering the room where he was waiting for her, the Princess bent down to touch his feet, but he took her by the hand and kissed her cheek.

One morning in August when H.H. was staying with me at the Guest House he appeared at breakfast wearing a bangle. It was *Rakhri* Day, he explained, when sisters give their brothers a bangle, generally of silk, as a token of affection, or more mercenarily for what had to be given in return. If a girl had no brother, she would perhaps adopt some near relative with whom there was no possibility of marriage, and they would become as brother and sister. When I laughingly protested that no one had given me a bangle, 'next year (said H.H.) you shall have one'. And next year it came, though I was now back in the Punjab. He had sent it on behalf of the Princess, by then his wife.

In India relationship is of such cardinal importance that an artificial one is almost as much respected as one of actual kinship. So it proved in this case, for from that day until his death H.H.

always called me 'brother' and my wife 'sister' and treated us and our children accordingly. Unfortunately I was not to keep the bangle long. With my marriage (in 1909) an ayah had to be engaged and it disappeared. But the tie between my family and H.H.'s, now represented by his eldest son, the present Chhatrapati, Maharaja of Kolhapur, has most happily remained to this day, so much so that he always calls me 'uncle'.

With the Princess's two brothers, aged eight and ten, I had almost too lively a relationship. One day H.H. brought them and their two young companions to see me. All four made a rush at me—it was not our first meeting—and like young monkeys clawed me arm and leg. I quieted them with bananas and mangoes, for which they had a passion. Having devoured them and thrown their skins on the floor, they chased me all over the bungalow. I had never seen English children so uproariously full of animal spirits. Coping with them in that climate was hot work. Yet I enjoyed it: I had not played with children since I left England, and never with children with whom I had not one word in common, since I knew no Marathi and they no English.

With the whole Court at their feet, the two Princes were inevitably spoilt. The elder, Raja Ram, with his curly hair and shining eyes, dearly loved to be petted, but only by the 'right' people. His brother, Shivaji, was the cleverer of the two, sometimes a shade too clever. They could quarrel fiercely and the smallest thing could touch them off—as, for example, when H.H. slept between them and each demanded that he should face his way. The elder was destined to succeed his father as ruler of Kolhapur, the younger to be killed pig-sticking when only nineteen.

Adult life at the Court was a much less lively affair. To all about him the Ruler's right to rule was divine and he was treated accordingly, even when it was the hour or two in the evening given to tennis at the Palace. As at Dewas, when he rose all rose; when he sat all sat; when he laughed all laughed. Only one of H.H.'s suite played tennis. The others sat there every evening with folded hands "as stiff as their walking-sticks".

There were two palaces, old and new. The new one gave one a fine view of the red-tiled town below and of distant hills. At sunset, outlined against a glowing sky, it recalled a modern German Schloss. Inside, East and West met in strange embrace. So at least it seemed from the suite of four rooms allotted to H.H. The first room was very small, but place had been found on its walls for two large lithographs of Edward VII exactly alike, neither in the place of honour. That was given to an oil painting of two Indian ladies in dreamy sentimental mood, one of them the Maharaja's late mistress "now leading a pious life in Bombay", the other, her sister, who shared the honours of another Maharaja's bed with his wife. A portrait of a former Viceroy, Lord Elgin, filled an odd corner.

The second room was larger. The two ladies reappeared with others recalling the shop window of a not too modest picture dealer. 'Bombay Beauties' adorned the third. Finally came the reception room with large mirrors and once more the King, this time with the Queen as well—two indeed of her. A less august pair were two nude women. With Lord Roberts, however, propriety returned.

All this was shown me while waiting to be taken on a shooting trip. This took us into the jungle-deep hills overlooking the Indian Ocean, south of Bombay.

That day we did thirty-six miles, the last twelve on ponies or mules, or donkeys according to our social status. Our party of over a dozen included H.H., the younger of the two Princes with a companion of his own age, three feudatory Chiefs of Kolhapur, and the Court Doctor "in case a tiger came too near". We caused quite a stir in the villages along our route. With their red-tiled roofs they were very different from the flat-roofed houses of the north. Very different, too, were the villagers who came out to greet us with horn and drum; the men, not tall and muscular like the Punjabis, but small, supple and strong, and at this season wearing nothing but a loin-cloth and a smock, some only the loin-cloth. The women, too, did not lag far behind, as they would have done in the Punjab, and with their red and blue skirts gathered round the hips they added colour and charm to the scene.

We were now in the heart of Maharashtra, the country of the Marathas, who at the call of the horn rallied to Shivaji's side when he decided to ride a tilt at the Mogul colossus. As we rode on, the country became wilder, and the jungle thicker. The hillsides bristled with stunted trees embedded in a grey-green stubble pretending to be grass, and all was thirsting for the monsoon which had still to break. At our journey's end I found two tents had been pitched for me a little apart from the Indian encampment and, as darkness fell, fireflies flickered "like flakes of gold in the blue of the night".

Next day a tiger kept us in a state of alternating hope and fear. For two hours we waited under a tree while the huntsmen went ahead to prepare machans* at vantage points where the tiger might appear. We were supposed to keep dead quiet, but with two lively boys amongst us we were in fact rather noisy. The long wait became so tedious that at last I took out a pocket edition of Musset's poems and began to read. H.H. was shocked—'If a book is brought on a shoot (he said) there is no luck.'

Moving on at last, we climbed a high ridge and came to a tree where two machans had been prepared, one above the other. I was given the higher, the Chief of Mhaisal the lower. 'You shoot first' (I said to him)—'I am sure to miss.' He nodded and the rest of the party went off to climb other trees. All was now silent, and I had leisure to look around. A clearing of fifty yards or so divided us from what seemed like an impenetrable jungle of tangled tree and bush. This sloped away down a ravine where far away 500 hillmen were gathered to beat the bush and drive any tiger lurking in it towards us.

For an hour the silence remained unbroken and after shifting my cramped position this way and that, I succumbed to the heat and dozed—to be startled into complete wakefulness by the cries of the beaters echoing up the ravine towards us. "Suddenly I saw something yellow just where the clearing began. By Gad, it was the tiger himself slinking along through the bush with his head close to the ground. I tapped the Chief gently on the head: 'the Tiger' I whispered, but he was too low down to see it—and then it was too late for me to fire: it had vanished into the jungle."

The beaters were now hard on its heels and wilder and wilder were their cries. There came a low growl, almost a grunt. The grunt turned into a muffled roar, and there he was again only forty or fifty yards from us. The Chief fired, and as the tiger plunged into the jungle I did so too. The beaters were now climbing trees as fast as they could, yelling and snarling to keep the enemy at bay. With confidence restored shooters and beaters gathered round our tree and a heated discussion began—was he wounded or not? Words were flying fast then there was another

* A platform up a tree with a screen of brushwood loopholed for rifle and eye.

roar. Once more a *sauve qui peut* up the trees. It was however a false alarm.

It was at this point that the gentle Master Sahib came up to me armed with a spear, and with him Wamand Rao* carrying a cane. Poising his spear firmly on the ground and speaking with the solemnity he considered due to the occasion he said—'You have done a heroic deed'! All I could say in answer to this ludicrous yet perfectly sincere compliment was to reply in kind—'With you two I feel I am safe.' It was certainly stretching a point for there had just been another scamper up the trees.

When I met H.H., he told me I should never have waited for Mhaisal to fire: who sees first fires first was the rule. I vowed I would never be so foolishly polite again. What H.H. did not tell me and I learnt only a month later was that my machan was the best placed of all and had been specially prepared for him as the guest of honour, but he insisted that it should be given to me.

The tiger proved to be wounded, and it was decided to leave him until the morrow. After a four o'clock lunch, with a panther in view we went off to a neighbouring valley. At dusk we came to trees where more machans had been prepared. A goat was tied up at a little distance below us as a bait. Even a heart of stone must have been moved by its bleating and struggles to escape. In time it seemed to accept its fate and it stood there in the moonlight gazing wistfully round. For over an hour we watched in silence but in vain. Next morning we heard that the goat had been killed. It did not go unavenged. A second attack on the panther, this time in full daylight with beaters, found me once more up a tree but now in the lower of two machans. Suddenly, there was the panther at the foot of the tree glaring at me and looking as if it would climb it. I fired and it fell dead, shot through the head. At such close range even I could not miss.

Meanwhile accounts had been settled with the tiger. This was done the day after it was wounded. Following up a wounded tiger on foot is only for the expert or the reckless. As we were neither one nor the other, this was left to the huntsmen, one of whom finally despatched it after a herd of cattle had been let loose to discover its lair. Great was the excitement when it was brought along to show us. It had been hit three times—I claimed none of

* See p. 157.

the three – and it measured nine feet from nose-tip to tail-end and took ten men to lift it on to an improvised stretcher.

It is doubtless absurd to grieve over the death of a creature whose life you have sought; yet, as it lay there with drooping jaw and teeth still clenched, it had a certain nobility. It had defied 500 men and now puny humans were pulling it about and measuring its length with a cord. Back to camp it was borne in triumph, with the beaters thronging round it and at their head two almost naked old men beating drums and a third clashing a cymbal. For them no sentimental questionings – their cattle were now safe.

For the tiro tiger-shooting is not to be compared with pig-sticking, as I found when another expedition took us to the banks of the Kristna, one of India's seven sacred rivers. Instead of sitting by the hour in a crow's-nest for at best a single shot, after wild boar one can be out all day on a horse and with any luck get gallop after gallop cross-country. The terms too between man and beast are less unequal, for a wild boar brought to bay can be a formidable opponent.

I never thought I should be enamoured of any sport, but from the very first I wrote of this one with enthusiasm: after my first day, for instance, when we were out from six a.m. until eight at night, "shooting is stupid in comparison"; and two days later, "it really is a magnificent sport and I will put up with any amount of heat for it". Yet it had its alarming moments: tearing across the sieve-like black cotton soil was a treacherous business, and the stony moorlands of the Deccan which followed were not much better. I took more than one toss, and once narrowly escaped tumbling into a large pit which suddenly opened in front of me when going all out after three pig. It was incidents like these which led me to write: "My cowardice frightens me; I suppose one can get rid of it by practice like any other bad habit; or perhaps the day will come when, as a cynic* hoped, cowardice will be a virtue."

On the other hand, one unforgettable day made me exclaim: 'By Gad! it really is the sport of sports.' The first pig had somehow fallen to my spear when we heard a shout that another had been seen climbing a low ridge half a mile away. We took the ridge at a nearer point and coming down the other side we saw him lolloping away across the moor. Knowing the Chief of Kagal to be a redoubt-

* A character in W. H. Mallock's *The New Republic*.

able pig-sticker I had decided to follow him in any chase as nearly as I could. In the tearing gallop which followed across the open moorland he was leading and I was close behind him. He was just about to prick the boar with his spear when it jinked and he was carried irresistibly forward in what was now the wrong direction. I just had time to change mine and overtaking the boar plunged my spear into his back so inexpertly that it broke. Given another by some kind person just behind me, I set off again. Meanwhile he had taken cover in some bushes. "He was dislodged and again I had luck. He came my way and I renewed the chase. When I was hard on his heels 5 or 10 yards away, he suddenly turned and charged. He gave me a blow with his head on the shinbone but my spear had found him again." After this he was soon finished off. I was told, perhaps flatteringly, that he measured thirty-five to thirty-six inches against a record of thirty-nine. It should of course have fallen to the Chief of Kagal but his luck was out and mine very much in.

Hunting with cheetahs was a speciality of the Kolhapur Court. One day we took out four, each in a blue coat and with a red eye cap. With us they were sufficiently tame to be caressed, but very different with deer. We were in a bullock-cart, and spotting three deer grazing, started circling round them pretending to be peasants. With each new circle we drew a little nearer until the crucial moment came when one of the cheetahs was stripped of coat and cap and let loose. Too far for a spring, he stalked across the red earth with his body stretched as flat as a kid glove and with the intent look of one about to kill. This time the deer escaped. But when a little later we got within fifty yards of them, he was again let loose, and in less than one hundred yards he had caught the biggest of the three. When we came up, he was lying there with a paw on its back and with teeth so deeply clenched in a hind leg that it had to be severed before he would release it. It was given back to him skinned and back he went into the cart, his face splashed with blood and jaw still quivering with excitement—not a pleasant sight, but when is it pleasant to see one animal kill another?

Like Dewas, Kolhapur had its Court Jester. He was a master of intrigue and a fox for his own interest. Yet he was generally welcome: he brought a breath of fresh air into the hot-house solemnity of Court life, as no doubt did his mediaeval counterpart in the West. Where, too, reading was at a discount, he was irresistible as a story-teller. He hated the Brahmins and once said so in public lecture. They returned the compliment with interest, and now he carried a pistol at his belt and never slept in the same place two nights running. A former Political Officer had made it very hot for him, and since then he classed Englishmen with Brahmins. Fortunately I managed to get on with him and was actually included in the guests at a feast he gave in honour of H.H.

Kolhapur also had its theatre and its command performances. One of these given by a company from Poona I attended. When I arrived it had begun. Master Sahib buttonholed me as I entered. 'The Maharani is here, Sir, and you should bow'—'bow', he repeated. 'But where, where?' I asked, and I took a hasty look round the house, a large corrugated iron building packed with turbaned heads. 'Her Highness is up there'—and he pointed to the first balcony, which was purdahed off. As I stepped down to the first row of the stalls, H.H. rose to greet me, the actors stopped, and attendants in red and gold shouted 'Make way—Make way.' Turning solemnly to that upper balcony and fixing my eyes on space, I bowed low to the unseen goddess. The play then continued.

Sixteen rather crotchety oil wall-lamps gave the stage its footlights, and a musician in each wing its orchestra, one with a harmonium, the other with half a dozen tom-toms. These he played with so frenzied a look that it expressed more than all the drums put together. The play was as simple as the stage. The Vizier kidnaps the King's son that his own may take his place. He then hires two murderers to polish him off in a forest. Entreaties, reproaches, tears—nothing will melt their hearts. At last he bares his neck. The blow is about to fall when there is a terrifying report and a friendly god in a white beard appears in luminous cardboard. Result—murderers terror-stricken, boy seraphic. The god disappears and a toe is cut off just to show the Vizier that his will has been done. Thereupon a neighbouring king appears, "looks about the forest as if it were an art gallery", spies the boy in a swoon and, being childless, makes him his heir. Reassured I left. But the boy was by no means out of the wood, for it was only midnight. As in Elizabethan days, the women were all played by men "wonderfully dressed up".

Our departure from Kolhapur—we had been there about a

month—was as ceremonious as our arrival, but we were a much larger party—six from Dewas, six children from Kolhapur, amongst them the little Princes, three or four courtiers, a doctor, and many servants including two huntsmen. As the train started, the order 'Present Arms' rang out, trumpets sounded, and bayonets glittered in the moonlight. H.H. was naturally depressed, and so were we all a little. In bed the younger of the two Princes hid his face under the blankets refusing to be comforted—he was attached to his sister and generally slept with her on the same bed.

We were in the Maharaja's spacious saloon. A bed was made up for me on a long couch. The others all slept on the floor, H.H. between the Princes; the Maharaja's niece, a girl of seven, a little farther on with two waiting-maids of about the same age and size at her feet; and in a corner, an orphan companion of the Princes called Nasrika, a boy with a thoughtful face touched with sadness.

Two durbars followed in Dewas, the first very formal to celebrate the King-Emperor's birthday and despatch a loyal telegram to His Majesty through the Viceroy; the second, in honour of the little Princes. This was a much more real affair and brought out the whole army with Court Photographer, elephant and band. I drove round to the Court House (H.H.'s residence) and found everyone in the most gorgeous dresses—the little Princes in green satin edged with gold, Nasrika and the Maharaja's niece in cerise and gold, H.H. in white and gold, and all of them adorned with pearls, emeralds and diamonds. "And I—*ma foi!*—walked into their midst in a dark suit and straw hat."

Most gorgeous of all was the elephant, with fine carpets swung across his back, silver frontlets plastering his forehead, and silver anklets encircling his forelegs. Red and blue stencillings decorated his trunk, and even his large flapping ears had been painted. When H.H. and the two Princes had climbed into the cream and gold howdah on its back and three men in scarlet and gold had balanced themselves on a footboard on either side, the procession started for the palace in the city. Today's 'new' palace had not yet been built.

There the proceedings were if anything more ceremonious than usual. As each noble and official made his obeisance to the Princes, he waved a rupee or two round their heads in token that he would willingly sacrifice his life for them. To each of his nine guests from Kolhapur H.H. presented a dress of honour varying in quality according to his rank, as was customary when entertaining persons of distinction for the first time. Which reminded me of 'To all of them he gave each man changes of raiment, but to Benjamin he gave 300 pieces of silver and five changes of raiment'.

The proceedings ended characteristically on H.H.'s part. He came to me with the two Princes and their companions. The younger Prince sprinkled me with scent, the elder dabbed some sweet-smelling paste on my handkerchief, H.H. gave me betel leaf and nut on a silver dish, the Maharaja's niece garlanded me, and the other children each gave me a nosegay—India at its most gracious. At the Prince's request I returned in their carriage, sinking into cushions of blue and gold as the Army once more presented arms.

CHAPTER 15

In and Around Dewas

IN the last three chapters, I have been living in the Courts of Princes. I turn now to their great nourishers, the peasants. In appearance the peasant of Central India was very different from the sturdy cultivator of the Punjab, but his gentler ways gave him an attraction all his own. One day out for a walk I came across one ploughing, with his wife at his side dressed in red and blue and decked with silver anklets. She had charge of the seed and trickled it into a long wooden tube open at both ends and attached to the plough in such a way that, as the black earth turned into a furrow, the seed fell into it.

I asked if I might try my hand at the plough. The first furrow I managed pretty well with the woman on one side of me, and with the man on the other prodding the bullocks and holding the guiding thong. But on the return journey, the furrow broke in pieces, something like this:

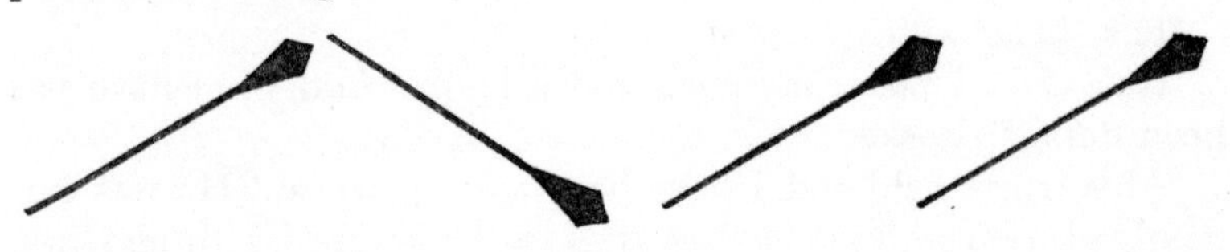

Ploughing was clearly not my vocation: even the woman laughed at my efforts.

An invitation to attend a wedding feast in a village twenty miles away gave me one afternoon in May a hot ride across a crumpled desolate country with one lovely sight repeated from village to village. The peasants were at work on their threshing floors. On some the bullocks were trampling out the grain; on others half-naked men were beating it out; but on most a man on a high wooden stool was throwing out the unseparated grain and chaff to the wind, and as the grain pattered on to the smooth mud-plastered floor, the chaff was blown away in a waving shower of gold. Did this beautiful sight perhaps inspire the imaginative Greek mind with the story of Danae and Zeus?

I would sometimes climb one of the flat-topped hills that broke the monotony of our plateau and would often stop for a word or two with passers-by. One afternoon I met a group of peasants who said that rain was badly needed to ripen one of their crops. 'We are in God's hands,' I said, repeating what I had so often said in the Punjab, and it had much the same effect. 'Yes, in God's hands,' they echoed, and they smiled as children do when something has been said to them which they really understand.

One of them, an old man with a white beard and full of life, declared he had only two acres and yet had to pay this, that and the other to the State. 'I am very poor (he said) and have not enough to live on. But you—you are rich: your pay is large, mine is small.' 'How old are you?' I asked. 'Seventy years perhaps.' 'You are a lucky fellow to have lived so long with nothing to eat.' That was quite enough to make the others laugh.

On one occasion it was the peasant who hailed me. He saw me running down a hill which I had just climbed and no doubt wondered at my unusual pace in a country where no one ever ran except perhaps to catch a train. 'Where are you going?' he cried.

'To the city.'

'Where have you been?'

'Up on the hill.'

'For shikar—for game?'

'No'—I had taken my stick and a book. 'And what have *you* been doing?' I asked.

'This is my field and I have been sowing wheat.' He was evidently pleased with the day's doings for he laughed with pleasure. I had a squash hat in my hand. He felt it, then made me put it on. He laughed even more and pointed to his blue turban.

'Yes (I agreed) that is more beautiful.'

'Get one,' he said: 'get one in the bazaar—a good one for ten rupees.' (13*s*. 4*d*.)

Looking into a village one day I came upon a peasant sitting idly and hugging a blanket thrown over his shoulders. Fever had laid him low. I told him to come and see me on the morrow and I would give him medicine. When he failed to appear, I went in search of him, but in vain. A neighbour however promised to give him the quinine I had brought for him. "And now here he is at my door with five others", all wanting to be doctored. As we saw at Rajanpur, malaria could have devastating effects.

Apropos of what I was to write many years later, I was already beginning to enquire into the conditions of the peasantry round me. For example, in both Dewas and Kolhapur they were said to be in the clutches of the money-lender and to borrow for their weddings at 25 per cent, and the women were thought to be wearing less jewellery, whether from increasing poverty or good sense was not clear. Village industries, too, were decaying and prices rising. My enquiries were far too superficial to be of any value but at least they show that some of the points which have been the subject of much study in recent times were in the air sixty years ago.

Life in Dewas itself, though completely uneventful, was not without its charm. "I dined tonight (says a letter) on the roof of the porch, in the full moonlight with the lake at my feet and the hill of Devi beyond. The air is full of scents and cool breezes, and overhead Orion is chasing the Pleiads across the sky."

Very pleasant, too, it could be to sit under a tree by the lake in the coolness of the morning, with clothes of many colours spread out on the bank to dry in the sunlight, and with grey and white squirrels darting through the grass and up and down the trees. "They are the most fascinating creatures (I write) and will reconcile me to this country if all else fails." At tea-time one of the more daring—or greedy—would come into my drawing-room, jump on to the tea-table and coolly nibble away at an oatcake; but if I moved before he had finished it, he would spring on to the floor with what was left and be out of the room in a flash.

Less attractive was the scorpion. One day my sice appeared with an agonised look on his face and the dead body of a scorpion in his hand. It had just stung him on the toe and the pain had already reached a shoulder. I called Master Sahib and a certain clerk was fetched. He inked the toe all over and having made a white line down the leg with ashes, he smeared them over the toe and as he did so he muttered some mantra to himself. In a moment the sice said the pain had left his shoulder and was now no higher than the knee. Fifteen seconds later it had sunk to the ankle, and in a minute or two it was down to his toe. The toe was then rubbed with some root and all pain vanished. All of which I saw with my own eyes and recorded on the day itself.

Delay in the coming of the monsoon was now causing acute anxiety to the peasant and all eyes were turned upon "a cruel white-hot sky". 'There will be famine' said H.H. 'Is anything being done about it?' I asked. 'Well, the Anushtan priests are there. They sit in the temples for 8 days with folded arms and pray. Sometimes, too, they fill a temple with water and shut the doors.' 'What! to flood out the god?' 'Yes, they are thinking of doing it in a temple in the city.' Very different from the Baluch remedy described in Chapter 9.*

Who—or what—ever was at work, the monsoon came at last, and with it torrential rain. With everything, even the roses in the garden, bursting into new life the usual magic change from torrid heat to springtime freshness followed. Less magical was the sound of low grunting like a pig's from a field I was passing on one of my before-breakfast walks. Treading stealthily across oozing red mud, I came to a small pond. A dozen frogs on the water's edge were basking in the sun and, as they did so, their flabby yellow bodies shone in the brilliant light. Others were diving in and out of the ooze or plunging at each other in amorous sport. And from bladders as large as grapes and a turquoise blue came an exultant chorus of grunts.

The monsoon at Dewas was very different from what it had been at Rajanpur. The almost daily rain kept temperatures down to the seventies; but it also made tennis, my chief recreation, a rare possibility. Instead, seated on the box of my victoria, I would take out one or other of the State's four pairs of carriage horses for an evening drive. From a carriage-and-pair I rose to a tandem and a four-in-hand. The tandem I managed pretty well after persuading the leader to stop looking round for a chat with the wheeler. But with the four-in-hand I never felt quite comfortable.

For eight weeks Indore had ignored us completely when one day, as H.H. and I were having tea together at the Guest House, a wire from Major Daly announced: 'Five persons coming to tea with you this afternoon.' I leapt from my chair. It was already four o'clock and I was in shirt and white drill trousers, "literally nothing more—no socks, no shoes, no tie". We had just finished all there was to eat and there was not even bread; only one cigarette, too, and three old cheroots. "For five minutes there was pandemonium—a note to Miss M. begging for a crust of bread; a mounted orderly despatched to the Court House for H.H.'s cigarettes; orders to the cook—'in heaven's name some cakes'; a

* p. 100.

call to the Bearer—'tea for five at once and socks, boots, coat and tie for the Sahib'. Even so I had forgotten to invite Miss M. Another note, and a call to the sice to take it."

When the car from Indore arrived, there we were, all three of us standing under the porch, H.H. in white, "Miss M. light and summery with a blood-red parasol, and myself cutting, I thought, quite a tolerable figure." A stoutish square-chinned lady descended from the car—'Lady Jacob', someone said. Sir Swinton, a distinguished engineer, followed. Luckily I had heard of him. The other three were soldiers, one of them Daly's A.D.C. Somehow the eight of us managed to squeeze round two little tea-tables. "Lady Jacob sat on my right, very gracious but silent and rather majestical. Sir Swinton was as unassuming as possible. We all liked him. After tea we went and sniffed the sweet briar in the garden, which Miss M. says is alone of its kind in India. Then they rushed away."

In both Rajanpur and Dewas I was largely cut off from the society of my own kind, but with a difference. In Rajanpur each day produced so much which had to be done that there was no time to feel idle, and little to feel lonely. Dewas gave me far more leisure, and for filling it threw me on my own resources. For this books were a great stand-by, and I was fortunate in having friends at home who realised this. One, for example, sent me Constance Garnett's translation of Turgenev's novels and short stories in fifteen volumes, week by week one volume, with two—*A Sportsman's Sketches*—in the fourteenth and last. I have never ceased to love Turgenev. The Book of Job was also a great discovery.

But the work that took me by storm was the *Iliad*. This I laboriously attacked in Greek, and had got no farther than the third book when I wrote: "Short of Shakespeare I have read nothing so poetically wonderful. I feel in a new world, a world of infinite light and colour, where men were both young and great, and life a harmony of great strivings. And what a roll of music runs through it all—the shakings of the earth, the roar of the sea and the thunder in the mountains. And then the softer melodies that sparkle through the deeper ones—the flowers by Skamander, the milkpails all bedewed, and the thrill when the old counsellors of Troy see Helen approaching, and they agree that the Trojans and Achaeans cannot be blamed for fighting so long on her account."

And I add, perhaps a little too caustically: "Why did they not tell us this at Eton? Six years too I spent there."

I was reading a play of Shakespeare's when a colonel "with the voice of a babe" came to me on a second visit. 'What have ye been reading?' he asked. 'Ah! Shakespeare! Now ye don't say so. Oh, a charming writer and so instructive. You're a lucky man to be reading that. Now, if ye come upstairs I can give ye the *Windsor Magazine*. I'm sure ye'll like it.'

More pertinent to my surroundings than either the *Iliad* or the *Windsor Magazine* were my attempts to understand the mysteries of Hindu philosophy. This brought me into close touch with one of the few intellectual lights in Dewas, the Superintendent of Education. Mr Shastri was a Brahmin with an imposing black beard and a strong tendency towards Theosophy. He had read widely and loved discussion, as my Scotch blood did too. In our many talks I learnt much about Hindu philosophy, though when they turned to metaphysics I could only flounder.

On one occasion we went for a drive together and for nearly two hours discussed such subjects as renunciation of the world, the problem of good and evil and the Hindu's attitude towards celibacy. At the end of our drive he thanked me warmly, exclaiming; 'A very ennobling talk'—not quite how an Englishman would have put it. Actually it had a curious effect on me: "I felt suddenly lifted into a new world in which this life seemed but a speck and world followed world ceaselessly."

On the more practical problems of life such as social reform he was always interesting. Women, he said, were the great obstacle to it. (Many years later this was still the case in the village.) And how could it be otherwise when almost to a woman they were opposed to education? Indeed, how was education possible when they were so often married by twelve? The intelligentsia of his generation, he declared, felt keenly the gulf between themselves and their wives. He himself had nothing in common with his wife and consequently talked very little to her. He had married her when he was only sixteen in deference to the entreaties of his father.

Apropos of the importance of education in India, H.H. told me that when his father died many Brahmins urged him to make his mother commit suttee,* and all but one were uneducated. Happily

* A Hindu widow's immolation of herself on her husband's funeral pyre.

the last fifty years have done much to reconcile women to education for their daughters.

India is famous for its Sadhus, men who wander up and down the country living on the charity of others and freed by their otherworldliness, real or assumed, from the restrictions of caste and the need to work for a living. In return for the charity, if they were genuine, they would expound their view of Hindu philosophy and explain to those who would listen how to distinguish between reality and illusion. From time to time one such, Atma Ram by name, would visit Dewas, and being of a sociable disposition he would join us at the tennis club and discourse on the nature of the soul. In what Western country would this have been possible at a tennis club?

Atma Ram was born in the Punjab and left it at the age of sixteen to roam over India. He had a fine Punjabi figure, well over six feet in height, very massive, too, with just a hint of stoutness. "When I spied him this evening (says a letter) he was wandering slowly through the fields, his long coat of pink muslin swelling in the breeze. A few minutes later he was at the club in our midst. All rose to greet him and hailed him 'Maharaj'." Great is the veneration paid by Hindus to a genuine Sadhu. There were about a dozen of us and we sat in a semicircle round him. At once he started talking about the soul, and after quoting something in Sanskrit he broke into a happy laugh. I could not follow what he said but it was a pleasure to watch him. His large eyes and whole manner radiated calm and contentment, and mustard-coloured socks and a pink parasol gave a whimsical touch to his appearance.

I asked him what he did all day. He said that he—his real self—was eternal and took no account of days. Could he tell me then what my real Self did all day, for I had no idea? 'You are living in ignorance: your real Self is steeped in the world—it sleeps,' was his unanswerable reply. At one point H.H. found himself sitting with his back towards him. 'Oh, Maharaj, my back is turned on you.' 'What does it matter? Light streams from your soul on every side.'

He spoke with great emphasis in a loud high-pitched voice, and when he had finished some exposition, throwing back his head he would show two rows of fine teeth and his whole face would shine with delight. At parting there was no shaking of the hand; instead he raised both hands in blessing shoulder high.

Some days later we found him at the club, pacing up and down the tennis court in a swirl of pink muslin, and as he did so swinging his pink parasol to and fro. On that occasion he declaimed against false Sadhus whose selves were still absorbed in matter. Another time I saw his sturdy figure coming towards me "with beaming face and the skirts of his pink muslin coat open to the evening breeze. We had not met for many weeks which was perhaps why he held my hand so long." I duly enquired after the health of his body. To him 'how are you?' was an absurd question because, as he had explained, the real 'you', that is, the soul, was eternal and therefore unchangeable. He turned and walked with me to the club in the gathering twilight. "We talked of God, but familiarly and laughingly as one may of a friend." He said that some were of the world, some of God: each had his task and the important thing was to do it. God, he added, was everywhere and in everything —"in my hand, which he took again, in my dog, and in my stick".

Another evening, again at the club, when India was suffering from drought and France from flood, I asked him why God had given too little rain to the one and too much to the other. His explanation was as simple as it was ancient. India had been given too little because Government had done wrong. Had they not allowed cow-slaughter, and did not the most precious things come from the cow—milk, butter, cheese, manure? I then asked him why the good man so often suffered even for doing good, and I put a case similar to the one in the first book of *The Republic*—the just man on the rack. The body through which we suffer, he said, was only the clothing, as it were, of the soul. The real self does not suffer, only the physical self and that is *Maya*—illusion. If, in fact, we do suffer, it is due to our actions in a previous existence, for which we are atoning here.

There was nothing solemn in Atma Ram's approach to these great mysteries: he was far too convivial for that. It was characteristic of him that later on he contrived to get himself included in the party which went from Dewas to Kolhapur for H.H.'s marriage. One day I went to the palace there to discuss certain difficulties with Master Sahib, and there I found the two together sharing the floor of a very small room. Except for a light pink scarf thrown delicately over his massive shoulders, he was bare to the waist. When tea was brought in, Master Sahib, an orthodox Brahmin, refused it, as I had found other Hindus do before; but Atma Ram, as a Sadhu freed from all caste restrictions, drank it remarking gaily that there was nothing in tea to keep two mortal creatures apart. Later I was to find him far from indifferent to port!

Underlying these uneventful daily-round doings, a change was taking place in my attitude towards life in Dewas. In July, when I had been there nearly six months, a light-hearted letter says: "I can find my way without difficulty to the right Club—J.B.'s is 200 yards away. I have the art of shaking hands 'au bout des doigts'. I know who is entitled to the whole hand, who to the fingers only, who to their tips. I am pretty well at the general bow, and I can take betel nut without a turn. I never laugh at the Army, and when the sentinel (at the Guest House) flashes his bayonet at me, I know that it is unnecessary to take any notice."

September produced a more serious letter. I had been away with H.H. for three weeks and was surprised to find how glad I was to return to Dewas. "These last few months (I wrote) Dewas has grown upon me—not in a sudden access of familiarity but by a slow and deepening intimacy. So I was glad to round the corner of the lake and see the old red-headed crane stalking in the long grasses between the islands. And I was glad to hear the temple bells again and look round upon my pictures and my books and to see the last copper lights of the sunset framed in the arches of the verandah."

CHAPTER 16

Politics and Friendship

IN previous chapters I have touched more than once on the social gulf between East and West. In Lahore both sides seemed to accept it as part of the scheme of things. In Rajanpur, with Dhalu Ram as the sole representative of India's emerging intelligentsia, it had little practical significance. Dewas was different. There I found myself on the Indian side of the gulf—to my great advantage. In a letter to Alfred Lyall I told him that in two months I had learnt more about India and Indian life than in the two years that went before.

It was curious, for example, to hear us spoken of as 'the Monkey People'. Nor was it altogether palatable to be told by a highly educated Brahmin—'you (that is, the English) are irritable, impatient, aggressive, and you love to kill'. There was much truth in this. On the other hand, "the better type of Englishman (I wrote) is always polite, often courteous (witness Abbott and Waring), but he is almost always the official and he is utterly lacking in sympathetic imagination. There are exceptions, of course, but that is the type." H.H., too, could be critical. 'We might have liked the English (he said) but we do not know them.' And with that gulf between us, what could we know of the Indians, "of their thoughts and doings, their wants and their aspirations"?

That we were called the Monkey People requires a word of explanation. It was due, said H.H., to a popular idea that we were descended from Hanuman, the Monkey God, and so fulfilled the prophecy that his descendants would one day rule India. However dignified the origin of the nickname, there was no flavour of respect in its common usage judging by the whispered remark of a Maharaja to H.H. during a Durbar at Indore in honour of the Prince of Wales—'When will this Durbar of the Monkeys end?'

One of the many lessons I learnt at Dewas was "that no people are more responsive to kindness than the Indians". Yet they were often treated as if the converse were true. H.H., for example, had had an unforgettable experience of Anglo-Indian discourtesy. At seventeen, when he was travelling by rail, a major and subaltern would not let him into their compartment though he had a first-class ticket. The station-master, whose help he invoked, with more discretion than valour, refused to interfere. The train started. Undeterred H. H. jumped on to the footboard, and only then did they let him in. On discovering who he was, they apologised, but would they have done so had he been an ordinary first-class passenger? "Too damnable," I wrote, and added – "H.H. says it happens often to others. No wonder we are not liked." The incident had one ludicrous consequence. The first time we travelled together he appeared in a khaki topee, on no one's head an embellishment but on his so disfiguring that at first I did not recognise him. Why not the becoming turban? I asked. He said a topee was a protection against insult: he would be taken for a member of the ruling race or at least for someone akin to it.

It was about this time that the tranquil surface of political life in the Punjab was rudely disturbed by an outbreak of seditious articles in the vernacular Press leading to riots in Lahore, Rawalpindi and Lyallpur, and to the deportation to Burma without trial of the two leading agitators, Lajpat Rai and Ajit Singh. The shock to educated India was profound, and even in our remote corner at Dewas "it caused deep indignation. 'Even I do not feel secure' said a mild cultured Brahmin to me." The sanctity of the law had been violated.

To me as an impatient young Liberal brought up in the full security of the Victorian age the deportations seemed at first "utterly deplorable; they will inflame the discontent not allay it" I wrote. Actually their immediate effect was the reverse. A month later I could write that the intelligentsia – Gokhale was an outstanding exception – "are now all protesting their loyalty as fervently as St Peter before the cock crew. It shows that Government has not much to fear yet." But I questioned the more important long-term effects: "the moderates are becoming extremists, and the extremists irreconcilable". And looking farther into the future I wrote in my diary: "India will become another Ireland", and in a letter: the danger "will come when Japan is stronger and we are in trouble elsewhere". Actually it was not long before Lajpat Rai became one of the heroes of the nationalist movement.

The troubles in the Punjab were symptomatic of a malaise which was just beginning to come to the surface. "I may be pessimistic (I wrote) but I do not think the English as a whole realise how widespread and how natural, indeed almost justifiable, is the discontent. I myself had only a glimmer of it until I came here." H.H. had told me much, and that he was able to do so was due to his close connexion with three important Courts—Kolhapur, Gwalior and Baroda. "Personally", says another letter, "I think we should act boldly and trust the Indians generously. But the Englishman will no more give up his prejudices than a hedgehog his bristles."

My strong reaction to the deportations led to an imprudent step. I wrote a letter to *The Times of India* (Bombay's leading newspaper) describing "what Indians had said to me rather than what I personally felt". It was returned with a long courteous letter from the Editor. He said he was convinced that Government was right; the situation had been very critical and he did not wish to do anything to embarrass Government. Only half the truth was known, and that the less important half. He agreed, however, with what I had written of the way Europeans treated Indians and said he would be glad to publish anything I wrote on that subject. A second letter from me signed 'Indian Civil Servant' followed and was published. More rashly perhaps I wrote a letter to the Indian-edited *Tribune* of Lahore* signed in the same way. The Indian newspapers were so inclined to speak of all Anglo-Indians as against them and of all Civilians as sun-dried bureaucrats that I wanted to show them that there were some "who had not bowed the knee to Baal".

Neither letter has survived—only references to their contents in other letters. For neither was I taken to task by Government; I had been careful not to transgress the regulation which allowed a Government servant to contribute anonymously to the Press, provided he kept 'within the limits of temperate and reasonable discussion'. The tone of my private correspondence was very different. "I have written", says one of the letters quoted above, "most petulantly and explosively, perhaps bumptiously seeing that I have been out here not 2½ years, as older heads are never tired of reminding me when I suggest that things are not as they should be."

One day at Kolhapur I was discussing these problems very frankly with the Chief of Mhaisal—when he said—'Put down your ideas about Indians now and lock up the paper for five years;

* See p. 118.

then put them down again and compare the two.' He thought that like others of my kind I should become "official and distrustful". 'Now (he said) we can treat you as a brother.' "When I left Rajanpur (says a letter) I was just beginning to feel it difficult to treat Indians on a perfect equality with myself. When one has ruled it is difficult to step down. But after a short struggle that has passed." At Dewas my position was very different: it was hardly official at all. "I am really H.H.'s friend and the friend of his friends. I have little to get out of them, and they even less to get out of me. So our relationship is almost natural, which is most rare in India."

If it was almost natural at Dewas, it was much less so at Kolhapur. Coming there as an unknown Englishman connected with the unloved Political Department, I was naturally distrusted and my many questions, put solely to learn more about India and its ways, did nothing to allay suspicion, as the following extract from a letter to my mother shows:

"Yesterday after a morning's shoot we were sitting over breakfast under a tree when we somehow began talking about politics, and even the Chief of Kagal joined in though he had purposely avoided me, as I subsequently discovered, in case I should ask him questions which he could not answer truthfully, for he hates lying though he believes in its necessity occasionally. To-day H.H. tells me that he (Kagal) had to lie because he thought that Major Daly had directed me to find out Kolhapur opinion on certain topics which affected Dewas. And another Chief, said H.H., had told me a heap of lies among a few things that were true. They blame H.H. for being so frank with me and say I have been too short a time in the country to be trusted."

It was a shock to find myself regarded as a Government spy. Throughout my time at Dewas no attempt was ever made to use me in that way. The letter just quoted shows what a sinister turn could be given by distrust to questions put in all innocence; also how deep in India was the well of truth. "There is the official attitude (says a letter) which records its views in fat blue-books and pompous resolutions; there is the Indian Press as biased as the Anglo-Indian; there are the Indians themselves, but not one in a thousand will be frank with you." To that H.H. was a blessed exception, and looking back I realise more than ever how fortunate I was in that respect.

An important aspect of H.H.'s character was his interest in politics. This caused me some concern for, as I wrote in September, the more I saw and heard of politics in Native States, "the more my stomach turns". "Heaven knows (I added) what will become of H.H. when left to himself. The danger is that the Oriental atmosphere may be too much for him. I am always telling him—'be frank'. It is the one thing I din into his ears. He is much franker than most (and especially so with me), but the last 6 years he has had to struggle for his balance and naturally he has been put to many shifts, never dishonourable so far as I know, but coaxing, cajolery and flattery and artful insinuation come a little too easily to him." On their lighter side politics for him could be no more than a game of wits, played with the subtlety and craft of the skilled fencer. The letter adds indeed—"He is never so happy as when he has a nut to crack with a high official, and the harder the nut and the higher the official, the better pleased he is." Of which an official visit he paid the Governor of Bombay when only seventeen is a good example.

He set out with a suite of three—his Commander-in-Chief, the Hereditary Controller of the Treasury and Master Sahib, his former Tutor. With an A.D.C. to meet him at the foot of Government House steps, the Political Secretary in full uniform at the top and a suitable amount of red carpet to walk on, all went well until they reached the hall of audience. There, through the open doorway could be seen the Governor sitting at the far end of the hall with a table in front of him. At that point H.H. stopped dead. 'Won't Your Highness go in?' said the Political Secretary; 'His Excellency awaits you.' 'I will just wait a moment,' he replied. And there, so he declared, he waited a full three minutes staring blankly into the hall while the governor sat on "as if he were the British Government itself". Result—the Controller of the Treasury horrified at the insult to the Governor—the Commander-in-Chief on fire at the insult to H.H.; and Master Sahib exclaiming to H.H. in Hindi—'What, will you make the Governor angry?' At last the Governor stood up. Even then H.H. did not budge in case the Governor stood fast. It was only when he was past the table that H.H. moved forward. 'And where did you meet?' I asked. 'Well, you see he took longer strides than I did and I went very slowly; so he was three-quarters of the way down the hall before we met.' Dignity outwitted indeed by impudence.

On that occasion he was master of the situation. But when his prestige as Head of the State was at the mercy of others, strong even passionate feelings could be aroused. One day he came to me in a great state declaring, 'I have been insulted before all my people.' That morning Daly had brought Miss M. back to Dewas and gone on without a word to H.H., who was standing with his entourage in front of his residence in expectation of a courtesy call. This he had some reason to expect since it was their first opportunity of meeting in Dewas itself during the two years Daly had been at Indore. As the Residency motor passed, he and his entourage salaamed, but the salaams were ignored. Judging by the pace at which the Residency cars used to be driven, I can well imagine that the salaams were not noticed. As to the failure to call, Daly probably thought a call on Dewas Senior would demand one on Dewas Junior. It was certainly not in his character to be rude.

Another time it was the Maharaja of Gwalior who upset him. Hearing that his car had broken down a mile from Dewas, we drove out at once to see if we could be of any help. As we arrived, he was just going off, and with no more than a salaam he went slowly by. H.H. was furious at this further 'public insult', this time from an Indian.

Of no one could it be said more truly than of the Ruler of an Indian State—*l'état c'est moi*. As such he felt compelled, like those in charge of any modern State, to keep himself informed of all activities within and without the State which might be prejudicial to it, or to himself as its head. Hence the elaborate spy system within the State, and outside it the bribing of clerks in Government offices to pass on confidential information affecting the State. In short, the interests of the State, whatever its size, were considered paramount and a sufficient excuse for all the measures (including lying) dignified nowadays by the label 'Intelligence'.

With this side of H.H.'s life I was in no sympathy, and in my ignorance of the world of affairs, I was perhaps inclined to take it too seriously. It was only later that I realised how usual it was for Governments to spy on each other, and what a sharp line could be drawn by some who served them between public and private standards of conduct and truth. When therefore H.H. told me one day that he had been sounding the clerks in his Political Agent's office to see if there was a source of confidential information he could tap, I was more critical than I would have been if I had known then what I have learnt since. Government offices were full of underpaid clerks who were only too glad to make money in this way. But sometimes they got caught in their own trap as happened, for instance, in the time of a former Resident at Indore. Suspecting his munshi of giving away secret information, the Resident one day gave him his confidential correspondence box to take to his First Assistant, who lived only a little distance away. The box, of which only the Resident and the First Assistant should have had the key, contained a note to the latter, who was in the plot, to say that the Government of India had granted the Resident six months' leave—a pure invention. A few days later there appeared a corresponding announcement in a leading Indian newspaper.

RELIGION

A realist in the world of politics, an idealist in the sphere of friendship, in the realms of the spirit H.H. was a mystic. Religion was in his blood. His father, grandfather and great-grandfather all 'meditated', he told me, for two or three hours every night, and in nothing was he himself so punctilious as in doing his Puja.* Every morning they took three-quarters of an hour and were a first charge upon his time. In later years they would take as much as four hours. One morning in the twenties I went to meet him at Delhi station, whither he had come to take part in some important official function timed, owing to the heat, for a very early hour. 'Anyhow this morning (I said) you have not done your four hours' Puja.' But he had: he had spent the night in his railway saloon and had started at 2.30 a.m.

What did such long devotions consist of? I can only describe what I saw one morning when H.H. said I might be present. The carpet was rolled up from a corner of the room and he was sitting on the stone floor dressed in white linen with a red border. In front of him was a low stool bearing a tiny image of the god Krishna, Shiva's symbol "about the size of two thumbs", two sacred books open with flowers on them, and a number of small bowls, containing water, rice, camphor or coloured powder. These were all offered in turn to the sacred emblems before him. A little silver bell rang and he bowed; and having bowed again, he rose with folded hands and walked solemnly round the stool. Sitting

* Devotions.

down, he bowed yet again and sprinkled the sacred emblems with water, rice and powder and, as he did so, incense was burnt and mutterings fell fast from his lips. Then suddenly they ceased. The whole scene recalled a Roman Catholic priest at the high altar, "only the ritual seemed more complex and it was all done more neatly".

This was a solemn occasion, and on such he would be so absorbed that he would not know whether he was being watched or not. But it was not always so. Religion entered so much into a Hindu's daily life, that it could easily lose the solemnity usually given it in the West. Once we climbed the Hill of Devi together. Custom obliged him to do Puja in a small temple which had been hewn out of the hillside to accommodate a scarlet-painted goddess with four arms. In he went and squatted down with a young Brahmin priest beside him. Together they chanted mantras* and, as they did so, H.H. shot an occasional glance at me "out of the corners of his laughing eyes". After ringing a bell, kissing the goddess's feet and sprinkling them with flowers and water, he emerged and we went gaily on up the hill.

One day speaking of the demands religion made upon their time, he exclaimed—'Every day, Sahib, every day there is something.' In early autumn, for example, came the rites due to a family's paternal ancestors, and specifically to the last three generations of the dead. For H.H. with responsibilities for two families, the one of his birth, the other of his adoption, this was an onerous duty. The two were so closely related that a single ceremony could well have done for both, but that neither might be jealous of the other each had its own observance and date.

The ancestors were venerated through the relatives who were present. H.H. touched their feet symbolically and sprinkled them with water. Amongst them on one occasion was an ordinary Maratha sepoy, and as H.H. venerated him, the sepoy, who was much the older of the two, threw a little rice over his head in token of blessing. There was much else besides this. The first day the ceremony took three hours, the next nearly four. Until it was finished, one might neither shave nor eat, nor all day touch meat.

These rites followed the Gokal Ashtami festival in honour of the god Krishna. Some have compared him to Christ. However that may be, what I saw did at least recall the Christmas celebrations

* Mystical incantations in Sanskrit.

in Rome in honour of the Ara Coeli's 'miraculous' image of the infant Christ. A shrine, says a letter, had been fitted up in the palace and there we all assembled to celebrate Krishna's birth. As midnight struck, the curtain which hid the shrine was drawn away, and there was the baby Krishna decked with jewels and with a menagerie of small animals grouped about him. We all threw rose leaves and red powder at him, much of which fell on my head, and in the courtyard the band played and the Army presented arms. A baby doll, with a coconut for its head, was now produced in a gold-embroidered cloth and given to the chief Brahmin, who nursed it "most professionally". After water had been sprinkled on its face and oil poured up its nostrils, it was given to H.H. to nurse. And that was all I saw of the celebrations that night. I heard afterwards that the Brahmins were annoyed (with some reason) that Miss M., who also was present, and I had not taken off our shoes. H.H. characteristically told them that next time he would himself wear shoes.

The celebrations lasted ten days. On the tenth, scenes from Krishna's life were acted, and "old Aryan games" played in the courtyard of the palace with H.H. seated on his cushioned throne and myself squatting on the ground beside him, this time shoeless. A game which went on endlessly and excited endless mirth, could hardly have been simpler. Krishna was now represented by a small boy dressed in green and gold with a peacock feather tiara on his head. To start the game someone took him into his arms and was given a ball. Picking out one of the many present, he threw the ball at him. If hit, the victim had to take over boy and ball until he could hit someone else picked out in the crowd. "Everyone laughed to see all the nobles and officials pelted in turn." When my turn came, rather unsportingly I fear, I discharged my obligation by proxy. Learning, however, that it was a great honour to be singled out in this way by the god, when pelted again I descended shoeless into the courtyard and duly received the god and then to everyone's delight pelted H.H.

From the palace we went in procession through the town with Krishna on the State elephant and H.H.'s other gods in a palanquin. Army and band led the way and H.H. and I followed on foot with the nobles and officials as usual behind us. From the town we made our way to the lake. There, facing a golden west, H.H. prayed to the gods. At one point all present joined in a rhythmic clapping to the clashing of cymbals while the Brahmins and H.H. chanted aloud. This lasted a full quarter of an hour and under the open sky was most impressive. Finally, a Brahmin waded into the lake with the gods and when up to his neck plunged them into the water and his head as well. And as he did so, everyone shouted and the band played the State anthem and a salute of five guns was fired.*

In mid-October came Dussera, one of the greatest of Hindu festivals. Traditionally it marked the end of the hot weather and the opening of the season for war. In the eighteenth century, when the Marathas swept over India, it must have had a very practical significance. Now, however, thanks to the Pax Britannica, the observance had only a token character.

One evening I accompanied H.H. and his suite up Devi's Hill. After due respect had been paid to the scarlet-painted goddess with the four arms, all joined hands and circled five times round a faggot fire. The fifth time swords were drawn and tempered in the flames. A Brahmin then stepped forward and tied a thread round each man's right wrist, in the old days to protect him from harm during the fighting to come.

Two days later came the blessing of the trappings of war—arms, banners, drums and every kind of transport including elephant and car. Two rams were slain, one by H.H., the other by his brother—not a pleasant sight, especially when the horses were led past and an attendant holding a bleeding head daubed each in turn with blood. H.H., who never left me out of any celebration, treated me less barbarically. Smearing a red powder called Kumku on my forehead (a mark of great respect) and offering me a rupee, he exclaimed—'Now you are my Guru.'† The ceremony recalled one I witnessed in Rome in the nineties when a Noah's Ark array of animals, including a pet monkey, were blessed and sprinkled, not with blood, but more pacifically with holy water.

In the evening came the inevitable procession through the town, very like the one in honour of Muharram, only more glorious since it was a Hindu festival and Dewas was mainly a Hindu town. H.H. was on the state elephant. Master Sahib and I followed with the younger on horseback, and the elderly in carriages. The State

* For a striking and far fuller account of the festival fourteen years later see E. M. Forster, *A Passage to India*, Part 3.

† Spiritual teacher.

band had new instruments, and whether it was due to this or to the bandmaster's pay being raised by two rupees a month, when I entered the courtyard of the Palace the band struck up the State anthem which they had never done before. At the Court House, H.H.'s residence, the procession halted. H.H. descended the elephant, squatted on the ground and worshipped 'the tree of victory', a shrub with golden leaves called Shamee. Its leaves were handed round to the more important persons present, and the crowd was left to scramble for the rest. This was a purely Maratha custom and went back to the days when those going out to fight and loot gave the leaves to their families as a symbol of what they would bring back. The State accounts were now solemnly read out by the Revenue Secretary. Vast sums were declared to be in the Treasury, and equally vast sums to be due to the State. The State's income was multiplied a hundredfold, and altogether one was made to feel that silver was nothing accounted of. Then the real accounts followed. But that was a dull modern innovation, only three years old.

By now the sun had set. The trees were a dark blur against a sea of gold. Above a half moon lay comfortably in a bed of white cloud. Around us were smoking torches, and every ten paces through the city we stopped, and a fountain of gold sparks leapt into the air from some magic pot in front of the elephant. At the Palace a durbar followed on the usual lines with some special features due to the occasion. Honours were conferred on a select few. Thus Master Sahib and Rajaramji each received a costly turban with the right to be preceded at durbars by a mace-bearer, and a Mutiny veteran was given a silver dish to be kept as a family heirloom. But most had not to receive but to give. All with any official status had to offer H.H. a small sum in token of allegiance to his person—the Revenue officials Rs. 15 each, other officials Rs. 5, and the village headmen one rupee. Each in turn waved his offering round the Raja's head and was then embraced. Most of them also touched his feet. All this took time; I had left the Guest House at four-thirty and only returned five hours later.

Dussera had its taboos as well as its 'blessings'. It had hardly begun when H.H.'s real mother went down with fever. He wanted to move her to his abode: the change, he thought, would do her good. 'Impossible at present,' she said. For during Dussera a Hindu's household gods may not be moved. How then could she be moved? If anything happened to H.H., it would be her doing.

What surprised me more than it would now after the last war's boom in astrology, was to find that a person of H.H.'s education and intelligence could believe that the stars influenced our lives. I have already related how the date for our departure to Kolhapur was fixed by the Court Astrologer.* At the time I thought that this was merely a concession to the orthodox. It was a surprise, therefore, to be told by H.H. one evening that he shared their belief. We were discussing the date for some ceremony which had to be performed in February. The stars, it seemed, would allow of only three dates—6th, 11th and 19th. H.H. inclined to the 19th because his own star would then be in the ascendant, but it was not perfect. The 6th would do too but at the cost of a plan to visit Ceylon. 'Then let it be the 11th,' I said. 'Oh, no, Sahib, that won't do: my star is bad for that.' I pointed out, rather mercilessly, I fear, that it was an insult to the Deity to suppose that he could be more favourable one day than another. 'Surely you don't believe that?' 'Well, Sahib, I do—I can't help it.' And in the India of those days few could help it, and the same applies to many today.

That H.H. could not help it "makes me see (I wrote) how little I can touch his mind. I like him so much that I am always regretting that our lives should have sprung from such different sources, that our ways should have lain so far apart, that they must lie so far apart again. After eight months I seem to understand him and we seem to be extraordinarily akin. Then comes one of those flashes, and I see that he belongs to a different world and that his life is not mine, nor mine his. 'Bapu Sahib (as I used to call him),† what a glorious sky!' I once exclaimed. 'Yes,' he answered with rather a drawl and then added laughingly—'I see nothing in it.' I tried to explain what it meant to me, but after a few words I gave it up. It was impossible. All that side of one's life must be a riddle to him."

FRIENDSHIP

I have perhaps been remiss in so far saying nothing about the more serious side of my appointment. I was H.H.'s tutor as well

* p. 159.

† One of his names before adoption.

as his guardian. That suggested responsibility for the development of his mind. Having never taught in my life and now left entirely to myself, I fell back on what I had 'read' at Cambridge. This, as already noted, was 'History', which sixty years ago very sensibly included both Economics and Political Science. All three were now grist to my mill, especially history itself. In this H.H. had a keen interest with, where India was concerned, far more knowledge than I had. The history of his own race, the Marathas, he had at his fingers' ends, and it was characteristic of his loyal nature that he would hear nothing against their doings in the past. This passionate feeling he had imbibed from his father. As a child, he would often sit by him for an hour or two listening to the ballads of his race and to the doings of his forefathers. He well remembered, too, how when his father heard that the Maharaja of Kolhapur, whom he regarded as the head of his race, wished to betroth his daughter to his son, he exclaimed—'Today my house is blest.'

Discussion, based on some stimulating book, seemed to me the best way of developing and enlarging H.H.'s alert and sensitive mind. We read, therefore, such varied authors as Mill on Liberty, Alfred Marshall on Economics, and Aristotle and Bagehot on Political Science. We even tackled some of Plato's dialogues—in translation of course. He was much impressed by the *Apology* and by the account of Socrates' death in the *Phaedo*. In *The Symposium*, an episode related by Aristophanes surprised him, but by that time we knew each other well enough to discuss it with perfect frankness. Aristotle's reference in *The Politics** to Ares' love-affair with Aphrodite made him exclaim he was thankful his fiancée was not fascinating!

Interested as he was in politics, he preferred Aristotle to Plato. He appreciated the terseness of his style and his astonishingly modern outlook, which made him particularly fruitful in subjects for discussion. These covered a wide field and one day ranged from government by the many versus government by the one to the nature of beauty and its relation to goodness. Some pictures of beautiful women led to a discussion on the Eastern and Western conceptions of beauty. He insisted on the importance of a moon-face with large eyes and a bold nose. Unlike my Baluch teacher, he thought Mona Lisa quite plain. We were both surprised to

* Book ii, 9.

find that Aristotle approved of abortion, though only 'before sense and life have begun'.* That led us to birth-control. On the principle of never hiding anything from him, I told him that measures for this purpose were becoming very common in the West. 'They are wrong,' he said; 'I could never use them: they are unnatural.'

All this was certainly not light reading, and even in the case of *The Politics*, when we got to the end of the first volume, the only one I had of Jowett's translation, he heaved a sigh of relief and closed the book with a snap. With no experience of how a young Indian Chief should be educated, it was a relief to find that my method of 'read and discuss' met with the approval of our Political Agent, Major P. T. Spence, of whom more in a moment. It was better, he thought, to let H.H. do as much reading as possible and not to trouble overmuch about the more practical side of his training. The tendency, he said, was to teach a young Chief this and then let him be. That could come later. Now was the time to catch the mind. This I endeavoured to do, but the mind proved more elusive than the heart, and I doubt whether I influenced it at all.

As Political Agent Major Spence was Daly's primary link with both Dewas States. The role was a very personal one and demanded special qualities on both sides if the Agent was to be regarded as a friend and not as watch-dog or spy. Neither I nor H.H. had any doubts about Spence: we both felt at home with him from the start.

Six foot in height and squarely built, he had a face in which opposing qualities seemed to meet. A bold well-shaped nose with long curving nostrils suggested both sensitiveness and strength. The lower part of the face was a little harsh but broke easily into a charming smile. His forehead was low with just enough room for three or four wrinkles. A moustache concealed his upper lip; the lower was roughly moulded and midway turned slightly outwards. In talking to Indians he was completely unaffected, and his face radiated with courtesy and interest. 'There is something royal in his manner,' said H.H.

Gifted with a copious mind, he poured out talk in a torrent of proverb, metaphor and slang. On his first visit to Dewas we talked for five hours every day about almost everything except books. Like many Anglo-Indians he had read much more in the

* Book vii, 16.

book of the world than in the world of books. He knew everyone's place in the Political Service with his pay and allowances, local and sumptuary, and spoke of most, meaningless to me, by their Christian names, or even more confusingly by their nicknames—Mickie this, Tubby that, or more simply 'Puffin' or 'Buster'. That side of his talk I found most exhausting. "It is refreshing now (I wrote) to hear only the frogs and the crickets."

On the other hand, when he drew upon his very varied twenty-two years in India I could listen to him all day. The touch of harshness in his face came out in his account of life on India's North-West Frontier, where justice to be effective had to be pitiless and swift. He had had ten years in Baluchistan and on one occasion had been saved by his wife from the sword of a fanatic. He came to Central India from a State ruled by a Chief notorious for his cruelties. He had been unable to curb them, and in speaking of them his face blazed with indignation and scorn. His time there, he said, had been the worst in his whole service.

Daly was a very different type. Tall and slender with sinuous nose, delicately chiselled lips, tapering chin and small blue eyes which could dance with glee, his whole appearance suggested a Renaissance courtier rather than an Anglo-India V.I.P. And even the wig he wore, with its auburn tint and parting down the middle, added to the impression. It was a highly intelligent face with nothing square about it, yet not without a touch of the masterful.

H.H. and I differed as to what lay behind all this. Daly had served under Lord Curzon and many Chiefs distrusted him as too apt a pupil of that great but hated Imperialist. H.H. was inclined to share this view and would have it that his marked courtesy of manner was no more than the mask of a well-trained diplomat and that basically he was unsympathetic and cold. To me on the other hand he showed nothing but kindness and trust.

After what has been said above it it is not surprising that H.H. had never been frank with him. In August when we were both staying at the Residency, wishing to draw them closer together, I advised H.H. to ask for an interview and then be as frank as possible with him. The day before the interview took place I told Daly how highly I thought of the boy, and incidentally I mentioned that he was always frank with those he trusted. The result was even better than I had hoped. H.H. "unbosomed himself" and Daly responded with more warmth than ever before. And when the question came up of who should be H.H.'s Minister when he got his 'Powers', Daly said at once, so H.H. told me—'I leave that to you: I trust you entirely.' Finally, when we left he saw us into our carriage, which he had never done before.

In October it seemed almost certain that H.H. would be given full charge of the State in the Spring. He would then require a Minister he could trust as his Deputy. The person he wanted was the Maharaja of Kolhapur's Chief Secretary. This took us back to the Deccan to see the Maharaja, but "after the most tortuous manœuvres" he very naturally refused to give him up. Back at Dewas we were driving home one evening from the club when H.H. suddenly turned to me and said—'Sahib, why won't *you* be my Minister?' I was taken completely aback. 'Surely, Bapu Sahib, you don't mean that seriously?' But he did. The suggestion, he said, came originally from the Chief of Kagal, his closest friend, whom I had met at Dewas and Kolhapur. 'If you like him so much,' he said to H.H. when our mission to the Deccan had failed, 'why don't you make *him* your Minister?'

I protested that the State could ill afford the charge, and even if it could, for much less he could get much more—an Indian, in fact, with twice my experience. He replied that the whole machinery of the State required overhauling, and for that he needed special help. I should have the courage, he said, to stand up to him if he did anything wrong. I should also be a shield to him in dealing with the officials who were too bad to keep. If he dismissed them through me, it would at least be a guarantee, he thought, that they had been impartially judged.

Much discussion followed and some days later I wrote, "He has made the offer in so handsome a spirit that I cannot find it in my heart to refuse him. Whether it is wise professionally I know not, but friendship becomes a farce if you will risk nothing for it. He says he will trust me implicitly and I can hardly ask more." It was indeed a noble offer, for his own people could hardly fail to resent the choice of a foreigner for what they would regard as an important post. The offer, too, was made unhesitatingly. When I told him I was consulting friends, he said—'I have not consulted anybody and I do not mean to.'

To cut a long story short, when H.H. went to see Daly (now Lieutenant-Colonel) about the proposal, he was told at once that it was out of the question. The Chiefs would never believe that I had not been imposed upon him and this might make some of them tremble for themselves. Elsewhere, too, there might be awkward comment. 'India for the Indians' was now a popular cry, and this cut right across it. H.H. was "obviously rather upset" but "as nice as possible about it". He said he wanted an Englishman at his side who would understand him. Left to himself, circumstances might be too strong for him. And then, as he put it, 'If I am treated badly, my blood gets up, and I begin to play tricks,' a remark tragically prophetic.*

It was perhaps surprising that he wanted an Englishman. He admitted that in the past he had rather disliked them—he had found them "stiff and cold"—and was still not without racial feeling; but since he had come to know my friends (he had met three), he had changed his mind about them, "a little".

His was a deeply complicated character, and it had often puzzled me. When I had been with him seven months, I wrote: "He is so contradictory—frank and suspicious, passionate and cold, tender and cruel, yielding and defiant, brave and timid, kind-hearted and vindictive. You should see (I added) the way his eyes start out of his head when he is insulted; then you should hear the tenderness of his voice when he is moved." The key to the contradictions was—were you his friend or not? If you were not, true Maratha that he was he could be suspicious, defiant and vindictive, and pride when outraged could make him passionately glacial. But, if he accepted you as a friend in the full sense of that overworked word, mind and heart would be open to you and nothing kept back, and on your side you could tell him anything about yourself without fear of being misunderstood, still less of being harshly judged.

That we quickly became friends was due, as I have shown, to my mother. But even she was put to a subtle test before he felt he could trust her. Here I cannot do better than quote what E. M. Forster relates in *The Hill of Devi*.† At first he (H.H.) thought that she had been set to spy on him, so he tried to trap her. Having imparted some trifling secrets, he said, 'You will not tell anyone about this, will you?' She replied, 'No, but I may tell my son, mayn't I?' If she had merely said 'No', he would have continued to mistrust her. As it was he knew she was 'frank'.

* See the Epilogue.

† p. 42.

He once said to me—'If you (the English) are the least bit suspicious of us, we Indians are a hundred times more suspicious of you.' When I had known him less than a fortnight, a little incident seemingly confirmed this. He had been kicked by a pony, he said; but one or two things made me suspect some more intimate trouble which he might well wish to conceal. I told him I had to see the Residency Surgeon at Indore about my eyes (this was true but not urgent), would he not accompany me? He came, and happily he had told the truth.

I had been prudent with some reason, for I had been told in warning of a young Raja who was suddenly found to have had three children by a waiting maid in the palace. But in this case prudence was a blunder, as I learnt six months later when our relationship was so firmly established that he could recall the incident with a laugh. He had of course seen through the little ruse, but had been so disturbed by the thought that I was going to distrust him that he wrote to his friend, the Chief of Kagal, and begged him "to come at once and advise him". He came on what I supposed was a purely friendly visit. 'Just arrange a shoot (he said to H.H.) and I will talk to him and see what he is like.' Well do I remember that shoot. We spent hours bumping over broken ground in a bullock-cart until I was nearly sick, but never for a moment did I realise that it was not the deer they were stalking. H.H. admitted later that this was the only time I had been 'diplomatic' with him.

The very day after my arrival in Dewas I had written—"I think we are almost certain to get on together," and less than a fortnight later: "I think there is something remarkable in him." These first impressions rapidly grew into a certainty. In March I wrote—"I like him more and more. He is always perfectly charming with me and his manners are irreproachable." In May, "I rarely feel the Guardian with him—I like him too much"; and in August—"We have not had one quarrel yet—nay more, not a single unkind word" since the misunderstanding of the first week.* In August, too, came the promise of a bangle which would make us brothers.† And finally in October the very seal of friendship—would I become his Minister?

* See p. 139. † See p. 161.

CHAPTER 17

The Grand Tour—Northern India

We were still in 1907 and had reached the end of October when we began a three months' tour, which was intended to give H.H. a bird's-eye view of India and her two neighbours, Burma and Ceylon. It was in fact an Indian version of the Grand Tour which young Englishmen of good family would do in the eighteenth century to round off their education. It had the sanction of the Government of India and was to be done under their auspices, and all concerned had been notified of our itinerary so that the ceremonial appropriate to H.H.'s position could be fully observed.

For H.H. the tour began uncomfortably. To oblige astrologer and priest he had to leave Dewas at 5 a.m., though our train from Indore did not leave till 3 p.m. 'I had to give in to them,' he wrote to my mother. I, on the other hand, was allowed to leave after breakfast—at my own risk. For H.H. there was worse to come. Udaipur was our first halt. Although Dewas was not to be compared with it in either size or importance, H.H. considered that he was entitled to be treated as an equal by the Maharana, as Udaipur's Ruling Chief was styled, on the typically Indian ground that in lineage there was little to choose between them. They both claimed descent from Vishnu, the Maharana through Rama, the hero of the Ramayana, and H.H. through Rama's brother. 'Do you believe in these claims?' I asked. 'Not in my heart, but as others make them, I must.' Accordingly, he fully expected that the Maharana would be at the station to meet him. At our last stop before Udaipur, when he had just got out his sword and puggaree and was considering what jewellery he should wear, he was handed a telegram to say he would be met by a second-class noble and a Mr So-and-so. With glittering eyes and lips curled in scorn he ordered the regalia to be packed away; and at Udaipur, as we left the station, he exclaimed—'When other Chiefs ask me how I was treated here, I shall be teased. I'm glad (he added) that the Maharana is not independent, that he is a British Protectorate (*sic*). They at least will treat us well.' And indeed they did, as we shall see later.

On our arrival H.H. was for refusing all hospitality from the Maharana and going to an hotel. I suggested that since we were hungry—it was after eleven—and the Maharana had doubtless provided breakfast, it might be as well to eat it. We were taken to a palace within the city walls and, as we arrived, a fifteen-gun salute echoed through the surrounding hills. Even this concession to H.H.'s dignity, as we learnt later, was due only to official pressure from above. The Maharana himself had actually left Udaipur to avoid meeting him. His heir-apparent (aged twenty-two) sent H.H. a message that he must not mind this as his father was 'old-fashioned'. He would have come himself to see H.H. but his father had forbidden him to do so.

Of Udaipur itself with its hill-girt lake and radiant island palaces I wrote in my diary—"it hardly seems of this earth: it has that torturing beauty which when most within your grasp is always furthest away".

At Jaipur again no Ruling Prince to meet us. But with two nobles instead, one even of the first class, and a cavalry escort of twelve for our carriage-and-four "the agony of our reception was not so acute". Even so H.H. was hardly less glum. The Maharaja had not troubled to flee from us, yet did no more than enquire after H.H.'s health; and as H.H. refused to be the first to call, the two never met. Our departure brought a second message from the Maharaja. H.H.'s reply was polite but pointed: 'Tell the Maharaja-sahib that the arrangements were good and that I am pleased. I regret that we had no opportunity of meeting, but doubtless if we come again, there would be no difficulty.'

By day Jaipur with its rose-coloured houses was full of charm, but at night it became a city of enchantment. Diwali, the loveliest of all Hindu festivals, was being celebrated in honour of Lakshmi, the goddess of wealth. It was an occasion when every good Hindu outlined his house, however simple, with the flickering lights of wicks in tiny earthenware saucers. Even the crest of a high hill overlooking the city shone with them, as if Lakshmi herself had touched them into flame. That night I found H.H. had just finished worshipping his jewellery and twenty-five rupees in coin. At Diwali, he said, all Hindus worship their wealth that they may have more.

On our way to Jaipur we stopped at Ajmer to allow H.H. to revisit its famous Chiefs' College, where he had had the last part of his schooling. This led to an interesting reminiscence. He related how after Curzon's Delhi Durbar (1902), and partly on account of it, a violent anti-English feeling swept through the College. Tilak's speeches were lapped up, and the English avoided. Till then he had done so much with them that many regarded him as on the way to becoming a Christian. Now he eschewed their company and refused to eat their food. It was at this point too that he took to doing Puja—were politics and religion ever kept apart in India? Never one to do things by halves, he carried his antagonism so far that friends warned him he risked being deposed for disloyalty. It is to the credit of my predecessor that with his appointment as guardian, H.H. became less uncompromising in his attitude towards the British. But religiously, he still refused to eat anything cooked by a non-Hindu. There came a day, however, at Kolhapur when he refused food cooked by a Muslim. The two Indian friends he was dining with—one of them the Chief of Kagal—had no such scruple and, to quote my diary, they "took him by the neck and forced some of the food down his throat". They told my predecessor what they had done, and after that H.H. could no longer refuse to take a cup of tea with him, as Dhalu Ram had done in my case at Rajanpur.*

It was at Ajmer, in the library of the Victoria Museum, that I came across a young Sadhu very different in type from Atma Ram, the Sadhu described in Chapter 15. Atma Ram had the simplicity of a child who somehow had found his way into the Kingdom of Heaven, while the Sadhu at Ajmer suggested a pilgrim still on the road there with an intellectual approach to his goal. At the moment he was studying the religion of the Greeks. The only book he could find in the library for the purpose was the *Encyclopaedia Britannica* in twenty-six volumes. He was proposing to work through the whole twenty-six, page by page, in his search for information on the subject. So far he had not got beyond '*Agnus Dei*'!

He came from Madura in southern India and was the son of a contractor. He had been educated by missionaries, and at the age of eight had had his ears well boxed for asking his master why he believed in the existence of God. At twenty-two, when in the employ of the local railway, he met a famous Sadhu and under his influence became a Sadhu himself. The next two years he spent

* See p. 82.

with his Guru,* and another two at Benares learning Sanskrit. From there he went to Mathura for a seven-year course at a Training College for Sadhus. The first year he studied the Vedas, the second the Puranas, the third the Bible. The Koran should have followed, but after three years his health broke down. Now he was making his way back to Madura.

With a fine forehead, clean-cut lips and a mass of black hair, and arrayed in a dark cloak he was a striking figure, and his earnestness was in keeping with it. His age was between thirty and thirty-five, but he looked much younger. He quoted the Bible and, speaking in excellent English, said that Christ was the finest example of a life of renunciation. He also spoke admiringly of St John the Baptist. We talked of many things. He disapproved of the missionaries' zeal for conversion but admitted his debt to them for his education. H.H. came in as we were talking and unlike himself was stiff and silent when introduced. He suspected him of being a government spy but later on, after hearing my account of him, agreed that this was unlikely.

At Agra we all went straight to the Taj. Whenever I came back to it, my first sight of it always left me spell-bound, and so it was on this occasion. The Indian reaction was more sober. 'It makes me feel more calm and serene,' said H.H. 'What Emperors the Moguls were,' exclaimed Rajaramji; and finally the devout Master Sahib: 'it teaches the mind the better things'.

It was at this point that the only serious contretemps of our tour occurred; and for twenty-four hours it imperilled my relationship with H.H. The villain of the piece was Madharao Sindhia, Maharaja of Gwalior, H.H.'s maternal uncle by adoption, and one of India's most important Ruling Princes. I had met him more than once and had even accompanied H.H. on a visit to Gwalior. My diary of that date (September 19) describes him as "bubbling with energy but entirely unreliable". This should have put me on my guard. But Gwalior was so near Agra—only two hours or so by express—that it seemed to H.H. a good opportunity for a surprise visit. He had little affection for his uncle but knew this would please him. It would also confirm the recent healing of an old quarrel between them. So off he went one Thursday evening, alone to ensure surprise, and promising to be back at latest by Saturday morning.

* Spiritual teacher.

Saturday came but no H.H. Instead, that afternoon I got this telegram from Sindhia: 'Tomorrow being my birthday anniversary please abandon Mathura trip (fixed for Sunday) and bring Dewas party here. Peshawar trip holds good.' The wire added – 'Rajasahib knows.' This proved to be untrue. We were due at Peshawar on Monday evening and to get there in time would have to leave Agra on Sunday evening at latest. It was tiresome enough to have to cancel the visit to Mathura, for which various arrangements had been made by the local authorities. Peshawar would be worse. We were to be met at the station by the head of the District, there was to be a salute of fifteen guns, and we were to see the Khyber Pass on Tuesday when it would be under special guard for the caravans linking India and Central Asia. That we had already changed our dates once would not make matters easier. For all of which as H.H.'s bear-leader I was responsible.

There were various reasons for our not going to Gwalior, and I wired Sindhia accordingly. I also wired H.H. – 'Join us Sunday Agra 18.47 train – shall never forgive you if not there.' In transmission, to add to the growing confusion, 'forgive' became 'forget'. A third wire cancelled the visit to Mathura. That evening came another wire from Gwalior, this time from H.H.: 'Maharaja urges and heartily wishes me to stay tomorrow for birthday. I tried utmost to explain my inability to stay. Now Maharaja told me that he wired you to come and bring Party instead of going Mathura. Our Peshawar trip remains untouched. Under circumstances think better to agree to Maharaja. Excuse this trouble and fickleness on my part. You can understand reasons.' This showed that in saying 'Rajasahib knows' the Maharaja's telegram had misled both H.H., and myself. "I should have scented the cunning underlying in this (says my diary) and gone off to Gwalior at once. That is my great mistake. But I trusted H.H. implicitly and I never thought for a moment that he could fail me" – after getting my wire quoted above.

On Sunday evening we went to the station to catch the Punjab Mail. It was running in two parts. The first came in – no sign of H.H. An hour passed and in came the second. Again no sign of H.H. "Gad! I was angry," says a letter. I went straight to the booking office: 'When is the next train to Gwalior?' I asked. 'At 0.50, but only 3rd class' . . . I then wired to H.H. – 'What on earth has happened? Arriving Gwalior at 3.4 this morning, meet me at station.' Finally, a wire to Peshawar to say we should arrive a day late.

At 0.50 I left Agra accompanied, most fortunately as it proved, by Rajaramji, who had friends he wished to see in Gwalior. I was still angry but he was as gay as ever. 'We, too, are rejoicing,' he said, alluding to the birthday festivities at Gwalior. 'We are rejoicing by the 3rd class Special. Ah! (he added) at Gwalior they play very bad tricks—very bad tricks indeed!' We reached Gwalior at 4 a.m. Again no H.H., only an almost deserted station lit by foggy oil-lamps, and outside it a carriage-and-pair waiting, it was said, for 'the Guardian Sahib'. I had intended, if H.H. were not there, to beard him at the palace. But Rajaramji suggested he should go instead: he knew the palace well and would be much less conspicuous. I agreed but said that if he were not back with H.H. by five o'clock, I should come myself. So off he went to the Palace of Victory, as it was called.

I shall never forget the hour that followed. The station was deserted except for two men asleep, one outside the booking office, the other on the station steps. It was very cold, and to keep warm I paced up and down with Orion and the Great Bear overhead. Two country carts staggered up on crazy wheels and discharged women and children into the night. As one by one the minutes crept by, I listened more and more intently for the sound of carriage wheels. At last, at ten minutes short of the appointed hour, I could bear it no longer and started moving slowly towards the palace over a mile away, and when at last five o'clock struck, I almost broke into a run. I had done about a half a mile when far away two lights flashed into the darkness, followed a little later by the sound of wheels moving at speed. It was a carriage and as it passed me I shouted and it stopped. Rajaramji's cheerful voice rang out—'He has come'—and there he was in his gala clothes. I told him that we would take the 6.20 back to Agra and advised him to go to the waiting room and sleep. I was too angry to say more. He had hardly gone off when another carriage drove up. Sindhia had sent his Private Secretary hot-foot to the station to bring us to the palace. I told him that all our plans had been upset and that we were returning to Agra at once; and, since I could not trust myself to speak calmly, I would say nothing more. So back he went to the Palace of Victory.

Dawn was now breaking and sitting on a station bench I heard

Rajaramji's story. As he entered the palace, which he knew well, there was a titter of surprised women's voices exclaiming from above—'Rajaramji has come.' He was told that Sindhia and his Court were celebrating his birthday in the Durbar Hall with a nautch.* He went straight there and whispered in H.H.'s ear—'The Sahib is at the station—come.' And he came—before anyone had realised why he had left the Hall.

Back at Agra, as he walked down the platform, I heard a peasant woman say—'The Maharaja has been brought back by force.' This was not fair to H.H., but a good example of how quickly fact gets distorted as it turns into history. His story was this. On Friday Sindhia said he would let him go on Saturday if he stayed another night. Saturday morning he agreed again to let him go. In spite of this he despatched the wire asking the rest of us to come to Gwalior, adding 'Rajasahib knows'. This, as I have said, was not true, for he told him only three hours later, and then H.H. had perforce to wait for my answer. On Sunday, after promising to make all arrangements for H.H.'s departure, Sindhia refused to let him go, even denying him transport to the station. At the same time he promised to let me know but did not do so. That evening there was a banquet in honour of his birthday, with covers for a hundred. H.H. proposed Sindhia's health, and in reply Sindhia greeted H.H., not as a nephew, but as a brother Chief. My wire telling H.H. to meet me at the station reached him only at 2.30 a.m. When he asked for a carriage to take him there, there were further excuses: first and last, in fact, every possible obstacle was put in his way.

At first I thought H.H. had acted very wrongly. "But (says a letter) we have talked it all out and upon my word I doubt if he could have acted otherwise: circumstances were too strong for him." The whole affair brought home to me how little I still knew of Indian ways. In India it seemed, an engagement had not the fixity that we had been taught to give it in the West. It might have to give way to a more cogent consideration—as in this case, for instance, to the paramount importance of family ties. To be rude to an elder relative was considered "almost unpardonable", and on this occasion it would have been very rude to have walked to the station, as at first I thought H.H. should have done when transport was refused. He had indeed been rude enough in leaving

* An entertainment of dancing and singing.

as unceremoniously as he did. There was a further point: Sindhia was not only a relative but also one of India's most powerful Ruling Princes. It was natural therefore that H.H., who was still only nineteen, should wish to avoid giving him offence. His mistake, if any, was to go to Gwalior alone, and my greater one to let him do so.

Mercifully, thanks to the firmness of our friendship and to his generous nature "within 24 hours after a most trying day, everything went on exactly as before". Some days later H.H. could write to my mother: 'I paid a surprised (*sic*) visit to Gwalior and met His Highness there. His birthday fell after 2 days of my arrival there and he simply did not allow me to go back. This caused a lot of disturbance in our plans . . . and all of us were put to great inconvenience, trouble and misunderstanding by it. . . . However everything ended all right as Mr Darling wisely and suddenly came to Gwalior and took me away. The whole thing is all right now." I had, in fact, taken the whole affair with unnecessary seriousness, as I found on reaching Peshawar. My abject apologies to the Deputy Commissioner, who received us at the station, were met with the unexpected remark–'Don't worry–we are used to that kind of thing with Chiefs,' or words to that effect. We were not even deprived of a sight of the Khyber. As we were too late for the caravan day we saw it by special arrangement two days later.

This gave us a memorable day. We were off at a very cold 8 a.m. in a little country cart drawn by two ponies. I took the reins, and before the day was done they had taken us forty miles–twenty up to Ali Masjid and twenty back. The return journey we did in two hours, and how they rattled us along the last five miles into Peshawar! The pass was specially guarded for us by sentinels posted on the hills overlooking the road on either side. At Jamrud, the entrance to the pass, someone pointed to the road winding away into the hills and said–not quite as seriously as H.H. took it –'If you are killed on it, there will be an enquiry, but if you are killed a hundred yards or more away from it, there will be no enquiry.' We had in fact come to where civilisation ended abruptly and before us lay a country where, to quote H.H., the people were 'very brave, savage and roguish'. The hills were sprinkled with what looked like little forts but were in fact homesteads built in this no-man's-land for security.

At Ali Masjid, some thousand feet above the plain we had left below and only fifteen miles or so from Afghanistan, we found a burn running through a grove of trees. There we spread our rugs and breakfasted. An Afridi sepoy joined us and I told him that I had with me 'a big Maharaja from Hindustan'. This was perhaps imprudent on my part and certainly tactless for it made H.H. uneasy: he feared it would get about and that we should be sniped at on our way back. Back on the plain below, he exclaimed with a sigh of relief: 'However much we may hate the British Government, it does keep order and that is a great thing.' A great thing indeed, and in those days it did it in this part of the world for the millions spread over the whole of India, Burma, Malaya and Ceylon.

For me Peshawar was only less exciting than the Khyber. We seemed to be standing on the threshold of Central Asia, with barbarism so near our doors that at sunset the city gates had to be closed and exit and entrance confined to a wicket gate. The bazaars too were "full of the most astonishing faces". Many times did I return there in later years but never, in spite of its growing sophistication, without an echo of that first thrill.

From Peshawar, with halts at Lahore and Allahabad, we passed on to Benares. There we must pause, for nothing we saw on our tour made such a deep impression on H.H. For him it was what Mecca is for the Muslim and Jerusalem for the Christian. 'All my strong feelings (he wrote to my mother) came to the top and compelled me to revere the place as if it was the only sacred place and where the Lord of the Universe resided. . . . One evening Mr Darling and myself rowed in (*sic*) the river and it was a magnificent scene. The Palaces and Temples of the Princes of India on the bank of that holy river made me simply wonder at the great power the river had over us. There I felt the Princes met each other in peace and no rivalry existed amongst them except in excelling one another in building temples and palaces in honour of the Hindu deities and on the sacred bank.' Altogether a splendid and stirring sight for a Hindu.

One of these palaces, built of vast blocks of masonry on the water's edge, belonged to the Maharaja of Gwalior, and there, through the courtesy of his uncle, H.H. lodged. It was as much temple as palace, and in one of its small courtyards I found a sacred bull at large. He indeed was allowed to wander where he would, but we could not cross from palace to temple without taking off our shoes, and this applied even to the temple-palace roof. There one evening, on the part which was not holy ground, we had tea with the river winding nobly below us. At dusk we embarked in a boat and, as darkness fell and the stars appeared, the sound of temple bells and chanted litanies came floating across the water to the beat of drums, and on the bank funeral pyres blazed and mortal remains "flew away in a cloud of smoke and sparks".

'Shall you acquire merit by coming here,' I asked H.H.

'Certainly.'

'But how? Is this spot really more sacred than any other?'

'Yes, it is the atmosphere: there is something different.'

'Do you believe (I continued) that washing in the Ganges will do you good?'

'It will wash away all my sins.'

'And mine too?'

'Yes, there is no difference.'

A further question–not recorded–was too much for his patience. 'It is no use discussing these things,' he said. 'I know that if you apply reason everything will fall away. But I want to keep my beliefs. They are too deep-rooted in me.' A wise last word in answer to my gad-fly questions. On that side of his life his English education had had no effect. He was intensely proud of his race and also of his faith, and there was no gainsaying the strength and firmness of their roots.

'I shall come here again (he said) and then I shall bring the bones of my ancestors.' Apparently when a person dies a small bone may be saved from the pyre to be thrown into the Ganges. H.H. had the bones of ten ancestors awaiting this final immersion. "Today (I wrote) all the hair cut from his head during these 8 or 9 years was thrown into the Ganges." This was done, he said, by the Chiefs descended from Vishnu. The barber, missing no opportunity of flattery, said he had also included some of mine, easier done then than now.

Early the next morning, when the sun was no more than temple-high, I was on the river and met H.H. in another boat sitting in a wicker chair on the roof of its cabin. He was reading the Bhagavad-gita aloud to Master Sahib and Rajaramji and was so absorbed that he did not look up until he had finished the chapter. We landed and I went with him to a temple which every pilgrim to

Benares must visit. It is said to be 2,300 years old; it is in fact only 150. H.H. went inside to tap a bell and offer rice and cash. When he came out he was followed down a narrow alley by a pack of Brahmins. Beggar women tried to join in the mêlée but were driven off by the men. At Benares, the Brahmin was certainly not at his best.

My boatman said I must visit the Nepalese temple, which was "jammed in with many others on the river bank". At the head of a flight of stairs a priest was waiting. Taking a long pole, he pointed to this figure and that, and so on round the temple. What I saw amazed me—"I have never (I wrote) seen anything more vividly and grotesquely lewd—the act of intercourse in all its stages. At times I feel as if I should like to blast the whole town and pour the dust into the river, so much it stands for all that is base in religion. Yet there is a kernel somewhere. It is the heart of India, the source of the great stream of its life, the point to which 250 millions look for redemption."

CHAPTER 18

The Grand Tour – Burma

AFTER a brief halt in Calcutta we embarked for Rangoon. The voyage put me to shame. The nursling of a sea-faring race, I was obliged to take to my bunk for twenty-four hours, whereas H.H., who as a good Hindu should have looked upon 'the black water' with horror, was unmoved. "You should have seen him (I wrote) squatting on his berth and doing puja with folded hands like a little image of Buddha. I could have shaken all the religion out of him," I added in a moment of green-eyed envy.

Burma fascinated me. In India, "you may travel across great spaces. You may pass from the plateaus of Malwa and the Deccan to the empty horizons of the Punjab, from the banks of the Indus to the banks of the Ganges, and still you are in the same land." But here was something different – Chinese with pigtails, Burmese with sunshades, monks in yellow robes, and best of all, women tripping along with the grace and assurance of a Parisienne. We had come from a country where women were shut up, or if allowed out, passed you furtively, veiling faces made to be seen. Now we were talking and laughing with them as we chaffered over their wares in market and bazaar.

Though their features were plain with noses "flattened on their faces", though too they used an ash-grey powder which was far from fragrant, I found them captivating. A letter explains why. "There is a *je ne sais quoi* in their gait, and in the poise of their lithe little bodies, an assurance that comes only of freedom. Then the clothes they wear: there I despair, I can only admire. From the waist downwards they wrap round them yards and yards of plain silk of the palest and most delicate colours – sunset greens and lemon yellows, rose and watered crimson, cerise and mauve. Above, a white cotton jacket – Heaven help us – fits closely to the bust, and round their hair, bunched up on top in a black and shining mass, they tie a scarf of pink silk with a flower or two peeping roguishly just above the ear."

In Rangoon our first visit was to the famous Shwe Dagon

Pagoda, which draws pilgrims from all parts of the Buddhist world to worship at a shrine said to contain a hair of Buddha himself. Clustered round it were scores of smaller pagodas with statues of Buddha in every possible pose—"Standing, sitting, lying; large as a colossus, small as a doll; grave and gay, foolish and wise, alive and dead; hundreds of him. Turn this way or that, he sees you behind and before; he smiles at you, he reproaches you, he ignores you. And in time I ignored him."

Meanwhile the little bells which adorned each pagoda tinkled in the breeze, mingling with the murmur of prayer. Fair forms glided noiselessly from shrine to shrine; monks in yellow robes passed by fan in hand, men in red skirts sank on to the ground in adoration, beggar children prowled about, and squatting under palm trees old women hawked their wares. But the most charming sight of all was a group of maidens kneeling at a shrine with hands folded in prayer, the thumb just touching the whispering lips, and the fingers clasping a bunch of flowers to be offered to Buddha. 'Doing as Rome does', I bought a few lotus flowers for my offering. A little boy of four or five in a long skirt took them from me and "like some Samuel of old" offered them to Buddha. Doing again as Rome does, this time literally as well as metaphorically, I lit a taper as a further offering. In this gracious atmosphere I could deny Buddha nothing.

In the bazaars Mammon can never have been worshipped with greater charm. Girls with long merry dark eyes unrolled their silks and laughter rippled around one. I had come across nothing of the kind in India. In the silver market there was the same temptation to buy. But what I found irresistible were the gongs. I was not so reckless as H.H., who bought a dozen, but more irresponsible. I tapped all I saw, and one day—we were now at Mandalay—we climbed one of its fort's wooden towers. At the top hung a gong. Instintively I seized its padded stick and sounded a loud note upon it, then another, and yet a third. There were shouts from below, but all in Burmese of which I knew only three words. It was clear however that someone was very much annoyed. Up came a man puffing with the ascent, and then we learnt that I had sounded the fire-alarm for the whole fort, which was largely built of wood, and that a fire-engine would certainly rush to the scene. But none came. Evidently it took more than three beats to wake it up.

The journey to Mandalay by train took twenty-four hours. It

was long since I had enjoyed one so much. Leaving the cosmopolitan Rangoon at night, we woke the next morning to the real Burma, with pagodas sprinkled on hill and plain, village houses on piles, and great stretches of golden rice fields sweeping up to wooded hills a misty blue in the morning haze. And in December what a climate! "like the loveliest of English summer days, and in the air something intoxicating that recalls the ecstasy of Italy".

I shall not dwell on the attractions of Mandalay and its famous fort, but one tiny incident I must recall because it suddenly brought back my schoolboy past. One evening I dismissed my carriage, a wooden box on wheels, and walked. As I rounded a corner of the fort and its lotus-leaved moat, there stole upon my ears from the Commissioner's house close by, the strains of the Eton Boating Song. A band was playing and Chinese lanterns shone in the dusk, and within there must have been dancers. A waltz has always affected me, and here was the one I liked best floating across the moat to where I stood looking at the last light in the west. In a moment I was carried back ten years to when torch in hand a thousand of us young Etonians sang it before the Queen in honour of her Diamond Jubilee.

Very different from the waltz was the Pwé, as the Burmese national dance was called. We were entertained to one by a Mandalay merchant. The three dancers were in various shades of pink finery and so slim that "I could have held all three in my arms". Thanks to the ash-coloured paste on their faces and its exotic scent this was not a tempting experiment. Of the orchestra of four one had a concertina with no sweeter notes than its Western counterpart, another a shrill penny-whistle played *con brio*, a third two tiny cymbals, and the fourth sat encircled with drums.

The dancing was of the Indian type. As the body swayed this way and that, with the chest thrust forward and the shoulders back, elbow and wrist came into play with a subtle twitching of the thumbs. With growing tension, lips quivered, eyes became dreamy and the whole figure taut with expectancy; and as the climax approached, the movement became faster, the gestures more ardent, and the orchestra more discordant. Each of the players sang, or rather shrieked in turn; and in the middle of it all "a rustic churl" got up, took off his pink skirt, wound it about his hips and began a dialogue with one of the dancers. "I don't know what he said but he was most entertaining and recalled the slave in a play of Plautus." Englishmen, they say, take their pleasures sadly, and H.H. is always throwing this in my teeth. But there is nothing more curious than the immobility of an Eastern audience watching a nautch and doing this by the hour. The Pwé, had we wished, would have lasted all night, but we had to catch a boat. So after an hour of it H.H. gave the performers thirty rupees and we left, with flowers in our hands and scented, and drove to the river. Wonderful was the moonlight on the water as we embarked; but even more wonderful was the blue light which filled the night sky, and to crown all across the river came the deep booming note of a gong.

After the women the Buddhist monks were the most striking feature of the human landscape. "In every street, in every tram you will see bald-headed men (like Elisha), in yellow robes, the right arm and shoulder bare. They are supposed to live on alms and at dawn you will see the younger amongst them going from house to house gathering fragments—rice, bananas, sweetmeats—into large black pots which shine in the sunlight."

We visited one of their many monasteries, an old gilded pagoda upheld by a forest of piles to protect it from Burma's torrential rains. Inside, a large room was divided by curtains into cubicles each containing a rug to sleep on, a long chair to rest in, with such other necessities as clock, rosary and cheroots, the latter beloved in Burma of both male and female. In this monastery at least life did not seem excessively ascetic. Close by was the chapel, another large room adorned with a statue of Buddha. As with Madonnas in Italy, one gets tired of seeing him everywhere. Yet how much more human he seems than the more prominent Hindu deities.

From monastery to village was a natural transition in a country where every boy had to have a spell in a monastery before reaching manhood. The village we visited was in Upper Burma and almost on the Irawaddy. We had some difficulty in finding the way in. It was seemingly on not too easy terms with its neighbours, for all round was a thick hedge about the height of a spear. Within the pale were dishevelled rows of wooden shanties with a very care-free look. After peering into the school, where all we could read was the superscription on a cardboard box marked 'Polo Cigarettes', we came upon a woman plying her shuttle through a woof of red yarn. She was bare to the waist and as we approached, she hurriedly concealed what certainly there was no danger in exposing. Another we found chopping up the stalks of Indian corn needed for the white long-leaved Burmese cheroot. She, too, was bare to the waist but unashamed. Though wrinkled with hollowed cheeks, when a naked babe was put into her arms, standing there and smoking a cheroot, she gave it suck. Here was the other side of Burmese womanhood.

As in an Indian village, many dogs were about barking incessantly but running away if you looked at them. Even more numerous were the children. We wondered who could be their mothers, for we saw few who seemed young enough for child-bearing. Several women were weaving and one was at her spinning wheel. Though we had scarcely a word of their language everyone was as pleasant as possible, meeting our ignorance with smiles and our gestures with soft-sounding words.

Two excursions from Mandalay must be briefly mentioned. The first was to Bhamo, only thirty miles from China. At Peshawar we felt we were on the edge of Central Asia. Here we seemed to be almost in China itself. The market place was full of Chinese—pigtails, baggy blue trousers and all. There was even a joss-house. In its innermost shrine sat Buddha in the company of a dozen ascetics "with pinched distorted faces". Each had a niche to himself and a lighted incense stick stuck in one of Huntley & Palmer's biscuit tins full of earth.

We reached Bhamo by train and ferry boat. The train took us through what seemed an impassable jungle, with not an opening to right or left, only a thick wall of shrubs, bushes, branches, and trunks crushed together in a stifling mass of disordered growth and all struggling for air and freedom. One of the Irawaddy Flotilla Company's luxurious steamers brought us back to Mandalay. We were forty-eight hours on board, and until near the end we had nothing on either side but undulating forest lying like a pall over the hills and smothering every rock and peak. At first I loved it; "there was something rich and splendid in this panorama of silent trees". But man's eye, or mine at least, was not made for monotony, and on the third day when the brown earth reappeared, I gave a gasp of relief.

Our second expedition took us by train into the Shan Hills to a spot so solitary that the substance of our meals had to come three hours by train. Our object was to see the Gokteik Gorge and the railway viaduct which spanned its river 1,500 feet below. The gorge was wide as well as deep and could hardly have been bridged —in those days at least—had not nature herself bridged it first. A swift stream had cut its way through the rock and arched it into a long winding tunnel. Upon this natural bridge 400 feet below rested the central girders of the bridge above. Seen from the bottom of the gorge, the viaduct soared into the blue sky "as light and frail as a spider's web". 'It is wonderful,' exclaimed Master Sahib. 'Nature and Art—look, there is thick friendship between them.'

Accompanied by a bearded German from Berlin, a tourist like ourselves, I explored the tunnel. 'It is like the entrance to the Hell,' he said as we entered it. Not inapt, for the air inside had a strange and rather evil smell. Birds (were they bats?) whistled unseen. The planks we trod on were covered with their droppings, and in one place there was a little pile of feathers where one had been plucked to pieces. The vaulted roof was well above us, but with its spiky stalactites piercing at us in the gloom, one had the feeling that it might suddenly crush us.

It was one o'clock and the sun was shining, so we bathed. At least three of us did; Master Sahib refused. Indians are extremely modest about their persons: even in his bath H.H. wore a loin-cloth. The question therefore was—how could the bathe be done? After much discussion H.H. borrowed a servant's loin-cloth; Rajaramji made do with his cotton pyjamas and I, feeling very indecent, with my under-pants turned round. The bathe was a merry affair but for one anxious moment when Rajaramji was knocked down by the swiftness of the stream, and was only saved from being slithered over jagged rocks by catching my hand at the critical moment.

The German proved an agreeable as well as an interesting companion. H.H. took to him too. 'He was so jolly,' he said, and contrasting him with Englishmen, added—'You are a dull race.' He was particularly impressed by his ceremonious politeness. When introduced to Master Sahib and Rajaramji he bowed lower than any European I had ever seen bow to an Indian. Indians too are extremely polite. "They will say anything rather than risk hurting your feelings. Hence they rarely say what they think. If I suggest something that H.H. may not care for, he will agree at once, but somehow he will work into it the barest suggestion that perhaps

I had not quite considered the matter. I know now what that means."

Back in Rangoon, on Christmas Day I paid a farewell visit to the Shwe Dagon Pagoda. At one of its many shrines my eye was caught by a young Burmese woman absorbed in her devotions. So exquisite was she in dress, figure and pose that I could not help exclaiming to an unknown elderly Englishman standing beside me, who was also watching her—'Isn't she charming?' 'She's my wife,' was the unexpected reply. I never paid a happier compliment. 'Well, have ye finished your prayers?' he asked, turning towards her. As they moved away, she did not reach much beyond his elbow. I remained to offer roses 'to the Lord'. But this time there was no 'infant Samuel' to take them from me, only two men whose one word, as they did so, was 'Bakshish'. And with it vanished the graciousness of the East.

Far worse was it with the West. I took a tram. It was full of Burmese—mild-mannered men in claret-coloured skirts with pink scarves wound round their temples; one woman, too, with a fillet of faded lilies adorning her jet-black hair. They, too, had been to the great Pagoda to fall at Buddha's feet and murmur his praises. One was pulling on coffee-coloured socks taken off, no doubt, to tread on holy ground; another was putting on European boots; a third was adjusting a sock-suspender—when a dozen men of a certain regiment got in; a noisy rackety crew, three of them drunk. Shouting at each other, they flung themselves on to the vacant seats while the Burmans huddled together to give them all the elbow-room they could. One of the three who were drunk, lolling across the seat opposite me with a dribbling chin, asked me—"Ave ye a cigar?'—'I'm afraid not,' I said; whereat he exclaimed, 'You're a bloody—' and the rest was lost in the noise of the tram wheels. 'A curse on them beggars!' exclaimed one who seemed to be in command, when some of the men made more noise than even he liked. Another clapped his topee on to the head of the woman with the faded lilies. Happily her charms were also a little faded, and she escaped further attention by slinking up to my end of the tram. When at last they got out, two of them insisted on shaking me by the hand, one of them remarking—'Don't often get the opportunity with a gentleman like you.' It was a scene to fill one with shame, but one must remember that the Army of those days was largely recruited from a much rougher type than the Army of today with its higher level of education and pay. Nor must one forget how stoutly that Army fought in the war that was to come seven years later.

The next day we left for Calcutta. We had been in Burma just over three weeks.

CHAPTER 19

The Grand Tour—India, Eastwards and Southwards

WE returned to Calcutta for one purpose only—an interview with the Viceroy (Lord Minto). On our first visit this had not been possible. In preparation for the occasion I bought boots and gloves and had my top hat ironed and my frock-coat pressed—the frock-coat was still the height of fashion. All I thought was in order when, only an hour before we were due to start, my Bearer announced that all my shirts were with the dhoby except one which I had already worn. The frock-coat too was found to have "an aggressive crease" down the front. There was nothing to be done but to hope that all eyes would be upon H.H. He indeed was resplendent in silk and gold lace with ropes of pearls round his neck.

In our anxiety not to be late we were far too early and the brougham, which we had hired "at a preposterous rate", had to pace slowly up and down the street outside the Viceregal gates. Inside Government House, we were escorted to the door of His Excellency's study. The door opened, and there was the Viceroy in a pink shirt with a white rose in his buttonhole sitting at a large table covered with books and papers. He stood up, shook us both by the hand and motioned H.H. to a low chair, myself to a high one. Conversation followed, but as I took no part in it I had leisure to observe His Excellency. He looked well past his prime and much bent. There was nothing impressive about his person, and little to attract one except the kindliness of his manner. Even this was somewhat abrupt, for he was evidently pressed, as well a Viceroy might be. He asked H.H. a few questions, complimented him on his English almost before he had opened his mouth—and so good-bye. The interview had taken perhaps five minutes. And for this I had carried frock-coat and hat several thousand miles and we had retraced our steps all the way to Calcutta instead of sailing straight to Madras.

The same day there lunched with us at our hotel a very different type of man, yet, like Lord Minto, an Old Etonian. He was a Cowley Father and had long been known to my family. He glowed with the fire of life—the life of the spirit. After lunch, I asked H.H. what impression this ascetic from the West had made on him. 'His religion (he said) is genuine: there is no doubt about that.'

'But what makes you think that?' I asked.

'I could see it from the way he treated the ladies. When they came into the dining-room he did not look up at all.' There spoke India and its purdah system.

The day before, New Year's Day, and H.H.'s twentieth birthday, we had been sucked into the swirl of Western gaiety. "All to-day (I wrote) I have been looking at horses—mares, stallions, geldings; Australians and Arabs; some walking, some galloping; men flying over hurdles, some with red ribbons, some with blue; the Viceroy walking about with an A.D.C. in gold lace; the Chief Judge with two massive daughters; people standing on chairs (to look at H.E.); a band playing 'Violets'; others at tea, and all apparently happy. So did the year open for the West."

The mood of the East was different. H.H. took me that evening to a Bengali theatre, where the play dealt with what followed the Battle of Plassey (1757). An actor in a pink shirt and red wig plus frock-coat, top hat and brown boots represented the Governor. There were many patriotic sentiments addressed to the Bengalis about dying for their country, and these were always applauded. Feeling against us (I wrote) was increasing. Everywhere I came across it—in Lahore, Burma, Southern India (the letter was from Madura), on board ship, and in the train. Master Sahib and Rajaramji travelled second class and would sometimes relate what their fellow-passengers had said. There was but one topic—Politics, whether it was Chinaman, Persian or Bengali.

One afternoon during a thirty-five-hour journey from Puri to Madras a pleader from Madras, who was a member of Congress, got into our compartment. He was "declamatory and fervent" and had a great argument with H.H. about the part the Chiefs should play in the India of the future. On my asking him what he disliked in the English, he said: 'They will not treat us as equals, nor will they trust us'—charges only too familiar, with much to be said on both sides. He added that the two races understood each other less and less.

From Calcutta we travelled south to Puri on the Bay of Bengal. It was one of India's great centres of pilgrimage and famous for the car of Juggernaut, which was kept within its temple precincts. With its semi-fortress walls, and gates open only to Hindus, the temple was very different from the Burmese pagodas which were open to the sunshine and to all. As at Benares, the atmosphere was highly charged with religion and H.H. deeply stirred.

This led one evening to a long discussion of what religion meant to him. His point of view was strongly coloured by the Bhagavadgita, which he read daily. His ideal, he said, was to attain a state of self-sufficing calm, unaffected by either pleasure or pain, through complete aloofness from the world. Only so would he cease to be like a candle flickering with every breeze—a metaphor taken from the Bhagavadgita itself. Only in this way could perfection be attained. I made the obvious remark that no one could be perfect and suggested that we should concern ourselves with the good around us, of which as yet we knew very little, rather than with the good beyond us, and that his ideal could only be attained by crushing the heart, which was the kernel of our being. To this he replied that the world around us was full of evil and that only by withdrawing from it could men obtain sufficient self-control to resist "the terrible, almost overpowering temptations of their lower selves". I did not share his pessimism, but then the Victorian world of my upbringing had been far more sheltered than his, and the world that lay before me had much more of value to offer than the world he must live in.

For me Puri's attraction was not its famous temple but the long foaming line of its sea-shore booming ceaselessly with the sound of breakers. Here indeed might Wordsworth have exclaimed:

> Listen! the mighty being is awake
> And doth with his eternal motion make
> A sound like thunder—everlastingly.

We did more than listen—we bathed. This time even Master Sahib was persuaded, but not H.H.: he was intent on higher things. Master Sahib said he must first be shaved. This presented no difficulty—H.H.'s barber was summoned and shaved my fellow-bathers as they sat on the sandy shore, Master Sahib bare to the waist. This done, we entered a very lively sea, Master Sahib girded with a thick loin-cloth, and myself in the lower half of my pyjamas, and on my head a solar topee, still considered a necessary protection against the Indian sun but in this case soon swept away by an outraged wave. So soft was the shelving sand, so warm and brilliant the sun that even the ascetic Master Sahib chuckled with delight. Not far away stood timid pilgrims ankle-deep in the sea's frothing edge, their hands folded in prayer.

From Puri we edged our way along India's eastern coast to Madras. There H.H. received an invitation to an evening party at Government House. Hearing that the Maharaja of Mysore was to be present, he felt he could only accept it if he were treated in much the same way as the Maharaja. This was a bold request for the Maharaja stood very high in the hierarchy of India's Ruling Princes. Fortunately Government House were most accommodating, and so we went. Admitted by the Private Entrée, we were shown on to the dais in the Banqueting Hall, where all the men seemed to be in uniform or in knee-breeches and silk stockings. I felt like the man without a wedding garment, for H.H. had of course put on his pearls and the Maharaja wore an exquisitely embroidered silk coat. Meanwhile the body of the hall was filling fast and East and West mingled together with pleasant smiles and occasional bows. Only a group of Indian ladies held together a little apart.

At ten o'clock a sudden hush fell upon the hall. Their Excellencies, Sir Arthur and Lady Lawley, were entering in a procession led by officers of the bodyguard. On the dais we craned our necks as far as curiosity and decency would allow. Sir Arthur, with Lady Lawley half a step behind him, advanced very slowly despite the encouragement of the band, and with some reason for he had a fine figure and bowed to perfection. "Never (I wrote) have I seen such bowing. You felt a tremor about the waist, then a movement passing up the spine and spreading over the shoulders till the neck relaxed a little and the gold lace collar suddenly unstiffened, while the head slowly, very slowly came forward but so imperceptibly that you felt rather than saw the bow."

After the usual formalities we were treated to a Musical Ride by twenty-five men of the bodyguard with torch-headed lances. They broke into two lines and it was fascinating to see them thread their flaming way in and out of each other in a maze of evolutions done by horse and man with the utmost precision. Some exciting rounds of tent-pegging with torch-lit spears followed, and an appetising buffet brought a delightful evening to an end.

From Madras we went yet farther south to a spot almost in sight of Ceylon. There we embarked in a little black launch full of pilgrims and were ferried across to the holy island of Ramesvaram, midway between India and Ceylon and second in sanctity only to Benares. H.H. also came as a pilgrim intent on visiting the temple built to commemorate the rescue of Rama's wife Sita from the clutches of Rawan, the demon king of Ceylon, who had abducted her.* As we steamed away, India's mainland slowly shrunk until it was no more than a narrow spit capped with palm trees. On landing at Ramesvaram we were taken by train a last eight miles to a tiny village dominated by the temple we had come to see. This the faithful believed to have been built by Rama himself, but was said by the less religious Fergusson (a well-known authority on Indian temples) to date from the seventeenth century. For want of other lodging we put up in a small and not too clean serai. A rug was spread for us on its verandah and on this we sat talking to two Brahmins who joined us, each clad in the ample folds of a saffron shawl which scarcely concealed the ampler folds below.

Conversation turned on an image of great sanctity in the temple. H.H. had heard that the Maharani of Nepal had been permitted to touch it and asked to be allowed to do the same. Impossible he was told: it was a privilege reserved exclusively for Brahmins. The Maharani had also been refused but got her way, so it was said, by threatening to use her forty followers for the purpose. This was no way for H.H. and he had to accept the rebuff. 'I was very angry at this,' he wrote to my mother. 'I did not therefore pay tips to Brahmins.' He expressed himself more forcibly on the spot. 'Who are these Brahmins?' he exclaimed, and he turned to the Brahmin Master Sahib, 'Who are they that they make themselves better than us? There are no true Brahmins now. I have been all over India and I find everywhere the same: they simply want money. They come between us and God. We Kshatriyas (the warrior caste) are their protectors and this is how they treat us. All right, I know what to do when I get back to Dewas: I will stop that 10,000 rupees I give them. I will not give them a farthing,'

* The story goes that to enable Rama and his army to cross the strait, the Monkey God and his monkeys built a stone causeway across it, which floated because Rama's name was inscribed on it.

and so on. This was too much even for the gentle Master Sahib. As we sat on the rug by the light of an oil lamp, words flew this way and that. The discussion would perhaps have been less lively had we not been so hungry.

We had arrived by starlight and dinner did not appear until ten o'clock. This was a strictly vegetarian affair, with mine set apart in the porch while the others went elsewhere, their strife composed. As only one bed was available for the four of us, I slept on my dinner table. For breakfast, after some doubt on the part of the Brahmins whether their vegetarian principles would allow me an egg, I was given three omelettes laid one above the other! A visit to the temple followed, and as at Puri, I was not allowed to enter the inner sanctuary. I was standing at one of its massive gateways when a cart bearing a huge block of granite appeared drawn by eighteen coolies. As they pulled, one of them intoned a phrase which the others caught up in antiphon, and still singing, they passed into the temple. Strangely mysterious was the sound of their voices as they penetrated farther and farther into the depths of what seemed another world. The incident, trifling in itself, gave one an inkling of the way enormous blocks of stone had been moved in the days when all had to be done with human labour.

Leaving H.H. to follow a day later, I pressed on to see a friend at Tinavelly. On the long train journey I had as my companion a young lawyer, the brother of a local Raja. I had never before met an Indian so entirely European in manner and dress. He spoke English fluently, lived in the English fashion, wore a solar topee, had no caste taboos about food, enjoyed dancing, and was so far unmarried because he had found no Indian girl whom he could love, and without love, he said, he could not marry. He would like an English girl, and the Raja, his brother, who at thirty-three was still unmarried, had actually wanted to marry one; but, "fearing an Eurasian dynasty" Government had objected. We talked of many things, amongst them of racial feelings, the unrest, Morley's proposals, and were the Government wise to rely on the landed classes rather than on the educated? A pertinent question for it was the educated classes who wrested independence from us.

The last part of India we visited was the Malabar State of Travancore on India's south-west coast. This gave us the most romantic journey of our tour. It was not the train journey to the small port of Quilon, though that showed us one of India's loveliest landscapes, but the last forty miles by boat to Trivandrum, the capital of the State. To reach it, we had to thread our way through a network of canals and small lagoons on the edge of the sea. Four long rowing boats were waiting for us at Quilon, one for H.H., another for myself with fourteen oarsmen, a third for Master Sahib and Rajaramji, and a fourth to pilot us along our winding way. We embarked by torchlight, which outshone the shy light of a young moon. With a shout the rowers bent to their oars and we sped away in the wake of our pilot, with H.H. and myself sitting on the roof of his cabin, H.H. in loin-cloth and shirt, I in pyjamas. The lightest of breezes kept us cool, and the palm trees on either side sprayed moonlight upon us. It was long before we could bring ourselves to leave so bewitching a scene for our beds. On waking we found breakfast awaiting us, for H.H. in one house, for myself in another—a good example of the influence of caste upon social relations with the orthodox Hindu. As our host, the Maharaja, was one of the strictest, H.H. thought it wiser for us to eat apart. At midday we glided softly to a landing stage to be greeted there by the State's Chief Minister with (to H.H.) a satisfying array of horsemen, officials and police.

The Maharaja was not present but was not long in calling. He was a frail shy-looking man past his prime, with a delicately chiselled nose and "a very vigilant eye". He spoke disjointedly as if struggling to keep his mind from wandering off, and the whole time "he twitched his fingers grazing their tips with his thumb". He was beautifully dressed in a velvet coat of Tyrian blue edged with gold, but in deference to the demands of orthodoxy for that day he was unshaven. Orthodoxy also required that we should pay the return call at 7 a.m. to allow him to have the prescribed bath after touching a European.

Of special interest to me at Trivandrum was Travancore's Christian population. Out of some 3 million they numbered nearly 700,000, most of whom claimed St Thomas as the founder of their Church. Many of them were fishermen, and on the beach one morning I found "scores of them mending their nets" in sight of a little white-washed church as humble as themselves. Insensibly my mind sped back 1,900 years to 'the sea of Galilee' and, as it did so, I was approached by one of them stripped to the waist with the curt request—'Sir, I want a rupee.' I felt inclined to reply with the apostle—'Silver and gold have I none', as indeed was the case at the moment. What I did was to show him an empty pocket.

In the train on our way to Tuticorin Master Sahib brought H.H. a copy of the New Testament which a missionary lady had just given him 'for the Prince'. H.H. started reading it. A little later I heard a loud laugh—'Ha—Ha—Ha—I like this story.' 'Which one?' I asked. And he read me the one of the woman taken in adultery. What delighted him was the discomfiture of the woman's accusers.

From Tuticorin we crossed to Ceylon. We were both beginning to feel we had travelled enough. A week later, therefore, we made for Bombay and Dewas. Bombay gave me a fitting climax to the tour. In the last three months I had seen many cities, great rivers too, and primaeval forests, but nothing more stirring than Bombay's roadstead at dawn. We arrived when moon and stars were still shining upon a sleeping city. In want of exercise after the long journey from Colombo, I walked to the Apollo Bundar, and there the roadstead lay open before me "with lights innumerable and dark shadows of monster ships". In the still air coils of smoke hung listlessly over black funnels, and a deep crimson stole into the sky above the hills beyond them. Slowly the crimson turned to orange, the orange to pale gold with rifts of green, and as the eastern sky filled with the full splendour of the dawn, the ships swung mysteriously round to welcome India's arch-enemy—the sun.

We would have pushed on to Dewas at once, but as when we started, the Court Astrologer had first to be consulted. February the 1st would have suited us well, but that was a Saturday, a day on which the stars never allowed H.H. to return from a long journey. He then suggested the 2nd, but that turned out to be "a fearfully unlucky day", recurring only once every twelve years. H.H.'s mother, the Rani, the Superintendent of the State, a well-educated Brahmin, all implored H.H. not to do anything so rash. And so the State entry took place on the 3rd, and the Grand Tour of 11,000 miles came to an end.

Speaking of it some weeks later, H.H. said what had impressed him most was 'the extraordinary power of England—from Peshawar to Rangoon, from Rangoon to the borders of China, and from Calcutta to Colombo'. He had also been struck by the patriotism of the English. 'Whoever it was, an official or a train-guard, they would none of them, whatever their wrongs, go against England. If only India were like this,' he added.

CHAPTER 20

Initiations – Return to Dewas

H.H.'s homecoming seemed to fill the air with happiness.

> Let us clap and let us sing (sang the schoolchildren)
> Let us form a merry ring;
> God has safe our Master brought
> Home with precious lessons fraught.

All, high and low, young and old, were out to greet him—the village headmen with their rupees (in every case remitted), the Brahmins with coconuts, the city fathers and tennis club with their addresses, the Army with their guns, and the State band only less noisy. A touching figure was his mother, who had been waiting for many hours since dawn in a tent pitched on the banks of the Sipra.

Before entering his capital, H.H. changed into his gala clothes by the roadside. We then drove to the palace in the State chariot. There, when H.H. had worshipped the household gods, the thronged courtyard smothered him with flowers. In the town we stopped for him to pay his respects to the Maharani, his grandmother. He told me to follow him. At the head of one of Dewas' many narrow stone staircases I was beckoned into the room where I had been received before. Looking round for the purdah screen which had been there then, I saw H.H. sitting at an old lady's feet. It was Her Highness herself. I bowed low and she motioned me to be seated. There was only the floor and I sat down accordingly. "She did not say much: it never is necessary to say much in the East. We overdo that." This gave me leisure to scan her face. She was a very austere-looking woman; and with her imperious air she reminded me of the great Demeter in the British Museum. Illuminations brought us back to the town after dark and rounded off a delightful day. Everyone had been happy and shown it so naturally that "I liked Indians better than ever". This I wrote exactly one year after my arrival in Dewas. And I added: "How I loathed the place then! Now I could hardly wish for anything better."

But there was the usual fly in the honey. Major Spence, our attractive Political Agent, had gone on leave and been replaced by Lt-Colonel N., a man with a good brain but a bully. Once, when the late Raja for some reason or other had placed his turban supplicatingly at N.'s feet, he kicked it away and "it rolled down some steps in full view of the Court". That at least was what H.H. had been told, and he had never forgiven him. Knowing his explosive temper, I viewed their first meeting with some apprehension.

This took place at the Residency on our way back from Bombay. We were spending the night there, and so was Colonel N. That evening he and H.H. happened to meet tête-à-tête. Luckily I came upon them before any damage had been done. But "things were going badly, and it was all I could do to keep the fire in H.H.'s eye from slipping onto the tip of his tongue". I put in a word or a wink as often as I could, and when H.H. was on the point of exploding I pulled out my watch and said it was time to dress for dinner, as fortunately it was, and the situation was saved.

What upset H.H. was the way N. talked about the powers he was shortly to get as a full-fledged Ruling Chief. He gave us both the impression that they would only be nominal. Yet later Colonel Daly assured me that it would be very much the reverse. N. had also refused to sanction a modest sum for a religious ceremony "as important to H.H. as Confirmation to the most ardent churchman". But what stung his proud sensitive nature to the quick was less what N. said than the way he said it. That evening H.H. was "terribly depressed". Like so many who are highly strung, he was inclined to despair when things went wrong.

SPIRITUAL POWER

The religious ceremony just mentioned must now be described, but to understand its importance we must go back to last August.

H.H. was no friend of the Brahmins: that the last chapter showed. He resented their century-old domination in the Maratha States, especially in his own. In their eyes he belonged to the lowest of India's four great caste-groups. As such he had to submit to their direction in all religious matters, and as already noted, these permeated a Hindu's daily life. Even in things temporal, thanks to the many offices they held in the State, they had an ascendancy in it which could easily weaken his authority as its Head. Not unlike Henry VIII in this respect, he was determined to have the last word in both spheres. But this would only be possible if he could establish his claim to belong to the warrior class, one of the three higher caste-groups. If he could do this, then in his own State he would be co-equal with the Brahmins and even the final authority in matters affecting his own caste-fellows, the Marathas. But first of all he must be formally invested with the Sacred Thread.* This could be worn only by members of one or other of the three upper caste-groups and would therefore be the outward and visible sign that his claim had been accepted. But this could only be done by the Brahmins, who hotly disputed his claim. To add to the difficulty at least sixteen were needed for the purpose.

To secure their assent thirty-four were summoned to a meeting in H.H.'s Court-room. Seated in the usual way, he reminded them that his family was one of the oldest in India and that its claim to belong to the warrior caste-group had only lapsed through the negligence of his forefathers. He would now ask all present to sign a document acknowledging his claim. After it had been read aloud, it was first presented for signature to the less influential lest they should be corrupted by the attitude of the more important. They signed readily enough. Yet, as the document went round, here and there I could see a hand shake, and one or two thought a little before signing. The first to refuse was the State Doctor. The Superintendent of the State did the same. Then came the ex-Superintendent. As a pensioner of the State he was expected to sign. On the other hand, as a Brahmin he ran the risk of being outcasted, a dreaded punishment. So he hedged. The claim, he said, had his sympathy but before signing he felt he must consult his brother. In all only four refused to sign. That was in August. By February, thanks to a favourable ruling by the highest Hindu authority of the region, and to some local measures, all serious opposition had been overcome and a date could be fixed for the ceremony.

Before however this could take place, the leading personages of Dewas had to be formally invited. One afternoon I was waiting at H.H.'s residence for his return when a messenger arrived from

* A triple cord worn next the skin, and normally across the right shoulder.

the Guest House to say that my presence was earnestly desired. There I found a Guard of Honour drawn up with the State band in attendance, and as the former presented arms, the band rolled their drums. On the steps under the porch, headed by Master Sahib, were a number of H.H.'s special friends, all in their finest clothes. In the drawing-room they told me they had come to invite me to be present on the morrow when the ceremony would be performed. A Brahmin stepped forward and muttering some Sanskrit verse put a pinch of rice into my hand. Master Sahib then suggested I should accompany H.H.'s friends on their further rounds. It would be, he said, an act of great friendship, and all would see how well we stood together. "And you (he added) are as his father (only 7 years between us!), and his father must certainly have done this." I pointed to my clothes—I was in a silk shirt and white flannel trousers—but he said they would wait while I changed them, and I could but agree.

Our first call was upon 'J.B.'* At his palace we were conducted to the Durbar Hall and there, as the Raja was away, we bowed to the Gadi† and left a pinch of rice at its foot. We were then taken to an empty room divided in two by a crumpled sheet behind which, after a pause, the Rani took her seat. Our invitation was followed by one to me to attend a religious ceremony of her own. "I accepted as one must in a country where no one ever says—No."

At the palace of the Senior Branch I found a very agitated H.H. 'What is one to do?' (he asked). 'There are three ladies (his grandmother and two mothers): if I talk to one, the other two get hot. There is no rest, and when the Maharani is angry I must go and lay my head on her feet.'

Master Sahib tried to dissuade me from coming farther. The important people, he said, had now all been invited: smaller deputations would be sent to the rest, such as Rajaramji and himself. 'There is much time-killing,' he warned me. But as they had invited me, I felt I must invite them. So off we went again. First of all to the house of the Controller of the Treasury. He himself was one of our party and actually in our carriage. Taking me courteously by the hand, he led me to a small room bare of all furniture except a chair quickly placed there for me. "But there was far too much dignity in the old man's ways for the room to

* The Raja of Dewas, Junior Branch.

† Cushioned throne.

seem bare." Rajaramji came next. A very steep narrow staircase led to an upper room as bare as the last. This time I insisted and like the others sat on the floor. Our visit was a short one, but there was time to make friends with his daughter of four or five, who came and sat in my arms. 'Ah! she is not afraid,' exclaimed Rajaramji in great surprise "as though even babes must feel that sundering gulf of colour". Other visits followed and I did not get back till nine o'clock. A time-killing affair indeed, but it had given me a further glimpse of the graciousness of Indian domestic life.

Now for the ceremony itself. It took place in the pillared courtyard of the palace. This was thronged and, seen from above, where Miss M. and I were sitting, it looked as if every head bore a different coloured turban. In the centre was a low brick platform under a canopy of green velvet brocaded in gold, and at each corner there was a pile of seven earthenware vessels. 'Why seven?' I asked the Brahmin Mr Shastri sitting beside me. 'It is a mystic number,' was all he could say.

H.H. now appeared as a warrior sword in hand, and sat on the platform with his feet tucked away under his knees. An ill-looking Brahmin squatted in front of him "as it were, preparing for a cock-fight", and as he did so a red curtain was drawn round them. The Brahmins then began their Sanskrit chant, and others showered rice. On and on went the chanting, and at last I asked my Brahmin friend—'When will it end?' 'Ha!' he exclaimed. 'An astrologer is sitting over there with an hour-glass. When he says the right moment has come, it will be over.' There was no mistaking the moment when it came: it was saluted with an outburst from guns, trumpets and drums and everyone clapped. The Thread had been given.

At this point H.H. disappeared into the palace to reappear wearing only a loin-cloth, but with a gorgeous mantle of purple and gold thrown over his shoulders. With him back on the platform the chanting was resumed, this time by four Brahmins, who wagged their heads without ceasing like the penny toys of my childhood. Every now and then H.H. would look at me with a smile or exchange a word with those around him. Numbers might be mystic, but no one seemed to feel the solemnity which our religious rites commonly inspire: religion was perhaps too much a part of a Hindu's daily life for that.

I was enjoying some children's delight in the scene when

Miss M. exclaimed—'Look what they are doing!' H.H. had disappeared under a blanket and with him three of the four Brahmins, whose heads could be seen bobbing under its folds. They were imparting to his ear a mantra of such sanctity that it was for the initiated only.

The next scene in the drama was preparation for the journey to Benares whither, according to Vedic tradition, the young warrior had to go as a scholar for the first stage of his education. Since he must beg his way thither, he was given a beggar's bowl and staff, and that he might not start empty-handed, he must approach his family and friends for alms. He went first to his grandmother, the Maharani, because traditionally the first offering must go to the Brahmins and he thought that she would not give him much. To his disgust she gave him five sovereigns.

The drama continued another two days and on the last ended at sundown when H.H. set out on his symbolic journey to Benares, staff in hand and with a small bag of food slung across his shoulder. Somewhat incongruously to Western eyes, he was wearing his jewels, perhaps to mark the fact that he was a prince as well as scholar. Even without them no one could have mistaken him for an ordinary scholar, for he had with him two servants, one carrying a tray of provisions, the other holding a red umbrella over his head. He was also accompanied by what seemed like a Greek chorus of nobles and officials to see that he did not miss the way to Benares, in this case represented by a small shrine 100 yards away. There the drama ended, and he returned to the palace to be photographed, and next day to feast 500 Brahmins.

TEMPORAL POWER

The Sacred Thread ceremony gave H.H. spiritual authority in his State. Now, when just over twenty, he was to be formally invested with the temporal authority of a Ruling Chief. As we have seen, the earlier ceremony was entirely of the East. The one now to be described was a starchy mixture of East and West, with everyone seated on chair or couch, with British officials in uniform instead of Brahmins in loin-cloths, and with the proceedings in English instead of in Sanskrit. Sharpest contrast of all, one ceremony dealt with the transient world of politics, the other with the unchanging ritual of an ancient past.

Over twenty English guests were expected and we had but four spare beds, and almost nothing required for them was to be had in Dewas. Great cases arrived from Bombay full of china, sheets, pillow-slips and towels; and the day before the Investiture five sets of bedroom furniture had to be fetched from Mhow forty miles away. The beds were brought but no pillows. I sent to the bazaar for some, but there were none. 'Make them,' I said, and made they were. More serious, four sets of camp kit were due from Allahabad. A clerk had been sent with four bullock-carts to fetch them from a station twenty-two miles away. On Saturday, two days before the ceremony, he wired–'Nothing arrived, what shall I do?' He could do nothing but wait. Monday morning, a bare hour before the first guests arrived, he appeared with eight chairs, four tea-tables and four 'indispensable articles', and when Colonel Daly drove up, all was in order, with moreover two speeches written for H.H. But it was 'a damned close thing'.

Colonel Daly, or the Honourable the Agent to the Governor-General in Central India, as he was styled, came of course officially. That is to say he was met at a fixed spot by both Rajas of Dewas–Senior and Junior–and arrived sitting between them in the blue and gold state coach already described.* Happily all three were of slender proportions. Otherwise, as Colonel Daly said, the question would have been–would it be more proper for each Raja to sit on a knee of the A.G.G., or for the A.G.G. to sit on a knee of each Raja?

At the Guest House, amongst the guests gathered there I came upon Maharaja Sindhia. 'Ha! my friend!' I thought as we bowed slightly to each other: 'you have not forgotten that night. Nor have I.' H.H. told me later that Sindhia had advised him to get rid of me as soon as possible. 'I am keeping him on as Adviser and Private Secretary,' said H.H. 'Wh-a-t!' he exclaimed in a voice of amazement and disgust.

That afternoon I drove round to the Court House. There in a tiny room I found H.H. and Bhau Sahib, his brother, dressing for the occasion. Two servants were decking them with jewels from trays lying on the floor. 'Oh, Sahib,' he said as I entered: 'Nothing but worry, worry, worry. You are the only one who has been nice to me today'–I had written him a short letter. Then he told me how he didn't know whether he would be able to make the speech I had written for him as Sindhia did not like it; "how the ladies

* See p. 142.

were quarrelling and he had got angry and said to them: 'If I do not see your faces again to-day, I think I shall be right.' " The question was—should his real mother sit above the sister of his grandmother, the Maharani, or not? Then Colonel N. (our new Political Agent) had made him go a mile farther than was right to meet the A.G.G. I admired his clothes and told him that really I thought very well of him. And then his eyes sparkled—'Sahib (he said), I have added one thing to the speech. Do you know what it is?' I could guess. 'And of his successor, Mr M. L. D——' he began declaiming.

It was now time to drive to the Palace in the heart of the town. (The 'New Palace' of today did not exist then.) We climbed into the state coach and were hardly out of the compound when H.H. discovered he had forgotten his cigarettes and said they must be fetched. " 'What, now?' I said. 'Oh, Sahib!' and he put on his most insinuating manner—'I shall not have another for an hour and a half.' A little further on we stopped again. He had forgotten his speech! A servant was sent for it. We entered the Palace as usual by a steep stone staircase just wide enough for two people to pass each other with the feel of the other's stomach."

I went into the Durbar Hall to take note of my seat. The day before I had gone with Colonel N. to see that no one's chair was set in the wrong place or even at a wrong angle, points which could be of great importance in India's political world. One such was how to seat the Maharajas of Gwalior and Kolhapur "without a growl from one or the other". Sindhia had the larger State and politically more influence, but Kolhapur was of nobler lineage and the social head of the Marathas, and in India lineage is almost everything. H.H. had no doubt that his father-in-law elect should have precedence. On the other hand, Sindhia was his uncle and he did not wish to have a fuss. A cunning expedient was suggested for solving the difficulty. It was arranged for them to share a couch placed immediately to the right of the A.G.G.'s chair. On the couch Sindhia was to be given the place of honour, that is to say at its right end, and Kolhapur at its left end would have the greater honour of sitting on the A.G.G.'s right. But when the two Maharajas reached the couch, Kolhapur "gigantic and massive in white, Sindhia in lilac", Kolhapur with great dignity bowed low and with arms outstretched motioned Sindhia to sit on the right of the A.G.G., Sindhia, "constrained to be his match in courtesy", did the same. Whereupon Kolhapur said out loud that others might hear—'A friend's path, do *you* sit there.' Adjured in this way, Sindhia could not refuse and sat down, the gainer perhaps in place but publicly vanquished in courtesy.

The last to arrive was the A.G.G. with his staff. By some strange difference 'J.B.' had to meet him at the foot of the stairs, and H.H. at their head. When all had taken their seats, the A.G.G. under an oleograph portrait of Queen Victoria, there must have been nearly 200 of us present. For some minutes we sat in silence listening to the boom of guns firing a salute in honour of the A.G.G. Presentations followed and in each case the gold mohr (about Rs. 15) offered as a token of homage to the Paramount Power was touched and remitted. Colonel Daly then rose to speak. Tall and slim with finely chiselled features, in his dark blue uniform, he looked more *distingué* and charming than ever. He spoke for twenty minutes and exceedingly well, "though there were indeed a few sentences which made me feel very uncomfortable". After alluding to 'the close interest' which the Viceroy took in H.H.—"here a silent chuckle at the thought of our five-minutes interview with him in Calcutta"—Colonel Daly turned solemnly to H.H. who rose—as we all did too—and presented him with the letter of Investiture in a claret-red bag.

H.H. was now on his feet with my speech half crumpled in his hand. He never referred to it once. He, too, spoke for twenty minutes and never faltered. "He chopped up a word here and there and sometimes clubbed two sentences together but on the whole it was a surprising feat: he was speaking in a foreign language and he had learnt the speech in less than three days, amid all the distractions of the occasion. There was one long paragraph, too long and too orientally phrased by far, which gave me a most embarrassing five minutes. I felt myself almost collapsing from my chair." Yet his last two words—'beloved brother'—were the only ones I remembered, "a rich reward for so easy a year".

In the evening twenty-three of us sat down to a State banquet in a large open tent by the Guest House. At first H.H. was not with us: he was entertaining his Indian guests elsewhere. But as prearranged, when the ices appeared, I sent him word by mounted orderly—there was then no telephone in Dewas—and ten minutes later he arrived and we drank Edward the Seventh's health, "the State Band doing wonders with the National Anthem". Then came H.H.'s second speech. This he had had no time to learn by heart. He would have to read it he said. But he didn't do so and "got through it somehow, murdering it a little here and there". In a charming reply Colonel Daly alluded to his 'engaging frankness'. That was indeed one of his best assets, but, as already noted, trust had to come first. So ended a notable day, of the happiest omen for the future—but omens sometimes mislead.

Those last four words are a comment of today. But at the time I was not without my fears. Four days before we met Colonel N. I wrote: "What will happen to H.H.? I don't know. He is very masterful and proud and inclined to fight. If he gets a Political Agent who misunderstands him and pricks his pride with tongue or pen, there will be trouble. He will never swallow even the suggestion of an affront and there are so many unimaginative 'Politicals' that I sometimes fear for him."

DEATH

The Investiture over, all was astir for an even more important occasion—the longed-for marriage with the daughter of the Maharaja of Kolhapur. But death came first.

Early one morning Master Sahib came round to tell me that H.H.'s sister, only five years old, was dangerously ill. A little later he returned to say that all was over. On reaching her mother's house I found that the slender body was about to be borne away to be burnt by the family tombs on the edge of the lake in front of the Guest House. Hearing that no one had ventured to tell H.H. what had happened, I drove round to the Court House. He came out to meet me with his usual smile. The next ten minutes were most distressing: he was one who felt both keenly and openly. When the first shock had passed, he said he must follow his sister to her end. I followed at a distance. I did not dare go near lest as a non-Hindu I went too near. When H.H. saw the little bundle in a red shawl lying upon the ground he fainted. As soon as the pyre was ready, the body was laid upon it under straw. It was not long before smoke began to find its way through the branches of the mango tree above, and as the flames leapt up there seemed "something holy and awe-inspiring in their devouring tongues".

It was then that someone begged me to come to H.H. who was in great agitation. I had lost sight of him in the crowd that had gathered round him when he fainted. I found him struggling in the arms of Master Sahib who wanted to take him away. I laid him down by a bank, and there we sat very quietly until all was over. He then went to see his mother. She had been, so he told me, most courageous and had not shed a tear. Was she perhaps too familiar with death, for this was her sixth child to go?

After breakfast I went round to see how he did. He was sitting in silence on a mattress in the verandah with one or two others by him. We did not talk much but once or twice an exclamation showed what he was feeling–'God gives us great happiness (a reference to his approaching marriage), but always (he said) with it a lash to counterbalance it; I cannot think what sin we have done.' 'Perhaps none,' I suggested. 'Then why this?' Why indeed!

In the evening I found him in a small inner room lying on a red mattress. As I sat there, many came on a formal visit of condolence. Without a word they entered, and without a word they left. I was reminded of Job and his three friends who 'sat down with him upon the ground and none spake a word unto him, for they saw that his grief was very great'.

CHAPTER 21

The Wedding

NOW came the wedding. For me the first step was to go to Baroda in my new capacity of Adviser and Private Secretary with a small deputation and invite the Gaikwar to be present. My two sisters, who had come out for part of the cold weather, were also with me. The invitation itself consisted of a gold-starred scroll folded into a common long envelope. This was enclosed in a red embroidered bag, and for further security and importance the bag was put into another of white muslin. We were most courteously received and after witnessing another cheetah hunt resumed our journey to Kolhapur.

At Poona we joined H.H. and his wedding party of 600. This included not only the State band but the whole army. A special train of twenty-four coaches took us on to Kolhapur. 'Next morning', to quote a letter home from my elder sister, 'it was most exciting. At 6.30 the train stopped to allow all the 600 to get out and change into their best clothes. You never saw such a funny sight. Two men stood in the luggage van tossing out tin trunks and Maratha hats onto the platform, where the trunks were duly unpacked and the travel-stained garments exchanged for something smarter. R. managed to get out her trunk and change in the waiting-room, while H.H. was getting into his gold lace and jewels behind a screen formed by a guard of honour! Malcolm donned his frock coat in the train, but I had nothing beautiful to put on, as my trunk was quite at the bottom of the van and there were a lot of packing cases on top of it.'

At our first stop in Kolhapur territory H.H. received a typical Maratha welcome from a large gathering of peasants, the women on one side of the line, the men on the other filling the air with the blowing of horns and beating of drums. The women had come in hopes of largesse on so auspicious an occasion and held out brass plates and little flickering lamps,* and when the train set off again, ran after us laughing and "showing us many shrivelled

* Signifying it seems—'now you are protected'.

legs and shining teeth"—all of which was repeated at our next stop.

Finally Kolhapur itself. There our reception was even more glorious than the one given us in May, with a dozen elephants to greet us and everyone in their wedding best, headed by the gigantic figure of the Maharaja enveloped in voluminous folds of blue silk sashed in gold. On our side the Dewas Army did a march-past to the strains of 'Oft in danger, oft in woe'. In the procession which followed the most remarkable object was an old railway saloon painted white and drawn by two elephants. It served two purposes. That all might see him H.H. sat on the roof between Kolhapur's two little princes. Inside, screened from masculine eyes, rode the Indian ladies of our party.

Outside all was gay, not so inside. The Rani, ever a stormy petrel, had been allotted a house just outside the palace, whereas H.H.'s real mother was with him inside it: after her recent loss he naturally wished to have her by him. This was not a point to appeal to the Rani. As his adoptive mother it was her right, she said, to be inside the palace; and at 6 p.m.—we had arrived at 10.30—her kit was still lying on the road outside it. H.H. suggested that the two ladies should exchange quarters. At the same time he made it clear that he would not sleep under the same roof as the Rani. In the procession just described she had taunted his mother with her 'unlucky feet'—had she not lost both husband and daughter prematurely? This had naturally roused his anger. On the other hand, to leave the palace as the Rani entered it was to give too open expression to his feelings of resentment against one who had become his mother by the binding tie of adoption. The affair threw the Dewas camp into a ferment. The Rani was furious and said she would go back to Dewas. Master Sahib, now Minister, got hot and said he would resign; Miss M. shed tears, and to add fuel to the fire, through some oversight, Kolhapur had omitted to feed the Dewas party.

Whether due to all this or not I cannot say, but the air became alive with sinister rumours. The hall built for the wedding ceremony would collapse in the middle of it; the bride would die five days later as a sacrifice to avert plague and famine from Kolhapur for three years, and H.H. would go out of his mind. There were others equally absurd. Through the usual busybodies they came to the ears of both bride and bridegroom. The bride half believed them, and H.H. himself was none too sure when his temperature suddenly shot up. The astrologers were sent for, and the horoscopes of both parties compared to see whether any disaster impended. All but one, who would not commit himself, said No.

Rightly or wrongly all this was set down to the Brahmins, with whom the Court was not on the best of terms. Indeed, as I wrote to Alfred Lyall, "In Kolhapur the Brahmin newspapers attack the Maharaja as their fellows in Poona the British Government." To guard against a possible act of violence—it would not have been the first in that part of India—the Maharaja's entourage were told to carry swords at every function and twenty-five police were set to guard H.H.'s tent night and day. Happily nothing worse occurred at the moment than a second attack of fever.

My sisters naturally wished to see the bride, and a meeting at the old palace was arranged accordingly. Hearing what we were about, Miss M. said that she and a friend would come too. This was annoying for it was obvious that a girl of fourteen could not talk to five people at once. Somehow, chiefly I fear by being rather rude, we shook them off. We were taken up a narrow creaking staircase and ushered into a room with a doubtfully white sheet spread across the floor and with just enough chairs for us all.

We were watching the lively scene in the courtyard below when we heard a rustle of silk. Looking round we saw a slender little figure in a beautiful sari of cerise and gold. A Brahmin doctor came with her to interpret. "She was very shy and as long as I was there said nothing. Even when I told her how well I thought of H.H., she hardly moved but sat with head bent low." After a minute or two I left, hoping she would talk a little to my sisters, but they fared no better. After all she was very young, and here were three of us from a strange new world with barely a word of her language between us.*

For any idea of what the bride was like I had to depend upon what H.H. told me of her as seen through the eyes of a lover. The gist of what he said is recorded in my diary. Although she was only just fourteen, everyone stood in awe of her except her father and her uncle, the Chief of Kagal. Master Sahib, who will say anything to H.H., was afraid of her and Rajaramji found her eyes awe-inspiring. Yet, said H.H., though many feared her, they all

* Cf. p. 160 for an earlier interview.

loved her. A girl of few words, she was slow to tell anyone her mind, but if necessary would make it up 'in five minutes'. She was very observant and knew whom to trust and whom not to trust. H.H. thought her deeply religious, but also very superstitious. Which, indeed, made it all the more courageous on her part to show no fear when she heard the rumour that she was to die within five days of her marriage. One further point H.H. mentioned. She was fond of authority and born to rule. 'If only she had been a boy', it was said, 'then Kolhapur would have gone mad with joy.'

Though it was still only March the hot weather had begun and my sisters felt the heat acutely. 'Kolhapur (wrote my elder sister) is the hottest place I have ever been in (except Khartoum) and in our tents by day the thermometer registers 103 – luckily it drops at night to 63, so there is something to look forward to, but whilst the sun is up, we hardly know what to do with ourselves. Whilst I am writing I see R. on one side in a dressing-jacket and petticoat and Miss M. in an adjoining room lying down in her petticoat bodice. I am in my pink dressing-gown, no shoes and stockings and my face looks like an advertisement for Pear's Soap I am so shiny and sticky.'

The catering was some compensation for the heat. A Captain O'Brien had been deputed to look after the Maharaja's European guests. 'He gives us champagne every night (continues the letter), cream in our porridge and coffee – such thick cream – and we have ices and delicious fruit: in fact he gives us such enormously rich meals, we don't know how to get through everything. Someone comes to dinner with us every night and they are very friendly, but the amount of scandal and gossip they are ready to pour into our (not unwilling) ears is extraordinary. Captain O'Brien, a delightful Irishman, says that in India you ought only to believe half what you see and nothing that you hear! Really if one believed everything life would be too tragic.'

The great day came and it started with a procession to the temple in the old palace. There in a pillared hall and amidst a great concourse of nobles and officials H.H. took his seat on the usual cushioned throne with the Maharaja in front of him. A servant was in attendance and with his help the Maharaja washed H.H.'s feet, first one then the other. He then offered him rice and wheat, pressed two coconuts thrice to his forehead and sprinkled him with water. 'Now,' said the Maharaja turning towards me—he had made me sit by him, 'he is a god.'

At this point I left to get ready for the wedding itself. This meant putting on a frock-coat, "that most barbarous emblem of our civilization, more barbarous than ever on a hot afternoon in March". I arrived back at the old palace just in time to see the head of the wedding procession entering the palace courtyard. The railway saloon and its two elephants, once more on show, had got stuck in the five-storeyed gateway erected in honour of the occasion, and standing there "very burly and very hot" in a crowd of liveried retainers, the Maharaja was urging them on to push behind.

My sisters were on the palace roof, and there I found them looking over the parapet and enjoying the sight of the procession making its way below. It was no common procession. In addition to the two armies, there were the falconers with their hawks, four bullock-carts with the Maharaja's hooded cheetahs prowling up and down their cages with long whisking tails, and of course all the elephants. On one of these in a castellated howdah sat H.H. between the little princes. As he passed into the palace courtyard, he gave us the happiest of smiles.

We now took our seats in the open corrugated-iron hall built on to the palace for the occasion. As ugly as a railway station and not unlike one, it was in curious contrast to the gorgeously dressed assembly within it. There Indian taste was impeccable. The principal guests were now arriving—a Maharaja necklaced in enormous pearls, an admiral from Bombay, a general from Poona, followed by the Governor of Bombay who drove up in a yellow coach-and-four.

Finally came H.H. himself. He took his stand in a throng of Brahmins with a red curtain drawn between him and the bride. Strict Hindu etiquette required that bride and bridegroom should not see each other until they were wed. When this moment approached, we all threw rice at H.H. and "there was a most awful din. I don't know how many bands played all at once. Blunderbusses were exploded in the courtyard, and all the Brahmins chanted with one voice." As the rice showered upon him, H.H. stood before the red curtain with head demurely bowed, and we all waited for the astrologer's signal that the auspicious moment had come. "The din must have lasted a quarter of an hour when suddenly the curtain disappeared and bride and bridegroom found themselves face to face. They sat down and Rajaramji, who had stood behind H.H., with a drawn sword—someone else doing the same for the bride, that no rival might snatch her away—could sheath it." Other ceremonies remained to be performed; but they were not for our eyes, and we came away.

On the morrow I took my sisters, who were due to sail for home a day or two later, to bid H.H. farewell. Before the wedding he had been "counting the hours to the decisive moment". Now he was "jubilant" and his eyes shone with roguish glee. He was full of what he had felt and done during the ceremony: how while pretending to be bashful, he had managed to steal a glance at the bride over the curtain; and how when it was withdrawn and the bride had unveiled herself a little, he had made her veil herself completely. After the ceremony, too, when the Maharaja asked him what he thought of her, he replied coolly he thought she would do.

When he had said good-bye to my sisters, he took me aside and in a voice full of feeling said—'Will you ask your sisters to tell Mrs Darling that if any arrangement for them was wrong, I hope she will pardon it'—a good example of his delicacy of feeling.

Three days later his high spirits had changed almost to despair. The Maharaja would not let him see his bride, and with some reason, for she was only just fourteen and "still untouched by womanhood. In India, too, passions have a vein of fire and the Maharaja himself boasts that though officially not allowed to see his wife for two years he achieved his purpose long before." Custom, all powerful in those days, was certainly on his side and entirely opposed to what H.H. called 'the English way'. Nevertheless, "it must be rather maddening (I wrote) to find you have married a kind of Selene who will only appear in dreams".

The matter was considered of such importance that the Maharani and the Maharaja's grandmother and three or four other ladies of the bride's family met one evening in council to consider what should be done. Their conclusion was that under "no circumstances must the two meet. Or let them meet and we will never see their faces again." To my surprise H.H. took this as final: I had still to learn how powerful women could be in India. The decision hit him hard. As he said to me: 'If I could only see her I would get to know her as a friend, but now they force me to think of her physically.' Personally, knowing him as I did, I should have trusted to his honour. His was no common clay.

The strain involved in all this helped to bring on an attack of fever so sharp that I spent one night at his bedside in the old palace. He had tossed about all day and his temperature had touched 105. Though I was as a child in medical matters, I knew that I could at least save him from the hands of his three doctors. "All day (says a letter) they had squatted at his side whispering and hobnobbing. One took his temperature, another felt his pulse, the third uncorked some medicine. And so it went on. They would not leave him alone, coming in and out and bringing others with them who also squatted round. In India when a great man is ill all, high and low, come and sit with him." In the evening I carried him up to a much larger room and kept out all I could. Two visitors could not be refused admittance—the Maharajah and his spotted terrier. They came after midnight. The last to leave was the faithful Master Sahib who sat up for a time stroking H.H.'s hot forehead. When he went off to sleep, and snore, behind a curtain which divided the room in two, I was left alone with one of the doctors and with a servant who massaged one leg while I massaged the other. The doctor was soon asleep in a corner of the room, and I was urged to sleep in a bed which had been prepared for me outside, but I refused as H.H. was very restless. In time the servant slept also. "I think I heard each hour except the fifth beaten out from a bar of clanging iron, and most of the quarters too." Meanwhile H.H. tossed this way and that "sometimes clutching my hand or flinging his arms round my head". Once at the night's chilliest point he threw everything off and there was the doctor sleeping peacefully with knees cocked up only a few feet away. However no harm was done and by tea-time the fever had left him.

One morning soon after this experience Rajaramji, H.H.'s ever gay Commander-in-Chief, breakfasted with me. As we stood a moment on the verandah before he went, he said I thought I liked Indians better than Europeans. I did not deny it of most Europeans I had met in India. 'And Mr Goodall (another of us from King's whom he had met at Dewas) likes Indians too. He is very nice gentleman, very nice. How many more (he asked) are there in this country from the same College?' I mentioned two more whom he had met. E. M. Forster he had not yet met. 'I don't know how it is,' he continued, 'but you all like Indians. I wish I could understand this.' 'We are very well educated there,' I said. 'Ah, that is it; and it must, I think, be (as he shrewdly added) some form of the climate when you went there,' meaning no doubt the atmosphere in the College.

H.H.'s illness gave me the opportunity to explore a part of the old palace, a long rambling building of many wings, only one of which I penetrated. It had rooms of all sizes, some almost large enough to be halls, others mere rabbit-holes, all linked together by narrow passages and pillared corridors with staircases of stone or wood, some marching boldly to the floor above, others tortuous and dark. One might see anything anywhere from a red silk chair to a sweeper's brush. At every corner someone would be doing something—"that something which in the East often is all the excuse for existence". At the entrance below men in uniform will be mounting guard, others sitting in half-darkness amid a litter of arms and equipment. Once past the guard a man may go anywhere. There is no one to stop him so long as he knows where the zenana begins. Sit in a room and one will see figures prying through the red window curtains. Look through them oneself, they will have disappeared.

At nightfall the roof becomes alive. Many will be preparing to sleep there now that it is so hot. Mattress after mattress appears with sheet and rug, or without either. "That bed by itself and tidier than the rest is for the Maharaja himself. Not far off some menial will stretch himself, perhaps on the stone itself. You hear voices, just there under old Orion: some nobles have flung themselves down together and are talking under the open sky."

The Maharaja had not yet appeared: he was busy with the poorer of his subjects in the corrugated iron hall below. He had announced that he would bear the expense of any marriage the parents could not afford to pay for themselves. The result was a remarkable sight. The men were in white and turbaned in orange and red, and with the light beating down upon them from dozens of electric lamps their faces looked "splendidly, diabolically dark"; and in their midst towered the Maharaja, head and shoulders taller than them all. As he stood there bare-headed in a cotton shirt hanging loosely over white jodhpurs, he seemed the simplest and kindliest of monarchs, and few would have guessed how subtle could be the brain within.

Twenty-four couples had been married and were filing past him to touch his feet. This was not an easy matter. When Hindus are married, the end of the bridegroom's sash (dupatta) is tied to a corner of the bride's sari. In this case—such was the India of those days—nearly all the brides were babes in arms, and it was the oddest sight to see mother and child bend to the ground so that the child might touch the Maharaja's feet. The bridegrooms had at least learnt to walk. Over a hundred couples had been married at a cost of about a hundred rupees each. "It is easy to see (I wrote) how much more popular the Chiefs can make their rule than we can ours, which is so mechanical and drab."

The culminating procession of the wedding was the Barat when, according to Maratha custom, the bridal pair went together to worship the family's household deity, and the bridegroom brought the bride to his own people and home. Till then, a week later, he had to remain a captive in his father-in-law's house and in token of his captivity wear an armlet of yellow cord.

The Barat procession was a night affair, and that gave it a very romantic character. At nine-thirty I drove to the old palace to see it and was soon entangled in its marshalling. Here in a narrow crowded street were the Kolhapur Horse in scarlet tunics and yellow breeches; men on foot armed with muzzle-loaders; huntsmen in jerkins of blue and gold; others with boar-hounds straining at the leash, and the cheetahs in their bullock-carts. When I came to the white-painted railway saloon I had to pick my way on foot through horses, elephants and men. At the palace, meeting no one I knew, I boldly entered. A lamp burnt here and there, but there was no sign of living creature until I came to the roof. There men and women were looking over the parapet at the gorgeously decked elephants knee-deep, as it were, in the crowd below, a scene lit up by little tongues of flame leaping hungrily from a hundred torches.

I was wondering what would happen next when an elephant larger than his fellows appeared moving majestically through the crowd. Seated on its back in a silver howdah were H.H. and a frail-looking figure veiled in white. Spying me on the roof, H.H. smiled and for a moment his teeth gleamed through the darkness. I took off my hat and with a low bow he disappeared through the palace gateway. He had come to pay his respects to the guardian deity of the palace. Hearing that there was to be a change of elephants, from a Kolhapur one to one from Dewas, I went down hoping to catch a nearer view of that little figure in white, my sister-to-be.* The Maharaja's brother-in-law had just carried her down from the Kolhapur elephant. As she stood for a moment in the midst of us all, one caught a glimpse under her white cloak of a cerise silk sari spangled with gold; and when she mounted the Dewas elephant the sari slipped up to a knee and revealed a very shapely brown leg. And that was all I saw of her.

Would I like to ride on an elephant with Shivaji Maharaj (the younger of the two princes)? asked H.H. 'Would I not?' but it was a very formal occasion and a dark European suit would look odd in the midst of so much splendour. The Maharaja was consulted, and since he made no objection I climbed up a green ladder and was soon comfortably seated in a silver howdah between Shivaji and another boy—the elder prince was ill. A Maratha noble sat behind us to watch over the prince, and when later on Shivaji went to sleep in my arms—he was only eight or nine—the noble kept digging him in the small of the back—exclaiming as he did so 'Maharaj Sircar ale—the Maharaja our sovereign lord has come'. But Shivaji did no more than look up for a moment and nod the next.

We were now moving along a narrow street packed with a crowd so orderly as they stood or sat that not a single soldier or policeman was needed to line the route. Never had I seen so many Indian women unveiled. The upper storeys of the houses on either side had been left to them. On every balcony and at every window they sat tightly pressed together. At a small window I counted six or seven, on a balcony seventy to eighty. It was delightful to watch their eager faces and to catch the gleam of white teeth through the smoke of the torches and the darkness of the night. As we moved along, fountains of tiny golden flakes spirited upwards from earthenware pots set across our path, and from above hissing rockets showered stars of many colours upon us, and from the crowd came an unending murmur of excited chatter. It was another example of the advantage the Chiefs had over us in popularising their rule.

It was just midnight when we turned into the palace allotted to the Dewas party. H.H. went inside with the bride to worship the guardian deity of Dewas. Symbolically he had brought his bride to her new home. Three days later he gave the Maharaja

* See p. 161.

and about 1,000 others a feast of Homeric proportions. And with that the marriage festivities came to an end.

Next day H.H. told me that the Maharaja would like to have me as tutor to the two princes—a pleasant compliment but an embarrassing one since I felt I must refuse. I could not expect a repetition of my singular good fortune with H.H.

A letter recalls a curious little incident connected with the wedding. When a Ruling Chief married, it used to be the custom to distribute largesse amongst his more important nobles and officials. The Maharaja of Kolhapur gave H.H. Rs. 10,000 for the purpose, on condition, so H.H. told me, that Master Sahib should receive so much and Rajaramji so much, and that "another person well-known to you whom you believe incorruptible" should receive Rs. 2,000 (about £130). 'Well,' said H.H., 'you had better give it him yourself and see what he says.' But he did not dare.

The Maharaja and his enormous bulk have often been mentioned in these pages, but little has been said about him as a person. For this I must draw upon my diary.

At thirty-three, his age at this stage, he was a baffling character. He looked heavy and stupid, yet his Political Agent admitted that more than once he had been outwitted by him. It was even said that he could listen to three reports at once and carry all three in his head. He would surround himself with fools and flatterers but not be taken in by them. The fonder he gets of a man, the more he will keep him at arm's length. Always treat a friend, he would say, as a potential enemy. Conversely, he would take to his bosom one whose secrets he wished to probe. An official, for instance, was accused of taking bribes. For three months the Maharaja gave him what seemed his full confidence, then suddenly dismissed him: he had discovered what he wanted to know. When, too, H.H. told him he wanted to get rid of a certain official, he offered to entice him away from Dewas with the promise of service in Kolhapur, and after a year he would dismiss him. In general, however, his policy was to keep everyone pleased and, superficially at least, he was kind to all, as he was indeed to me.

If in some of this there was an echo of Machiavelli's political philosophy, behind it lay a deep distrust of his fellow-creatures in the presence of great power and wealth. Personally I seemed to see in his face a profound indifference to a life which gave him almost too much. Did this perhaps explain his love of riding a vicious horse for the stimulus it gave to a large and sluggish body? Or was it, as H.H. thought, an outlet for feelings which he considered it impolitic to show? Feelings he certainly had, for he was devoted to his daughter, and when he saw H.H. off from Kolhapur, he wept. But, said H.H., 'not even his brother, the Chief of Kagal, who served him day and night, could say how deep they were'.

However this may be, the Maharaja was undoubtedly a remarkable figure and, as the social head of 30 million Marathas, an important one. On ceremonial occasions a Maratha would be expected to touch his feet with the head and H.H. would always do this after prolonged absence. So would most Maratha Princes, he said, though Sindhia would probably do it with his hands, and the Gaikwar not at all.

H.H., though proud of his Rajput descent—an ancestor had left Rajputana in the sixteenth century and come south—was first and last a Maratha with, at this time, a romantic devotion to the Maharaja as the descendant of Shivaji and Head of his race. He once said to me that whatever might be his personal relationship with the Maharaja, rather than let him get into any political trouble, he would himself take the blame if that were possible. To marry his daughter therefore satisfied not only his heart but also his pride.

CHAPTER 22

The End of a Beginning

VISIT TO GOA

WHEN H.H. announced that he would not be leaving Kolhapur for another ten days, I decided to have a look at Goa. The first thirty miles I travelled in the 'special' which was taking H.H.'s party, including the Army but not the Rani and her retinue of fifty-four, back to Dewas. It was curious to see their relief at leaving Kolhapur. They had been away only three weeks and already, like the Greek host in their tenth year before Troy (I was still reading the *Iliad*), they were sighing for their 'dear home'. Master Sahib, on the other hand, was in high spirits: he had at last secured the bride's dowry—nearly £6,000—from the Kolhapur Treasury.

The Goa expedition was not a comfortable one. The journey to Marmagoa, Goa's port, took twenty hours, the journey back twenty-two, with more than one change in the middle of the night. The heat, too, was insufferable, the hotels the dirtiest I had seen in the East; only two or three times could I get an iced drink, and there was very little I could eat. "I am very glad to have been there (I wrote), though nothing will ever induce me to go there again."

Everywhere I found the oddest medley of East and West. The people wore either nothing but a bit of cloth hanging, as Loti says, 'à peu près ou il faut'—or a mixture of anything to be had from the junk shops of the West—black coats over white trousers, white coats over black trousers, or check suits topped by a dusty old billycock or a faded straw. The Church in biretta and cassock added further variety to a scene set in the midst of countless palm trees with everywhere bays, inlets and lagoons embosomed in softly wooded hills.

After a night at Marmagoa, four men, all Christians, rowed me across the estuary dividing it from New Goa. Behind me at the tiller squatted an urchin in a coral necklace and not much else, and overhead a large wrinkled sail flapped languidly in the breeze.

We came to shore in a tiny creek where the palm trees grew almost to the water's edge. A short drive inland, and it was not long before we were jolting through New Goa to the Hotel Crescente, its best hotel. Gloomy as had been the account of it, the half had not been told me. It was not the bareness of my room with its two spotted spittoons, but the dirt. The mattresses were a thing of horror and the so-called bathroom, no more than a cellar. For breakfast—it was now eleven o'clock—a dish of four cold fried eggs was laid on a tablecloth only less dirty than the table. The butter I did not dare touch. There was no ice, of course, but there were at least some small bananas and of these I ate half a dozen.

At two o'clock a carriage with two diminutive ponies took me to Government House to call on the 'Viceroy', as Murray's guide-book styled him. It drew up at a two-storeyed stucco building with a low archway, under which stood a sentry in a slouch hat amusing himself with a rifle. I hailed him but without the slightest response. Passing into a small open court adorned with a pillar or two and some potted flowers, I might have been in some third-rate Italian Palazzo. I gave my card to a mean-looking orderly and an officer in white appeared. He informed me stiffly that His Excellency was sleeping but would see me on the morrow at two o'clock. By that time however I was on my way back to Kolhapur.

I drove on some miles up an estuary so lovely that I felt repaid for all I had endured. Cresting a hill, I came suddenly upon a sight of Old Goa, which Albuquerque seized in 1510. Once a town of some 200,000, all that remained of its former glory was a number of churches "within a bell's note of each other", all half buried in the palm trees, which had swallowed up everything else of note. Four men, one in a check suit and shoeless, the others "just not stark naked", showed me round as many of them as I wanted to see. They differed little from each other. All were white-washed and this in Goa's sunlight gave them outside "an incomparable brightness". Inside there was much heavy gilding with endless pictures of miracles and martyrs.

In the cathedral, a building of fine proportions, a score of priests were at Vespers anda sepulchral Gregorian chant echoed down the aisle. Now and then one mopped his forehead and another spat, but not one raised his eyes from his book to look at me though I had approached close enough to look at them. Although there was little in these churches to inspire one who was not a Catholic, there was something impressive in the way they had held their own in the rising tide of jungle round them. When England's turn comes, I wondered, what will survive to mark our brief passage through India?

THE NEW RÉGIME AT DEWAS

On our return to Dewas I took up my new duties as Adviser and Private Secretary. It was a pleasant change to have regular work again. There was plenty of it, for it soon became evident that the whole machinery of the State needed overhauling. Never, for instance, had I seen an office in greater confusion than that of the Head of the Police, and in another I found two men employed on work which at their own reckoning took only thirty-one hours a month. H.H. had already told me that this kind of thing was general. There was no supervision, he said, and everyone 'did exactly as he liked'. The District Magistrate would take six months over a petty criminal case and was so incompetent that the Superintendent of the State would often have to dictate a judgment for him. Nearly all the officials, too, were corrupt. Some exceptions were mentioned, amongst them the Superintendent who did no more than 'push his friends'. On the other hand, H.H. thought Dewas was no worse than most small States.

A letter describes a normal day under the new régime. "I am called at seven. At 7.30 the tandem comes round—I am getting very skilled in keeping the two ponies from looking at each other! I am back by halfpast eight unless I inspect something. Today I had an hour at the school and then went on to the hospital. At 10 H.H. and I breakfast together, and that lasts a full hour, for it is then that we discuss the questions that have come up the day before. Master Sahib (now Diwan Sahib)* sometimes appears. and that means more discussion." "We are a triumvirate," says another letter. "H.H. is almost—I was going to say a sleeping partner. But he is not that quite: only he leaves all the routine work to Master Sahib and myself. I inform him only of the weightier matters, and upon these we have not differed yet. Master Sahib does the work of ten Ministers but he has no administrative experience and nature perhaps hardly intended him for a ruler."

"From twelve till three he and I sit together to hear reports. I

* To avoid confusing the reader I continue to refer to him by his old title and not by his new one of Diwan Sahib.

suggest what should be done and he turns it into an order. At three o'clock I return for tea. By four I am back in office, the last two days in my capacity as High Court of Appeal! By six the day's work is done. It all keeps me very busy and the long hot Eastern day slips quickly away."

What I enjoyed most was touring the countryside and being once more amongst the peasants. This took Master Sahib and myself to a remote tract at the foot of the hills which supported the Malwa plateau. The roads were little more than two deep ruts made by the to-ing and fro-ing of the peasants' bullock-carts, and the fields all boulders and stones yet bearing crops. The area was suffering from drought and we had come to see whether relief works were required to keep the peasants going until next harvest. Little need be said about our doings as they were on much the same lines as the towns described in the chapters on Rajanpur. But two small incidents are perhaps worth recording. At one village with thirty to forty villagers round us, we were asked to stop the village servants, who must have been tanners, from killing a sheep and burying its head on a track used by the cattle going in and out of the village. This, it was believed, would lead to the death of the cattle passing over the spot, in which case the tanners would be entitled to their skins. Nothing we could say would persuade either party of the contrary. The second incident was an odd one. We were staying at a Rest House, and one afternoon, with nothing to do but shun the heat outside, I started learning the invocation to Urania in *Paradise Lost*. "I was declaiming that marvellous blank verse" when in came the watchman in charge of the Rest House, a black-bearded Muslim, with a cup of tea. Having placed it before me, he stood there with folded hands. "A whim seized me and I gave him the whole passage." 'Is it your Bhajan?'* he asked. 'Yes, certainly it was.' Then, he said, he would like more. So I read him the description of God's ascent to the Heaven of Heavens. This led to a further question—'With your Bhajan will Christ wash away sins and then there will be salvation?' All this from a man paid only a few rupees a month. Missionaries, it seemed, had been there. For all that he was still a Muslim.

My first tour had taken me amongst the aboriginal Bhils. My last, early in May, took H.H. and myself to a Rajput townlet which still had about it a touch of mediaeval enchantment. Horsemen

* A prayer or hymn in praise of God.

armed with sword and dirk met us at the station (only a year old) and with tattered minstrels singing lustily in front of us and a throng in motley turbans coming along behind us, we entered the little town, and winding up a steep hill passed through an old gateway into a fort overlooking the plain below. My room was a long pillared hall divided into three aisles, "each about a spear's throw in length". Morning and evening a band of hooded women would come and sing old ballads to us as we ate. They belonged to a caste which had been given land by the State for singing to its Head whenever he came there.

One evening I had been reading the parting of Hector from Andromache when in they came and began to sing. "Now (said H.H.) they are urging the men to go out and fight, and 'a woman tells her husband that if he comes back victorious she will be the proudest of women, and if he dies, she will do Suttee'."

Another day when we were at breakfast in the pillared hall, a servant in a blue velvet waistcoat came in and whispered something in H.H.'s ear: 'Oh! I have forget,' he exclaimed, pushing back his chair. 'Today the ancestors have to be worshipped.' This had already been done in September. Why it had to be done again I do not remember. Three Brahmins came in, and a priceless cloth was spread for H.H. to sit on. This he did with his bare feet tucked away under his knees. With a Brahmin on either side and one facing him, the ceremony began. An earthenware jar was placed upon a heap of wheat, and on its mouth was set a large pumpkin. It was very hot—the temperature in the room was 94°—and "it was thought the ancestors would like something refreshing". The more normal offerings—red and yellow powders, sweetmeats and flowers—followed while a Brahmin "darted nimbly like a squirrel through the branches of the family tree". The ritual was soon finished and H.H. returned with a smile to the breakfast table.

H.H. AND MYSELF

With the approach of my departure for England on a spell of leave, H.H. came to stay with me at the Guest House, and we had much interesting talk, some of which is recorded in my diary. For instance, one morning at breakfast we had been discussing Court etiquette when he jumped up and demonstrated how subtly graded was his way of greeting those around him. In each case it varied with rank, kinship or station. As already mentioned, he would touch the Maharaja of Kolhapur's feet with his head. But if anyone else's feet had to be touched, it would be with the hands only. Such cases however were exceptional.

Normally the hand would oscillate between knee and chin with every possible variation of level and pace. For one person it would be raised three times, for another only once; for a third from the knee; for a fourth from the waist; for a fifth from the chest, and so on until it was hardly raised at all. The bow, too, could add to the niceties of the art. The greetings indeed seemed almost as subtly varied as the gesture in an Indian dance. If, said H.H., a dozen Indians were present, he would probably greet each in a different way, and however slight the difference, it would not pass unnoticed. In his mind's eye in fact it would be impossible for him to regard them all as equal; rather would he see them as rungs in a ladder.

Another day, over tea, we had a very personal talk. This time the question was how he should be treated. He said he preferred the society of his own people to ours. With his own, his position was clear and readily recognised. With ours, it was liable not to be understood. Was it not the case, I suggested, that apart from a few very high officials he considered himself the social superior of all Englishmen he met out here? This he admitted. And when, flinging tact to the winds, I added that in his heart of hearts he considered himself my superior, with a mischievous and slightly embarrassed laugh he replied: 'Not when we are in a house like this, but on official occasions perhaps. I have sometimes felt that then I did not treat you quite well enough.' I assured him that this was not so, though I knew well enough that even at our friendliest he could not look on me as quite an equal. 'Well (he said) we have a feeling that the English in this country do not belong to the most aristocratic class' (no gainsaying that). And with a disarming naïveté he added: 'If I went into society in England and the room was full of dukes and peers, then I should feel at my ease.' I told him that he had a very high sense of his own importance, at which he laughed, but it was natural enough considering his position and background.

At dinner, we returned to the subject. He said he was astonished how well I had read his character—we had touched on other points as well but not recorded. I told him that when I first came to

Dewas, I had instinctively regarded him as my inferior, but now that I knew him well, that was of course absurd. Somehow we passed on to our mutual relationship. What I had said to him at tea had shown him, he said, that I knew much more of him than he did of me; though even so he thought he knew me as well as he did his best friend, the Chief of Kagal.

The two talks could hardly have been franker. Yet he took all I said in the best possible spirit. "The deeper you go into him (says a letter), the richer the reward." But one thing puzzled me. 'He is (as my diary notes) almost the kindest man I have ever met'; yet when his face is in repose, which it rarely is, 'a surly, almost sulky expression' would come over it. I asked him why this was so when he was usually so gay and his gaiety seemingly so effortless. At heart, he replied, he always felt depressed: the feeling was indeed one of his earliest recollections. He had often wished to die, life seemed 'so empty'. I wondered at that because everyone seemed to like him and that must make life comparatively pleasant. He admitted that people often told him they liked him, but he did not believe them. In fact, with a very few exceptions, he never felt sure of anyone's liking. 'But one class I know likes me—the cultivators. I never doubt them.'

CONCLUSION

At first, as I have noted, I hated Dewas. I had grown too fond of Rajanpur with its taste of independence and power, and during the first three months my mind was continually reverting there. The sight of Sirius one evening sending his last flicker into the lake in front of the Guest House recalled the nights on the Indus when the stars were mirrored in its stream. I longed to return. But (says a letter to A. C.) "I am not to be pitied, for in my most foolish moments I see quite clearly that this is a great opportunity and that I shall never—in India at least—have so peaceful a life again. (This proved true.) It is purely uneventful, as uneventful as the stars are to us. You say (I continue) that as you grow older you find more place for the affections, and certainly this is the supreme wisdom. I cannot complain. There is H.H." And indeed there was.

There was India too. I had not long been in Dewas when I wrote: "One thing only can make life worth living out here, and that is India; but save in the rarest moments to me it is only that peninsula they colour red on the map 6,000 miles away from the white cliffs—what lecturers call 'the brightest jewel of our Empire'." With now some knowledge, however superficial, of its ways and of its two great communities—Hindu and Muslim—it had become most attractive. The attraction had been of slow growth but "when it seizes you", I wrote, "it is like a vice". And so it was when the time approached for my first leave home.

When H.H. became the Ruler as well as the Head of his State, it was arranged that I should stay on three months to see him into the saddle. As the months ebbed away, he made it sufficiently clear that he would like me to stay on at least another three months. At the same time he made it even clearer that he did not wish to disappoint my mother, who was naturally looking forward to my home-coming. As to myself, I had become so attached to H.H., and overhauling the State was proving so interesting, that a three months' delay in my leave would involve no sacrifice on my part. But was it fair to burden the State any longer with a yearly salary of about £600 which it could not well afford? Like H.H. too, I felt the strength of my mother's claims. The question was finally settled by a cable from her bidding me stick to what had been fixed. "I am torn in two (I wrote) between my duty to you, the best of mothers, and my duty to almost the best of my friends. But of course your claims are paramount, so I come." And come I did, with a letter to her from H.H. which he gave me when he saw me off from Bombay on May 16, 1908. I shall perhaps be forgiven if I quote it in full:

My dear Mrs Darling,

This letter I have written a few hours before Malcolm starts for England. Of course the great thing of that is that he will see you, his Sisters, and friends. To me it is hard luck when I most needed one whom I consider to be one of the only two best friends in the world. On this subject I think it is better not to deal any more because I assure you I always think that mothers' claims are above comparison to those of friends.

Now I thank you very much indeed for all your kindness and sympathy to me when you were at Dewas and by letters from England. As for what I owe Malcolm I cannot in any case write. Suffice it to say that he has been to me more than father or brother and above all a staunch true friend and well-wisher. He worked himself in my cause all through. Mother, it now grieves me that I must part with him and you can picture to yourself what a state of grief and utter depression I am in. Please, I need hardly write, do not allow Malcolm to brood over Dewas affairs. It counts on his mind and will make him dejected.

Yours ever sincerely and affly.

Tukojirao Puar.

So ended my apprenticeship for the thirty-two years of service in India which were to follow.

Epilogue

THIS ends my account of H.H. as he was during the time I was with him at Dewas. I add a brief note on his subsequent career.

It began hopefully. He was created Maharaja and a Knight Commander of the Star of India, and Her Highness bore him a son.* Then came disaster.

His marriage proved a failure; his State became insolvent; his relations with the Government of India deteriorated, and in 1936 he died in exile at Pondicherry, officially disgraced.

Mistrusted, mishandled and publicly humiliated in the eyes of his subjects and fellow Chiefs, he reacted with the desperation of one mortally wounded in his honour as Ruler and Prince by a Power far greater than his own. We have seen how inflammable was his pride. We have also seen how responsive he was to consideration and trust. Of that side of his character the officials concerned, with their bureaucratic lack of imagination, seem to have had no notion whatever. To quote *The Hill of Devi*† 'they were impeccably right and absolutely wrong'. And so died one of the most lovable and generous of men almost literally of a broken heart.

* His Highness Major Vikram-Sinharao, G.C.S.I., now (by adoption) Chhatrapati Maharaja of Kolhapur.

† E. M. Forster, *op. cit.*, p. 171.